Myths and their Meaning

Max J. Herzberg

ALLYN AND BACON, INC.

Boston   Rockleigh, NJ   Atlanta   Dallas   Sacramento   Warrensburg, MO
London   Sydney   Toronto

Editor   Rita R. Riley
Designer   Virginia Pierce
Photo Researcher   Susan Van Etten
Preparations Services Manager   Martha E. Ballentine
Lead Buyer   Roger E. Powers

Library of Congress Catalog Card Number   83-70387

ISBN   0-205-08001-4

Printed in the United States of America

7 8 9 91 90 89

Preface

The stories in this volume from Greek, Latin, Northern, and Celtic mythology are not only entertaining in themselves, but important because of their varied influence. They have furnished inspiration and subjects for poets, painters, and sculptors. They have suggested figures of speech, designs, comparisons, and allegories to orators, editorial writers, advertisers, craftsmen in glass and pottery, engravers, and workers in tapestry. Scientists have called on mythology for names for plants and animals and stars. Mythological figures may be seen on postage stamps, in trademarks, and in the names of business products and enterprises. Everybody ought, therefore, to know mythology, not only for the pleasure it gives, but for an intelligent appreciation of our art, literature, and environment.

Myths are wonderful stories, rich in surprising incidents, unusual characters, and hidden meanings. To present them entertainingly and effectively is the object of this book. To do this, a careful study was made to determine which myths are most valuable to the man in the street, to the average reader, to the student of literature, and to the teacher of the classics, both English and Latin.

To help fix these stories in the minds of students and to show how important mythology is in life and literature, many novel exercises have been provided in the **Practical Applications** section. This section usually begins with examples of how myths have influenced literature all through the ages and the general examples are followed by specific literary references. Suggestions are made for both oral and written compostion work which can be used as classroom activities or as stepping stones for developing individual creative writing and speaking skills. The **Word Studies** unit shows how many English words have derived their meanings from the stories and legends just studied. Word Pronunciation exercises are offered as a springboard into dictionary work focusing on using the pronunciation guide in the text or in a dictionary, thus improving skills in pronouncing other unfamiliar words. **Questions for Review** are in chronological order and cover every major point brought out in the reading. They provide a good check on comprehension and retention of the facts. Each chapter ends with a suggested **Reading List** that is more than adequate. The readings can be assigned selectively for reinforcement of the lesson or for special student reports.

The numerous illustrations have been drawn from such sources as the great galleries and museums of the world, famous tapestries, movies, illustrations to books, advertising, and vases and jewelry of ancient and modern times. They afford in themselves a pleasing education in art.

A special section at the end of the text provides additional review material: References to Mythology in Literature, Composition Work, Word Studies, Comprehension Exercises and Suggestions for Special Projects.

Contents

THE OLYMPIC COUNCIL

Greek	Latin	Realm	Symbols
Zeus	Jupiter (Jove)	King of the gods and ruler of mankind	Eagle, oak, thunderbolts,
Poseidon	Neptune	God of sea, horses, and earthquakes	Trident,[1] dolphins, horses
Phœbus Apollo	(Same)	God of sun, music, poetry, and medicine	Lyre,[2] arrows, sun chariot
Hermes	Mercury	Messenger of the gods, god of commerce and theft	Winged cap, winged sandals, caduceus[3]
Ares	Mars	God of war	Sword, shield, dogs, vultures
Hephæstus	Vulcan	God of fire and of workers in metal	Anvil, forge
Hera	Juno	Queen of the gods, wife of Jove, and patroness of married women	Pomegranate, peacock, cuckoo
Demeter	Ceres	Goddess of agriculture	Sheaf of wheat, poppies, cornucopia.[4]
Artemis	Diana	Goddess of moon and hunting, patroness of maidens	Crescent, stag, arrows
Pallas Athena	Minerva	Goddess of wisdom, war, and weaving	Ægis,[5] owl, shield, olive tree
Aphrodite	Venus	Goddess of love and beauty	Doves, sparrows
Hestia	Vesta	Goddess of hearth and home	Hearth fire

OTHER IMPORTANT GODS

Greek	Latin	Realm	Symbols
Cronus[6]	Saturn	Father of Jupiter; among the Romans, god of agriculture	Sickle
Bacchus Dionysus	Liber	God of wine, drama, and revelry	Ivy, grapes, leopards
Hades Pluto	Dis	God of the under-world, minerals, and wealth	Cerberus, cypress, the bident[7]
Eros	Cupid	God of love	Heart pierced with arrow
Pan	Faunus	God of nature	Goats, satyrs
Eos	Aurora	Goddess of the dawn	

GROUPS OF DEITIES

The three Graces, the three Fates, the three Furies, the nine Muses, the dryads, the naiads, the Nereids, the Oceanids, the oreads, the four Winds, the Hours, the fauns, the satyrs, the sirens, the Hesperides, the Pleiades

[1] a three-pronged spear
[2] a musical instrument played like a harp
[3] a winged staff with two serpents twined around it
[4] the horn of peace and plenty
[5] a breastplate on which was fixed the head of Medusa, a woman with snaky locks
[6] not to be confused with Chronos, the god of time
[7] a two-pronged spear

INTRODUCTION

To the mean person the myth
always means little;
to the noble person, much.

John Ruskin

A prehistoric wall painting from the Lascaux Cave in France

Meaning of Myths

Great are the myths.

Walt Whitman

Birth of Myths

If one goes back in imagination to the dim beginnings of time, when true religion had not yet enlightened man, nor had science explained to him the causes and origins of things, one may watch the birth of what we call *myths*.

In the brooding darkness of forests—on plains where the sun shone blazingly—in cave-homes that barely protected their inmates against the ravages of saber-toothed tigers or gigantic bears—in houses perched insecurely over the waters of lakes—in the damp depths of rank jungles—on mountainsides and by the seashore— everywhere, man looked out upon a mysterious and dangerous world.

He asked himself. "Where does the sun come from, and what is it?" and he answered his question by saying, "The sun is a boat (or a chariot), and in it sits a dazzling god who guides it over the sky." Puzzled by the moon, early man explained that white luminary by thinking of it as another boat or chariot, in which sat the sister of the sun god.

"What lurks behind the terror of thunder and lightning?" he inquired; and to resolve his puzzle came the image of a great god enthroned in the skies, whose voice was the thunder and whose messenger was the lightning. When the sea broke forth in disastrous tempests, it was because the blue-haired deity of the waves was enraged. When the grain and the trees bore seed in due season, the Earth-Mother was gracious; when famine came, she had been angered, and must be appeased with sacrifices and prayers.

Many other questions puzzled these primitive dwellers on the earth—the origin of fire, the fashion in which various animals and plants came to be, the reasons for one man's prosperity and another man's troubles, the nature of death and the problem of an afterworld.

To answer questions such as these, men of ancient days devised myths—those in this book, and many others. For long ages the myths were not written down. They were handed down by word of mouth from father to son, from one generation to the next. Often they were greatly altered by those who received them; and a clever storyteller or a poet with fine imagination would add touches here and there that others in their vicinity would at once accept. So it usually happened that the versions of the same myth, as told in different localities, would differ from one another. Sometimes a great poet, like Homer, would take a myth and tell it in his own way, and thereafter his form of the story would be the one that everybody accepted. With such great poets one reaches the stage where the myths were finally written down.

All nations have had their myths. Although resemblances may be traced among them, they are so different in details, that as a whole they form the world's most wonderful collection of stories.

Why Myths Are Studied

Why do we study myths? For at least four reasons. These stories are still studied because they have had such a deep influence on all great literatures. It is especially true that the myths of the Greeks and Romans have profoundly affected English and American literature. The great writers in our language have been fascinated by the stories that these ancient peoples told. We can hardly understand Shakespeare, Milton, Keats or Lowell without being familiar with the myths of Greece and Rome.

The gods, the demigods, and the heroes of myth play their part in music also. The very word *music* pays tribute to the Muses, and many of the myths tell how musical instruments were first invented. Numerous compositions for instrumental or vocal performance have been inspired by the ancient figures whose stories are told in this book.

The story of Orpheus and Eurydice was the theme of the first opera ever written, and it has since then been a favorite subject of musical composers. Perhaps the most famous treatment of this story is that by Gluck, with its famous solo and duet: *I have lost my Eurydice* and *Orpheus and Eurydice*. Other tales that have attracted musicians are those of Medea and Jason and of Iphigenia. Among composers who have handled themes from mythology are Massenet, Offenbach, and Purcell.

But perhaps the greatest of all musical geniuses who have turned to the treasure house of mythology for material is Richard Wagner, who in many of his operas employs the myths of his native land—particularly the story of Siegfried. The second half of the cycle of four operas, *The Ring of the Nibelung,* tells the adventures of that great hero.

Moreover, myths have had a potent influence on other arts. Great painters and sculptors of all ages, like great musicians, have found in these ancient legends inspiration for their finest achievements. The illustrations in this volume testify eloquently to this inspiration.

Then, these stories are in themselves often both beautiful and entertaining. They still appeal to our imagination today. Often there may be found in them a kernel of allegorical truth, but they may be read for amusement, for their striking plots and remarkable characters.

Finally, they are an important link with the past. They are often our only source of knowledge as to how our distant forefathers regarded the world around them and how they explained its innumerable phenomena. Often, too, we may be surprised to find that because the ancients used a certain idea to explain some puzzle in nature, we today may still have a word that preserves that idea. Our language is full of terms that go back to these old myths, and that can be explained only by learning the myths. Thus, for example, so common a word as *janitor* goes back to *Janus,* the two-headed god of gates whom the Romans worshiped. The name of *June* is derived from *Juno,* queen of the gods among the Romans; while *Thursday* comes from *Thor,* god of war among the old Germanic tribes. We praise food by saying it "tastes like ambrosia," which was the food of the deities on Mount Olympus; and our ideas of the underworld are very much like those of Homer and Virgil. We are bound to the past in innumerable ways, and it is well to know the old myths in order that we may understand our own times.

Where Myths Are Found

Myths are found in many kinds of writings. There are, first, the ancient documents in which they first occur. In reading Homer, Virgil or Ovid one may see the myths in the form in which they crystallized among the peoples that devised them. Similarly, the *Eddas* of the Scandinavians, the *Sacred Books of the East,* and similar productions give the myths of other nations and races.

Scholars have always collected old stories. Geoffrey of Monmouth, an English writer of the twelfth century, told some of the legends, which the Celts related concerning their ruler, King Arthur, and his famous knights. Later scholars collected stories of the Indians, Eskimos, African tribes, and the bushmen of Australia.

Poets and storytellers of all nations use myths for many purposes. They retell them in their own language—in prose, verse, short story, epic and play. Dante has Ulysses, the Greek hero, tell part of his story in the *Inferno*. Shakespeare reworks certain episodes of the Trojan War in *Troilus and Cressida*. Goethe tells the story of *Iphigenia in Tauris* and Racine that of *Andromache*. William Morris recounts in a long poem the adventures of Jason in search of the Golden Fleece, and several novels have been written about Helen of Troy and about King Arthur's knights.

But the poets make even greater use of myths in their references and allusions, in their similes and other figures of speech. Hundreds of lines are quoted in the course of these pages to make this fact clear, but one can prove it by turning to almost any of the English poets and to prose writers like Charles Lamb and John Ruskin. Their pages are starred with characters in Greek and Roman myths.

In everyday life, as has already been suggested, we employ a great many words based on these same myths. Later on we shall study such words as *martial, volcano, cereal, mercurial, Wednesday, Saturday, museum, labyrinth,* and many others. Two other points may be made here. Rather oddly some persons still *swear* by the Greek and Roman gods. For we still hear people say, "By Jove!"—and Jove, or Jupiter, was the chief god of the Romans; and we occasionally hear someone say "Gemini!"—the Latin word for *twins,* referring to the twin gods, *Castor* and *Pollux,* rulers of boxing and wrestling.

In advertising, also, there is frequent recourse to mythology. An automobile may be named after a Roman goddess, or the figure of a swift runner in Greek myth may be placed on the hood. A cement may take its name from an ancient giant, a pencil from the graceful goddess of love, a process for treating a tire from the god of the forge. It is interesting to observe in how many different ways the writers of advertisements recall these old stories.

Moreover, mythmaking still fascinates modern writers. They may not believe, as the ancient myth makers did, in the tales they tell, but they are delighted with their creations, and their readers are often delighted too. Joel Chandler Harris put myths into the mouth of his Uncle

6

Jupiter (Greek: Zeus), king of the gods and ruler of mankind

Aurora (Greek: Eos), goddess of the dawn

(top left) Jupiter seizes Ganymede to serve the gods

(bottom left) A satyr, a woodland deity known for revelry and merriment

(top right) The Titan Prometheus, friend and rebel—Rockefeller Center, N.Y.

(bottom middle) Diana (Greek: Artemis), goddess of the moon and hunting

(bottom right) Pluto, god of the Underworld, and Cerberus

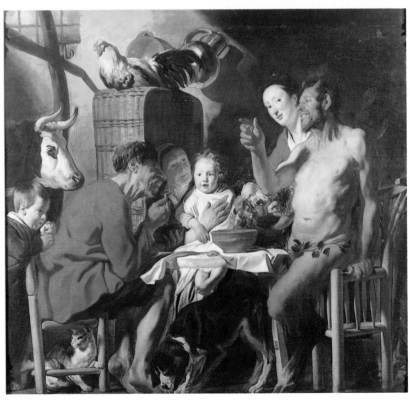

Mercury
(Greek:
Hermes),
messenger of
the gods
-Rockefeller
Center, N.Y.

Venus
(Greek:
Aphrodite),
goddess of
love
and beauty;
and Mars
(Greek: Ares),
god of
war—Botticelli

Bacchus,
god of wine,
drama, and
revelry
—Caravaggio

(left) **The Delphic Sybil—Michelangelo**
(right) **Aeneas and Queen Dido**

Theseus and the Minotaur

(left) Perseus with the head of Medusa

(top left) The head of the Gorgon Medusa—Caravaggio

(bottom left) Hercules slays the Hydra

(below) The Centaur—Botticelli

(top) King Arthur's Round Table
(bottom left) Lancelot saves King Arthur's life—Walter Crane
(below) Lady Guinevere—William Morris

Detail of the head of Odin

(above) Head of a Celtic god, bronze
(top right) Pendant usually identified as a Valkyrie
(middle right) Thor, the thunderer, Norse god of war
(bottom right) Pendant representing a Valkyrie offering a horn

Only eyes with special vision can see
the "Little People" of the Celtic Fairyland.

Remus; Lord Dunsany has told tales of the gods of Pegana—his own invention; and Sir James M. Barrie's Peter Pan is familiar to everybody—the name recalling quaintly Pan, the Greek god of nature.

A *myth* is an account of the deeds of a god or of a supernatural being. It relates a supposed historical event, or it serves "to explain some practice, belief, institution, or natural phenomenon" (Webster). Races, nations, tribes, or localities often have their own myths.

Mythology is the system of myths told by a given race. The word also means the study of myths in general.

Polytheism is the belief in many gods, such as is found in all mythologies. These gods may be thought of as human in form (as among the Greeks and Romans), as animal in form (as among many Indian tribes), as combining animal and human forms (as among the Egyptians), or as creatures of fantasy (like the Chinese dragons).

PRACTICAL APPLICATIONS

Myths in Literature

William Wordsworth, in his poem *The Excursion*, has a famous passage, quoted below, in which he endeavors to explain how myths arose in ancient Greece. He imagines the shepherd listening to a distant strain of music and in awe inventing a beardless god who played a lute; he imagines the hunter turning the moon into a goddess, accompanied by her nymphs, the stars; he imagines the traveler thanking the naiad, deity of the fountain. Similarly he explains the origin of the oreads, nymphs of the mountains; the zephyrs, rulers of the west wind, wooing their favorites with gentle breezes; and the satyrs, gods half goat and half man, with their monarch, Pan himself. Read his account carefully.

Once more to distant ages of the world
Let us revert, and place before our thoughts
The face which rural solitude might wear
To the unenlightened swains of pagan Greece.

—In that fair clime, the lonely herdsman, stretched
On the soft grass through half a summer's day,
With music lulled his indolent repose:
And, in some fit of weariness, if he,
When his own breath was silent, chanced to hear
A distant strain, far sweeter than the sounds
Which his poor skill could make, his fancy fetched
Even from the blazing chariot of the sun,
A beardless youth, who touched a golden lute,
And filled the illumined groves with ravishment,
The nightly hunter, lifting a bright eye
Up towards the crescent moon, with grateful heart
Called on the lovely wanderer who bestowed
That timely light, to share his joyous sport:
And hence, a beaming goddess with her nymphs,
Across the lawn and through the darksome grove,
Not unaccompanied with tuneful notes
By echo multiplied from rock or cave,
Swept in the storm of chase; as moon and stars
Glance rapidly along the clouded heaven,
When winds are blowing strong.

> The traveler slaked
His thirst from rill or gushing fount, and thanked
The naiad. Sunbeams, upon distant hills
Gliding apace, with shadows in their train,
Might, with small help from fancy, be transformed
Into fleet oreads sporting visibly.

The zephyrs fanning, as they passed, their wings,
Lacked not, for love, fair objects whom they wooed
With gentle whisper.

> Withered boughs grotesque,
Stripped of their leaves and twigs by hoary age,
From depth of shaggy covert peeping forth

In the low vale, or on steep mountain side;
And, sometimes, intermixed with stirring horns
Of the live deer, or goat's depending beard—
These were the lurking satyrs, a wild brood
Of gamesome deities; or Pan himself,
The simple shepherds awe-inspiring god!

Begin today to make an *Album of Mythology*. Collect as many references to the myths of ancient times as you can. Where the reference occurs in a magazine or a newspaper, and it is permissible for you to do so, clip the article or the advertisement containing the reference. Underline the exact words neatly in black or red ink. Where it is not feasible for you to cut out the clipping, copy the reference neatly on a slip of blank paper.

Gather these references and when you have a dozen or so, paste them carefully in a blank book (if possible, one with unruled pages). Arrange your references in groups; for example, put together all references to Jupiter, to Siegfried, and so on. Add to them from time to time.

Your *Album of Mythology* can be made still more attractive if you also make a collection of pictures to use as illustrations of the references. Some pictures you can find in newspapers and magazines. Others you can purchase inexpensively. Still others may be had by asking your friends who are traveling to send you picture post cards showing scenes from mythology or figures of the gods. Or, perhaps, you may be fortunate enough to do your own traveling and make your own collection of pictures.

At intervals through your book insert appropriate quotations, either taken from your own reading or selected from the numerous quotations that you will find scattered throughout this volume. Prepare a dedication page, on which you inscribe the book to someone of whom you are fond or who has helped you in your work.

Often the most practical way of preparing this *Album* is to secure a loose-leaf notebook binder, preferably one that will hold pages 8½ by 11 inches. You can then use ordinary typewriting paper of a good quality on which to paste your clippings and illustrations and to write your quotations and inscriptions.

Word Study

1. Show how a knowledge of mythology will help you to understand the following words: *janitor, June, Thursday, ambrosia, Gemini.*
2. Give a definition of *myth, mythology, polytheism.*

Questions for Review

1. How did myths originate?
2. What facts did they help to explain?
3. How were myths handed down?
4. Are myths confined to any one nation or race?
5. Why do we study myths?
6. What poets have been influenced by them?
7. How do myths help us to understand the past?
8. Where may myths be found?
9. Are myths employed in everyday life?
10. What are some words that are explained by myths?
11. How does advertising employ mythology?
12. Do modern writers ever invent myths?

PART ONE:

MYTHS OF GREECE AND ROME

On desperate seas long wont to roam,
Thy hyacinth hair, thy classic face,
Thy naiad airs have brought me home
To the glory that was Greece
And the grandeur that was Rome.

Edgar Allan Poe: To Helen

The feeding of Jupiter. After being secretly conveyed to the island of Crete, the infant Jupiter was cared for by the nymphs, Ida and Adrastea.

1 How The World Began

The horde of Titans, Earth-sons born in ancient days.

Virgil

Coming of the Gods

According to the ancient Greeks there was at first *Chaos*—a vast, seething confusion. There were no limits or bounds in the world, there was no plan or outline. It was all a tremendous disorder, but in it were hidden all things that now exist.

Gradually, after a long lapse of ages, Chaos ceased to be mere darkness and confusion. It resolved itself into two great beings, two majestic deities—*Gæa*, or Mother Earth, and *Uranus*, or the Overhanging Heavens. But a constant memory of Chaos remained and still remains in *Night*, the mysterious darkness in which Chaos lived.

From the marriage of Gæa and Uranus many children were born. Some of the children were very beautiful; others were terrifying monsters. The former were called *Titans*. They were twelve in number and of great size and strength; like men, only much grander. Among the most famous of them were *Oceanus* and *Tethys*, who ruled the sea; *Hyperion* and *Thea*, deities of the sun and moon; *Rhea*, later known as the "Great Mother"; *Themis*, guardian of law and justice; *Mnemosyne*, goddess of memory, and *Cronus*, youngest and most powerful of them all. The monsters born to Gæa and Uranus were of two kinds. Three of them had each a hundred hands. Three others had each only one eye. The former were called *Hecatoncheires*, the latter *Cyclopes*.

Now Uranus hated all his children, but above all he hated the six monsters, and he therefore confined them in the lower regions of the earth, called *Tartarus*. Mother Earth, to whom none of her brood was hateful, was angry at the imprisonment of six of her children, and she called upon the Titans to help her against their father. None would help her except Cronus (whom the Romans held to be the same as their *Saturn*). He took a sharp sickle and slew his father. From the blood of Uranus sprang the *giants*, more like men than gods, who wore the skins of wild beasts, and who were fierce fighters. From his blood sprang, too, the *Furies*, or *Eumenides*, whose hair was writhing serpents.

Having overthrown his father, Cronus seized the rule of the world. He took Rhea to be his wife, and divided his empire among his fellow Titans. But his own reign came to an end in time. He feared that a fate similar to that of his father would overtake him, and so he swallowed each of his children as it was born—three daughters, *Vesta*, *Ceres*, and *Juno*; and three sons, *Pluto*, *Neptune*, and *Jupiter*. At least, he thought he had swallowed Jupiter, but when it came to the turn of their youngest born, Rhea cunningly substituted a stone in place of the infant.

Jupiter was secretly conveyed to the island of Crete, and there the nymphs Ida and Adrastea fed him on the milk of the goat Amalthæa. When Jupiter attained full growth and strength, he resolved to conquer Cronus. With the aid of Gæa he managed to make Cronus disgorge the five deities he had swallowed; and then with the help of these he made war on the ancient god. On the side of Cronus were ranged almost all the Titans; on the side of Jupiter were not only his brothers and sisters, but also the hundred-handed and the one-eyed monsters, whom Cronus, like Uranus, had confined to Tartarus. The Cyclopes, in gratitude for their release by Jupiter, forged for him the thunderbolt and the lightning. The Hecatoncheires, on the other hand, provided him with the shock of earthquakes as a weapon.

On one mountain stood the old gods, and on another the young gods. For ages the war lasted, and every time a battle took place the whole earth shook with the tread of the divine warriors and the air resounded with their tremendous battle cries. Jupiter hurled thunderbolt on thunderbolt. The forests burst into flames, the rivers boiled, the very skies were scorched. At last the Titans could withstand the might of Jupiter no longer. They were hurled in fire from their mountain stronghold. The young gods pursued and overcame them. Most of the Titans were confined in Tartarus. The son of one of them, *Atlas*, was assigned the task of bearing the world on his shoulders forever. Another Titan's two sons, *Prometheus* and *Epimetheus*, who had refused to take arms against *Jupiter*, likewise escaped imprisonment; and for a time Prometheus was the chief adviser of Jupiter.

Now the gods divided the world among themselves. To Jupiter (Greek: *Zeus;* also called *Jove* by the Romans) was given the overlordship of gods and men, and he was to rule as king on their mountain stronghold, Mount Olympus. As his queen Jupiter chose Juno (Greek: *Hera*). Neptune (Greek: *Poseidon)* was assigned the government of the ocean. To Pluto (sometimes called *Hades)* went the sway of the underworld. Vesta (Greek: *Hestia)* became goddess of hearth and home, Ceres (Greek: *Demeter)* goddess of agriculture.

14

Four Ages of Man

Meanwhile, on the face of the earth, the races of mankind had already come into being. As ancient stories tell, several races of men succeeded one another. In the *Golden Age* of Cronus life was an eternal springtime. The soil brought forth so profusely that all toil was unnecessary. Men were both happy and good; old age came slowly. They dwelt always in a kindly out-of-doors, and knew neither strife nor poverty. When death at length came to them, it was like a peaceful sleep.

Next came the *Silver Age*. Jupiter created the seasons and made labor necessary. Hunger and cold prevailed, and houses had to be built. Man in that age showed courage, but he was often overbearing and forgot to pay due reverence to the gods.

The Age of Silver was followed by the *Age of Bronze*, in which men learned the use of arms and made war upon one another. Last was the *Age of Iron*—an era of crime and dishonor, when the gifts of the gods were misused and mankind sank into utter degradation.

Bound up with the history of mankind in these early ages is the wonderful story of Prometheus. The name of this Titan means "forethought" or "foresight," just as that of his brother, Epimetheus, means "afterthought" or "hindsight." In other words, Prometheus by the powers of his mind could tell beforehand what was going to happen. For a time Prometheus was the chosen counselor of Jupiter, who relied upon him for help in all things. Yet in time a quarrel arose between them, and all because of mankind. For when Jupiter beheld how men fell away from their former glory in the Silver Age, he swept them off the face of the earth, and resolved to create a new race. He called upon Prometheus for assistance, and the Titan took clay from the banks of a river in Arcadia and molded it into the likeness of the gods and breathed the breath of life into the images that he made. So a new race was born.

Yet these men were feebler than the men of the two preceding ages, and they came into a world that demanded more of them than had ever before been demanded of men. They had to struggle against the changes of the weather. The earth would not bear food for them unless they first tilled the soil, and around them were dangerous wild beasts. It seemed as if this race would perish unless help came.

Prometheus, looking down upon them, saw what was happening.

"Come," he said to Jupiter, "let us give these poor creatures the blessed gift of fire. With fire they will not need to fear the cold. With fire they can make themselves tools and weapons."

But Jupiter feared that if he gave this great gift to men, they would think themselves the equals of the gods, so he refused to grant the request of Prometheus. The Titan was deeply grieved, and at length resolved that he would no longer dwell with Jupiter but would make his abode with men. So he left Olympus, and carried with him, hidden in a reed, the gift of fire. Prometheus taught men how with fire they might make weapons to fight wild beasts and contend with their enemies, and how with fire they might contrive tools for all handicrafts and trades. It was in this age that tin and copper were first mixed in the furnace to make bronze. Prometheus likewise taught men how to subdue the ox, the ass, and the horse. He showed them how to write, build ships, reckon the course of the year, and cure diseases.

Dowry of Pandora and Punishment of Prometheus

So men prospered. And as they prospered Jupiter was more and more displeased. He finally settled on a cunning stratagem to overcome Prometheus. With the help of his son Vulcan (Greek: *Hephæstus*), lord of the forge, and of the other gods, he devised a most beautiful woman, named *Pandora* (a word in Greek that means "all gifts"). Each of the deities bestowed some grace or beauty upon her. Jupiter sent Pandora to Prometheus, and with her went a great box, such as men use for

16

Pandora's box

storage; the box was carefully sealed. Prometheus, suspecting a trick on the part of Jupiter, refused to accept either the woman or the box; so Jupiter sent her to Epimetheus, who had been warned by his brother against the wiles of Jupiter. Epimetheus, however, won by the beauty of Pandora, accepted her as his wife.

"This is my dowry," she explained, when Epimetheus inquired what was in the box; and together they broke the seal and opened it. Immediately a cloud of evils flew forth—all the diseases and troubles and worries that still afflict mankind. Too late, they tried to put the lid back again. But only one spirit remained in the box: *Hope*.

Jupiter was, of course, discontented with the result of his stratagem. He had, to be sure, inflicted upon mankind many ailments and cares, but Prometheus was still unpunished. So he commanded two giants to seize Prometheus, and he made Vulcan, who obeyed unwillingly, bind the Titan fast to a great crag in the Caucasus Mountains. There Prometheus was left, and each morning came a fierce eagle (or vulture) that consumed part of his body, which each night grew whole again.

"Yield to me," commanded Jupiter, "and you shall be released."

The punishment of Prometheus

But never would Prometheus yield to Jupiter or give up his devotion to mankind. He gazed, moreover, into the future, and saw that one day a deliverer would come to him, and this deliverer would be a descendant of Jupiter himself. He saw, too, that on another day Jupiter himself would be overthrown, and the ultimate God, the true God, would be installed as ruler of the universe. Therefore, he bore his torments unflinchingly.

Jupiter, in the meantime, had made up his mind to get rid of men by wiping them all out by means of a great flood. Prometheus warned his son Deucalion that this was coming, so Deucalion and his wife Pyrrha took refuge on Mount Parnassus. When the surging floods overwhelmed the earth and all its inhabitants, this pair was saved, for Jupiter at last took pity on them and remembered their blameless lives.

When the waters receded, Deucalion and Pyrrha sought a temple of the gods. There a mysterious voice spoke to them and said, "Repeople the earth with the bones of your mother." Deucalion interpreted this to mean stones. He and his wife veiled their heads and, as they walked along, they cast stones behind them. The stones that Deucalion cast became men, and those that fell from his wife's hand became women; and these, according to the ancient legends, were the ancestors of all the beings that people the earth today. Deucalion was the king of those that lived first, and he taught them many useful arts.

PRACTICAL APPLICATIONS

Myths in Literature

From the earliest times poets and other writers have been especially delighted to tell the story of Prometheus and Pandora.

Prometheus was the subject of many ancient dramas,

one of which was the *Prometheus Bound* of Æschylus. Later he was treated in poems by Byron, Longfellow, Lowell, and others, and in plays by Shelley and William Vaughn Moody. Prometheus has appealed to our imagination particularly as the great benefactor of mankind—he who first brought fire from the heavens; and also as the great rebel—who dared to outface the tyranny of Jove and was willing to suffer endless torments for having done so.

Similarly, the story of Pandora appeals to us because it gives an ingenious explanation for the presence of evils and diseases on earth, and because the figure of Pandora herself, despite the troubles she brought, is an attractive one. Milton, wishing to praise Eve, describes her as even "more lovely than Pandora, whom the gods endowed with all their gifts."

The fall of the old gods and their replacement by the younger dynasty of Jupiter and his fellows has been treated by no poet more magnificently than by John Keats in his *Hyperion*, which pictures Saturn, after his overthrow, sitting quiet as a stone,

> **Deep in the shady sadness of a vale**
> **Far sunken from the healthy breath of morn,**
> **Far from the fiery noon, and eve's one star.**

Specific Literary References

From the numerous references in literature to these and other myths, a group of lines has been selected, in the exercise that follows, for you to examine and explain. As you study the famous masterpieces of literature, as you read stories and novels for pleasure, as you examine advertisements and listen to intelligent conversation, you will come across many similar references, which the myths in this and later chapters, will help you to understand.

What do the following references mean? Where a word or phrase is italicized, explain only the word or phrase.

1. The rock, the vulture, and the chain.—*Byron*
2. It was the Titans warring with Olympus.—*Carlyle*
3. To whom the *Golden Age*
   Still nature's laws doth give.—*Drayton*

4. Even the Titanic strength of Valeries's car was hard put to it not to falter on the heavier grades.—*Hughes*
5. Or lacks she the Promethean fire?—*Lamb*
6. Prometheus, beautiful, rebellious one!—*Mackaye*
7.   Who first taught
   In the beginning how the heavens and earth
   Rose out of Chaos.—*Milton*
8.   *Chaos,* that reigns here
   In double night of darkness and of shades.—*Milton*
9. When went there by an age, since the *Great Flood,*
   But it was famed with more than with one man?—*Shakespeare*
10. Even the blood of giants, which were slain
    By thund'ring Jove.—*Spenser*
11. And next told he of stones by Pyrrha cast.—*Virgil*
12.   The horde
    Of Titans, Earth-sons born in ancient days.—*Virgil*

Suggestions for Oral or Written Composition

1. Give a talk on the myth of Prometheus, in such a way as to prove what Byron says of him, that his "only crime was to be kind."
2. If you were to prepare a script for a movie entitled "The Four Ages in Four Scenes," what facts would you list for each scene?
3. Write a playlet, entitled "The Coming of Pandora." The first scene shows Prometheus warning his brother against the gifts of the gods. The next scene shows the coming of Pandora and the opening of the box. (How will you show the escape of the evils that torment mankind?) The final scene shows Epimetheus and Pandora, living in the happiness that Hope gives them. In their conversation they tell what has happened to Prometheus.
4. Why has Thomas A. Edison been called "the Prometheus of our times"? Give a talk comparing the Titan and the inventor.

Word Study

1. The words and phrases we use in everyday speech still bear many traces of the ancient myths studied in this chapter. See if you can tell how the following words came to have their present meaning:

   chaotic—shapeless, disordered, confused
   titanic—enormous, very large
   geology—the science of the earth
   Cyclopean—huge, massive
   cereal—a grass yielding grain
   Olympian—heavenly, godlike

2. Look up the following names in a mythological dictionary and practice the correct pronunciation. (The pronunciation of many of these words is given in the index.)
   Chaos, Uranus, Titan, Oceanus, Cyclopes, Ceres, Prometheus, Epimetheus, Poseidon, Demeter, Pandora, Deucalion.

3. What does *Dora,* the common name for a girl mean? What does the expression *Golden Age* signify? What do the names *Prometheus* and *Epimetheus* signify?

4. Give the Greek name for *Jupiter, Neptune, Vulcan.* Give the Roman name for *Demeter, Hera, Hestia.* What was Pluto's other name?

Questions for Review

1. What was Chaos?
2. Who were the first gods?
3. What name was given to their beautiful children? to the monsters that were born to them?
4. What happened to Uranus?
5. Who became the chief of the gods?
6. What did he do to his children?
7. How was he overthrown?
8. Who then became the ruler of the gods?
9. Who were his brothers and sisters?

10. On what mountain did the new gods live?
11. What Titans helped the new gods?
12. What were the four ages?
13. How did Prometheus help mankind?
14. How did Jupiter punish him?
15. How did Jupiter send evils on mankind?
16. How did he seek to wipe out the human race?
17. Did he succeed?
18. How was the earth repopulated?

Reading List

Poems and Plays

Byron, George: *Prometheus—The Isles of Greece*
Henderson, Daniel: *Prometheus in New Jersey*
Keats, John: *Ode on a Grecian Urn*
Longfellow, Henry Wadsworth: *Epimetheus—Masque of Pandora—Prometheus*
Moody, William Vaughn: *The Firebringer—The Masque of Judgment*
Rossetti, D.G.: *Pandora*
Taylor, Bayard: *Prince Deukalion*

Novels and Descriptive Works

Church, A. J.: *Three Greek Children*
Davis, W. S.: *A Day in Old Athens—A Victor at Salamis*
Hall, Jennie: *Buried Cities*
Lamprey, Louise: *Children of Ancient Greece*
Mills, Dorothy: *The Book of the Ancient Greeks*
Mitchison, Naomi: *Cloud Cuckoo Land*
Sheepshanks, Richard: *Hector and Achilles*
Snedecker, Caroline D.: *The Spartan*
White, Edward Lucas: *Helen*

Marriage of Jupiter and Juno

2 Gods of The Sky

Hence! Wilt thou lift up Olympus!
Shakespeare

On Mount Olympus

In the northern part of Greece lies a mountain range, separating the regions called Macedonia and Thessaly. At the eastern end of the chain looms *Mount Olympus*. Its height is about 10,000 feet, and its summit is covered with perpetual snow. Here, the ancient Greeks believed, Jupiter had fought against the power of Cronus; and when his reign was established, it was on Mount Olympus that he held court and conducted the councils of the gods. He lived in a magnificent palace, and nearby were the mansions of the other important gods. Daily they came to Jupiter and sat around him in solemn conclave; or else the younger gods danced before him and entertained him with song. Their food was *ambrosia*, their drink *nectar*. They were shut off from the view of men by a wall of clouds, at the gates of which sat the *Hours* as guardians.

Some of the gods were constantly thought of as living in this home in *the sky*. Others, again, were thought of as the gods of *nature or the earth* proper; and still others were associated with *the underworld*. Of each of these three groups we will speak in turn.

Jupiter, Juno, and Vesta[1]

Three children of Cronus dwelt on Mount Olympus, although sometimes indeed their errands brought them on visits to man.

Jupiter, called the father of gods and men, was the founder of kingly power, the patron of rulers, and the establisher of law, order and justice. All good and evil sprang alike from him. To every mortal he assigned his earthly share of sorrow and prosperity. He was armed with thunder and lightning; the shaking of his shield produced the storm. He was the god of weather, especially of rain. A great eagle crouched before him waiting to be his messenger. The oak, monarch of trees, was sacred to him; and some believed that by listening to the whispering of its leaves, one might guess the mind of Jove.

Beside him sat his wife and consort Juno. When she spoke her mind, Jupiter listened to her with respect, and she knew all his secrets. Yet she was inferior to him in power and had to obey him. She was the goddess of marriage, and her appearance was that of a beautiful and majestic woman of middle age, with a wide forehead, large and attractive eyes, and a grave expression commanding reverence. Her head was adorned with a crown, and a veil hung behind her head. The peacock, in its gorgeous array, and the cuckoo, herald of the springtime, were sacred to

[1]See the table of the gods on pages viii and ix.

her. Her constant attendant was *Iris,* goddess of the rainbow. Juno was not very amiable, and was jealous of Jupiter, whose favorites she sometimes persecuted.

Vesta, the sister of Jove, was the goddess of home fire and the hearth; she was the guardian of family life. She was wooed by several of the gods, but Jupiter decreed that she must forever remain unmarried. Her sacred fire burned on every hearthstone; and inasmuch as a town or village was actually an extended family, there was in every ancient Roman and Greek community a public hearth, blazing with the holy flames of Vesta and tended by her priestesses, the Vestal Virgins. When emigrants set forth to found a new settlement, they took with them part of the fire from this hearth and used it to kindle the hearth in their new homes.

Children of Jupiter and Juno

One of the most important of the gods was a son of Jupiter and Juno—*Mars* (Greek: *Ares*), the god of war. He reveled in battle and slaughter. He appeared in full armor, a long plume floating from his helmet. Often he rode at high speed in his war chariot, drawn by four fiery steeds. Dogs of prey and vultures accompanied him; his symbols were a spear and a burning torch. His sons were Terror, Trembling, Panic, and Fear.

Another son of the royal gods was *Vulcan,* already mentioned as god of the forge. He presided over fire in many of its manifestations, from the smithy to the volcano, but especially over fire in its practical uses. He was himself a skilled workman and the patron of artisans; all the palaces on Mount Olympus were his handiwork. The workshop of Vulcan was usually on some volcanic island—Etna, for example; and when the volcano was in eruption, the people nearby would say in awe that Vulcan was at work. One legend related that he attempted once to interfere in a quarrel between Jupiter and Juno, and that the former in wrath hurled him from heaven. All day he fell, and at sunset he finally landed on the island of Lemnos. Ever after he was lame. He was represented as a vigorous, bearded man,

Research this painting of Aeolus and Vulcan by Piero di Cosimo.

holding a hammer or some other tool. He wore an oval cap, and his right shoulder and arm were uncovered.

Another child of Jupiter and Juno was *Hebe*, goddess of youth and cupbearer to the other gods. In later ages she was married to the great hero Hercules, and her place as cupbearer was taken by the youth *Ganymede*, snatched from the plains of Troy by the eagle of Jove.

Other Children of Jupiter

Jupiter had numerous other children, some of whom had important duties to perform.

Latona (Greek: *Leto*) bore to Jupiter twin children. They were assigned the charge of the sun and the moon.

Phœbus Apollo, god of the sun, was pictured as driving the flaming chariot of the luminary of the day across the sky. He was, too, the god of song, music and prophecy. He led the choir of the *Muses*—nine maidens, themselves the daughters of Jupiter and Mnemosyne, the Titaness who presided over memory. To Apollo was attributed the invention of the flute and lyre. From the bow that he carried went forth flaming arrows of plague and pestilence. Yet he was, too, the god of healing, and the father of Æsculapius, the first physician.

His sister *Diana* (Greek: *Artemis*), goddess of the moon, guided her silvery chariot over the sky at night. Like Apollo she was armed with a bow, quiver, and arrows. The sudden deaths of women were attributed to her shafts. But she was, likewise, a goddess of healing, and also of the chase. She was often represented as a huntress, with hunting dogs and a boar's head at her side. Sometimes she was shown in her chariot, drawn by four stags with golden horns. As goddess of the moon she appeared with a robe that reached to her feet, a white veil on her head and a crescent moon rising above her forehead.

Dione was the daughter of Oceanus and Tethys, the Titans who preceded Neptune in the rulership of the ocean. She bore to Jupiter the goddess of beauty, *Venus* (Greek: *Aphrodite*). Some fables related that Venus was born of the foam of the sea, and that the waves carried her first to the island of Cythera. She is therefore sometimes called "the foam-born" and sometimes "the Cytherean." She surpassed all gods and all mortals in beauty, and she had moreover the power of granting beauty to others. She possessed a magic girdle, and if she granted the use of this girdle to another goddess or woman, immediately that person became an object of love and desire. Her husband was, oddly enough, the lame god Vulcan. The myrtle and rose were sacred to her; her chariot was drawn by doves. Often she was represented with her son *Cupid* (Greek: *Eros*), who carried arrows of two sorts: some tipped with lead to produce hatred, some tipped with gold to incite love.

Minerva (Greek: *Pallas Athena)* was said by the Greeks to have sprung armed and full-grown from Jupiter's head. The legend may be an allegory explaining Minerva's realm, for she was the goddess of wisdom. She was the preserver, too, of states and governments. Rulers who displayed wisdom were particularly under her care. She was a patron of the fine arts, and was especially interested in weaving. She was usually represented as carrying a staff and wearing a breastplate called an *ægis*. On this ægis hung the head of a monster called the *Gorgon*, a woman with locks of snakes who had the power to freeze to stone those who gazed at her. Like Diana, Minerva watched over maidens.

Atlas, the Titan on whose shoulders Jove placed the burden of the heavens, had seven daughters called the *Pleiades*, who, according to Greek legend, were transported to the sky as stars. The eldest of them was named *Maia*, and to her and Jupiter was born a son *Mercury* (Greek: *Hermes*). He had a most curious mixture of qualities. His chief duty was to act as the messenger of the gods, and he was spoken of as "fleet-footed Mercury." Even as a child, however, he had a tendency towards thievishness, and was the patron of thieves and other rascals. As the messenger of the gods, he became the guardian of travelers; and as the herald of the gods, he became the god of oratory. He it was that conducted the shades of the dead to the underworld. All gymnasiums were under his control, and little heads of the god, called *herms*, were erected on posts alongside roads and at doors and gates. He was represented as a graceful youth. Among his symbols were a hat with small wings, that enabled him to go invisible; a staff (the *caduceus*) intertwined with snakes that was the sign of his authority; and winged sandals.

Minor Deities of Olympus

The Muses, who have already been mentioned, each presided over a distinct realm: *Clio*, over history; *Euterpe*, over lyric poetry; *Thalia*, over comedy; *Melpomene*, over tragedy; *Terpsichore*, over dancing; *Erato*, over love poetry; *Polyhymnia*, over religious poetry; *Urania*, over astronomy; and *Calliope*, over epic poetry. To them, called by the poet Pindar "the black-haired Nine," would pray poets and others who wished inspiration.

To the three *Fates* even Jupiter himself was obedient, for their decrees ruled both gods and men. They were represented as spinning at a great web, and in their hands were shears, with which they cut the thread of a life where they pleased. *Clotho* did the spinning, *Lachesis* assigned each one's fate, and *Atropos* moved the fatal shears.

On Mount Olympus likewise dwelt *Dike,* goddess of justice; the three *Graces,* the four *Seasons, Nemesis,* the spirit of just anger and punishment, and *Victoria* (Greek: *Nike),* goddess of victory.

The Greeks believed that in certain places and by certain means, the gods made their will known to mankind through *oracles.* The most famous of these oracles was located at Delphi, which was on the slope of Mount Parnassus. Here was located a temple of Apollo, and at the center of the temple was the oracle—a fissure in the earth, from which came volcanic vapors. A priestess or sibyl sat on a tripod over the fissure, and the words that she spoke after inhaling the vapor were regarded as the revelations of Apollo. Many great treasures—the gifts of those who had consulted the oracle—were to be found in this temple. Another oracle, sacred to Jupiter, was the grove of oaks at Dodona. Here questions might be asked of the ruler of gods and men, and the rustling of the leaves, as interpreted by the priests, would be his reply.

PRACTICAL APPLICATIONS

Myths in Literature

Due honor has been paid to the gods of high Olympus in our literature and our language, but some of these deities have, naturally, been greater favorites than others.

Undoubtedly more poems have been written about Apollo and Venus than about any other ancient god. The shining god of poetry and light, and the lovely goddess of beauty, have won constant allegiance throughout the history of literature. There is, for example, Shelley's *Hymn of Apollo,* in which the god himself speaks:

> **Then I arise, and climbing heaven's blue dome,**
> **I walk over the mountains and the waves;**
> **Leaving my robe upon the ocean foam;**

> My footsteps pave the clouds with fire; the caves
> Are filled with my bright presence, and the air
> Leaves the green earth to my embraces bare.

Others who have written about Apollo are Jonathan Swift and Keats. Poems in which Venus appears have been written by Chaucer, Shakespeare, and Swinburne. Her son Cupid is likewise a favorite of the bards.

Juno, prominent in Homer and Virgil, has not attracted modern poets, but her name occurs in a fine passage in Shakespeare, where it is coupled with that of Venus:

> Violets dim,
> But sweeter than the lids of Juno's eyes,
> Or Cytherea's breath.

Jupiter is the subject of few poems, but he is referred to many times, as are also Mars, Pallas Athena, the Muses, Vulcan, and other inhabitants of Olympus. A celebrated discussion in prose of Pallas Athena is Ruskin's *Queen of the Air.* The moon goddess Diana, on the other hand, has proved very attractive to many writers; for example, to Keats in *Endymion,* to Maurice Hewlett in *Artemision,* and to Ben Jonson in the *Hymn to Diana—*

> Queen and huntress, chaste and fair,
> Now the sun is laid to sleep,
> Seated in thy silver chair
> State in wonted manner keep:
> Hesperus entreats thy light,
> Goddess excellently bright.

If one leaves the realm of pure literature, one will still find many references to these gods. Newspaper articles and editorials make much use of these ancient gods. There are many references, for example, to something which is born in full strength or maturity, "like Minerva out of the head of Jove." In cartoons the figure of Mars may often be seen. In daily speech, too, we make constant use of the ancient gods, and we speak of some man as an Apollo and some woman as equal in beauty to Venus or one of the Graces;

or we remark playfully that so-and-so is a victim of Cupid. Science, likewise, makes use of the gods, particularly in naming the planets—Venus, Mercury, Mars, Jupiter, Neptune, and others. In advertising, the names of deities are employed both in naming products and in the text of advertisements. Painters delight to employ their imagination in representations of the gods and of scenes from the stories that deal with them, as the illustrations in this volume indicate; and many musical compositions go back to these mythical persons and stories for their inspiration.

Specific Literary References

In the passages that follow a selection has been made of references to the deities of Olympus. See if you can explain them.

What do the following references mean? Where a word or phrase is italicized, explain only the word or phrase.

References to the Major Gods
1. So saying, the goddess spread a table, loading it with *ambrosia* and mixing ruddy *nectar.—Homer*
2. And, just beyond, on light tiptoe divine, A quiver'd Dian.—*Keats*
3. *Jove* heard his vows, and better'd his desire.—*Keats*
4. Juno's proud birds are pecking pearly grain.—*Keats*
5. Turn to some level plain where haughty Mars Has legion'd all his battle.—*Keats*
6. Foot-feather'd Mercury appear'd.—*Keats*
7.   Her hovering feet, More bluely veined, more soft, more whitely sweet Than those of sea-born Venus, when she rose From out her cradle shell.—*Keats*
8. Jupiter himself cannot please all, whether sending rain or withholding it.—*Latin proverb*
9. Hence had the huntress Dian her dread bow Fair silver-shafted queen forever chaste, Wherewith she tam'd the brinded lioness And spotted mountin pard.—*Milton*
10. Wedding is great Juno's crown.—*Shakespeare*
11. Juno, within whose care are marriage bonds.—*Virgil*
12. In port and speech Olympian.—*Whittier*

References to Lesser Deities
  1. The matchless Ganymede, divinely fair.—*Homer*
  2. And joined with the nymphs the lovely Graces.
                    —*Horace*
  3.   Hebe bring
     A full-brimm'd goblet.—*Keats*
  4. As large, as bright, as color'd as the bow
     Of Iris.—*Keats*
  5. For when the Muse's wings are airward spread,
     Who shall delay her flight?—*Keats*
  6.   The Seasons four
     Join dance with shadowy Hours.—*Keats*
  7. Spin, spin, Clotho, spin!
     Lachesis, twist! and Atropos, sever!—*Lowell*
  8. The Graces and the rosy-bosomed Hours.—*Milton*
  9. I'll have nor worse a name than Jove's own page,
     And therefore look you call me Ganymede.
                    —*Shakespeare*
 10. O for a *Muse* of fire that would ascend
     The brightest heaven of invention!—*Shakespeare*
 11. Begin, O *Clio*, and recount from hence
     My glorious sovereign's goodly ancestry.—*Spenser*
 12. She dished out the potpie with *Olympian*
     impartiality.—*Wylie*

Suggestions for Oral or Written Composition

   1. Give a brief description of the geography of Greece.
Is the country mountainous? Are there many seaports?
Does the country naturally fall into sections, or is it unified?
What are the chief cities? Where is Mount Olympus
located? How high is it?
   2. Imagine yourself transported in a dream to Mount
Olympus. You wander to and fro and gaze in awe on the
palaces of the gods and on the gods themselves. Give an
account of what you behold.
   3. You are (let us suppose) writing a novel of ancient
Greek life. One of your characters writes a hymn in prose
to one of the high gods of Olympus, a deity to whom he or
she is particularly devoted. Introduce into this hymn some

of the god's qualities as mentioned in this chapter. Select for the subject of the hymn any god you please.

4. In this same supposed novel another character pays a visit to the oracle at Delphi. Find out as much as you can about this oracle, and then have your character write a letter to a friend, in which he or she tells what happened to him/her and what he/she saw.

5. Which of the gods of Olympus do you personally like best? Why does this deity attract you? Give an account of the god or goddess you select, including both the details in the text and any others you can find in an encyclopedia or other book of reference.

Word Study

1. How did the following words come to have their present meanings?

   martial—of a warlike disposition
   iris—of an appearance resembling the rainbow; a play of prismatic colors
   vulcanization—the application of heat to rubber or other substances
   museum—a collection of works of art or other objects of interest
   nemesis—a just or deserved fate
   nectar—a delicious or inspiring beverage
   Parnassians—a group of butterflies that inhabit, for the most part, mountain regions.

2. Look up the following names in a mythological dictionary and practice the correct pronunciation. (Check the index in this book also.)
   Iris, Hebe, Ganymede, Latona, Artemis, Dione, Aphrodite, Pleiades, Cleo, Nemesis.
3. The names of what three months are derived from persons mentioned in this chapter?
4. Explain the origin of the following words: *jovial, vestal, volcano, mercury, calliope.*
5. The name "kewpie" was once used for a certain

kind of doll. The name of what diety suggested the term?

6. Can you think of any other names used for advertising that are derived from persons mentioned in this chapter? Or can you find symbols used in advertisements that recall the old gods and goddesses?

Questions for Review

1. Where was Mount Olympus situated?
2. What children of Cronus dwelt there?
3. What was the realm of each?
4. What were the symbols of each?
5. Who were some children of Jupiter and Juno?
6. What were their realms and symbols?
7. Who were some other children of Jupiter?
8. What were their realms and symbols?
9. How many Muses were there?
10. Name one of them.
11. How great was the power of the three Fates?
12. Who were some other inhabitants of Mount Olympus?
13. What were oracles?
14. Where were two famous oracles situated?

Reading List

Poems and Plays

Arnold, Matthew: *Euphrosyne*
Blake, William: *To the Muses*
Doolittle, Hilda ("H.D."): *Hermes of the Ways*
Keats, John: *Ode to Maia*
Lowell, James Russell: *Hebe*
Schiller, Friedrich von: *The Gods of Greece*
Shelley, Percy Bysshe: Homer's *Hymn to Mercury*
Taylor, Bayard: *Masque of the Gods*
Tennyson, Alfred: *The Talking Oak*

Europa and the Bull—painting by Titian

3 Stories of Jupiter and Minerva

Jupiter is wheresoever you look,
wheresoever you move.

Lucan

Europa and Her Kin

Jupiter was the chief figure in one romantic episode, which brought in its train a number of important events and consequences.

Europa was a princess of Asia, the daughter of the king of Phœnicia. She shone preëminent among her attendant maidens as Venus did among the Graces. The son of Cronus beheld her, and he fell in love with her. He wooed Europa in the fashion of a bull, lovely and mighty to behold. He

36

came into the flowering meadow where Europa frolicked with her maidens, and when the rest fled, he cast his spell on the princess so that she was not afraid. She approached him and he lowed gently, and he bowed himself before her feet and showed her his broad back. Smiling she was tempted, and sat down upon the back of the bull. Scarcely was she seated, when he rose from the ground, moved towards the neighboring seashore, and leaped easily into the waves.

In vain she called to her companions, in vain she implored the seemingly gentle bull to return to dry land and permit her to escape. Over the sea, suddenly smooth before him, he swam with powerful strokes, and never a wavelet wet the hem of the maiden's garments. Around him frolicked the monsters of the sea, and bevies of sea nymphs rose from the waves and greeted him joyously.

"Whither do you bear me?" at last the maiden cried in awe; and the bull answered her in deep, immortal tones, bidding her to be courageous.

"Behold, I am Jupiter," he said, "and love of you has compelled me to wear this semblance. But Crete shall presently receive us and shall be our bridal chamber—Crete where I myself was born."

So he said, and so it was. It was from this Princess Europa that the whole continent received its name. Three sons were born to Europa—Minos, later king of Crete, Rhadamanthus, and Sarpedon. After their death the two former became judges of the shades in the underworld.

An interesting story is told of Minos while he was still a ruler of Crete. He had as one of his servants a man named Dædalus, who was a skilled mechanic and worker in metals and an ingenious inventor—the forefather, so to speak, of all inventors. It was Dædalus who devised for Minos a complicated series of tunnels and windings, called the *labyrinth,* in which was confined the Minotaur, a monster half man, half bull.

Later Dædalus lost the favor of Minos, who imprisoned him and his son, Icarus. But Dædalus set his mind on finding a way to escape. Finally he devised a pair of wings for himself and a pair for Icarus. He fastened them to his own shoulders and to those of the boy, using wax as the binding material. Then both triumphantly flew away. Swiftly they skimmed through the air, and closer and closer they came to the mainland. But Icarus, flushed with excitement and exhilaration, soared even higher towards the sun—despite the cries and warnings of his father. At last he flew so high that the heat of the sun melted the wax, and off dropped the wings. The lad plunged downwards into the sea and was drowned. The sea into which he fell was later called the Icarian Sea. Dædalus escaped without harm.

When Europa was carried off by the bull, her father commanded her brother Cadmus to go in search of her and not to return until he had found her. But Cadmus sought for months and years in vain. Then an oracle of Apollo told him to follow a certain cow wherever she wandered, and to build a city at the point where the cow finally rested. Cadmus obeyed, and at last on the plain of Panope the cow stood still. Cadmus, wishing to offer a libation to his patron goddess Minerva, looked nearby for water. Soon he came to a spring from which gushed a crystal-pure stream. But a dragon guarded the fountain, and no sooner had Cadmus's servants dipped their pitchers into the water than the dragon darted upon them, killed some with its fangs, and crushed others in its folds.

Then Cadmus himself gave battle to the dragon and finally slew it, not knowing that it was sacred to Mars. The god of war was angry and Cadmus was obliged to serve him for eight years. From the dragon's teeth, sown over the ground by the command of Minerva, sprang armed men, who became subjects of Cadmus. He built the city of Thebes, and to him was ascribed the introduction of the alphabet. He and his wife Harmonia were eventually changed into serpents. He never saw Europa again.

Œdipus

The descendants of Cadmus continued to suffer from the hatred of Mars, even though he had forgiven Cadmus for slaying his dragon. But of all these

What moment in the life of Oedipus and Jocasta does this portray?

descendants the greatest misfortunes afflicted Œdipus.

An oracle warned Laius, king of Thebes, on the birth of a son, that the infant, if allowed to grow up, would endanger both his throne and his life. So Laius ordered a herdsman to kill the child. But the herdsman, in pity, merely pierced the infant's feet and left him on a mountain. There another herdsman found the child and took him to King Polybus of Corinth. The king adopted the child as his son and called him Œdipus, or Swollen-Foot.

When Œdipus became older, he too consulted an oracle and learned, to his horror, that he was destined to kill his father, whom he thought was Polybus. To avoid the decree of the gods he hastily left Corinth, and in a chariot with a single servant, set off to wander through Greece. Once, on a narrow road, he met a man in another chariot who haughtily ordered him to give way. When Œdipus refused, an attendant leaped out of the other chariot, and killed one of Œdipus' horses. Then Œdipus, in great anger, slew the man in the chariot. It was Laius, and unwittingly Œdipus had killed his father.

When Œdipus came to Thebes itself, he found the city in deep distress. A monster called the Sphinx, half lion and half woman, stopped all travelers and asked them a riddle. If they could not give the right answer, the Sphinx killed them. But Œdipus fearlessly approached the Sphinx. "What creature is it," the Sphinx asked, "that in the morning goes on four feet, at noon on two, and at night on three?" "Man," replied Œdipus, "who creeps on hands and feet in childhood, stands erect on two feet when full grown, and in old age needs the help of a crutch." The Sphinx, chagrined, threw herself off a cliff and was killed.

In gratitude the Thebans had Œdipus marry their queen Jocasta, widow of Laius. Only when a plague afflicted the city did Œdipus and Jocasta learn through an oracle of the crimes he had committed. In horror Jocasta committed suicide and Œdipus blinded himself. For many months Œdipus, accompanied by his faithful daughter Antigone, went begging through Greece. At last the gods released him from life.

Callisto and Her Son

In Arcadia lived a beautiful maiden named Callisto with whom Jupiter fell in love. She bore to him a son named Arcas. When Juno saw how happy Callisto was in the love of Jove and in the growing handsomeness of her boy, she felt bitterly jealous. At last her anger and envy went beyond all bounds, and she changed Callisto into a bear.

Disconsolately Callisto roamed through the woods of Arcadia in her new and awkward form. She dared not mingle with the other bears, for her fear of them was as great as when she had been a human being; and yet she fled from the hunters, since naturally they would pursue her at sight and slay her if they could.

One day, however, she caught a glimpse in the distance of her own son Arcas, grown now to splendid manhood. Her love and yearning overcame her, and approaching him with clumsy gait, she stood on her hind legs and sought to embrace him. But he drew back in mingled wonderment and alarm. As the bear persisted in following him, he raised up his spear and was about to kill the strange but terrifying animal. As the spearpoint was about to enter Callisto's breast, however, Jupiter, looking down from the heavens, saw what was happening and in pity stayed the spear of Arcas. Then he snatched both of them from the earth and placed them as constellations in the heavens. One is the group of stars that we call the Great Bear, Callisto; and nearby is the Little Bear, her son Arcas.

It is said, in ancient legends, that Juno complained bitterly to the gods of the sea at the way Jupiter had treated her rival and her rival's son; and these gods granted to her as a special favor that the Great Bear and the Little Bear should never come into their waters. Hence it is that these constellations constantly circle the pole, but do not sink into the ocean, as do the other stars.

Baucis and Philemon

Sometimes Jupiter, although first of all a god of the wide heavens and usually thought of as abiding always in his wonderful palace on Mount Olympus, visited the earth and mingled with its inhabitants in human guise. His purpose in such visits was to discover whether men truly observed the dictates of hospitality, for not only was Jupiter the Thunderer and the king of gods and men; he was also the god of hospitality, and those who were cruel or unkind to strangers incurred his wrath.

Once Jupiter, disguised as a humble traveler and accompanied only by Mercury, visited the land of Phrygia. They sought shelter for the night at one house after another, but everywhere they were driven away with harsh words and contemptuous remarks.

Darkness had long since fallen, and the two immortals were on the point of giving up their quest in despair, when they came to the house of an aged couple named Baucis and Philemon. It was a lowly cottage, thatched with straw and with reeds from a nearby marsh, but here Baucis and her husband had dwelt together since they were wedded, and they had always been contented.

When Baucis and Philemon heard the knocking at their door they quickly opened it and bade the strangers welcome. Gladly they granted the request of the two travelers that they be allowed to remain for the night. They hurried around the humble home, gathered sticks to replenish the fire, brought forth such homely fare as they possessed, and prepared it for the strangers.

As the strangers stretched forth their hands for the food, a strange thing happened. There came suddenly to be more of it, and it gave out a wonderful fragrance. Then, suddenly, the gods revealed themselves in all their splendor, and the aged couple fell on their knees and begged forgiveness for the wretched food they had laid before them. Jupiter, however, bade Baucis and Philemon arise, and he led them to the summit of a neighboring hill. When they looked back at the valley in which they had lived, the old people saw to their astonishment that it was now a great lake. Even as they wept at the fate of their neighbors, another miracle happened—a great temple rose beside them out of the ground. Jupiter entrusted the care of this temple to them. Baucis and Philemon died many years later at a ripe old age. Their deaths came at the same time and Jupiter transformed them into trees, an oak and a linden, which the peasants worshiped as symbols of the duties of hospitality.

Two Contests of Minerva

Pallas Athena (called by the Romans Minerva) once engaged in a contest with Neptune to determine which should have the honor of naming a newly founded city in Attica. Each was so eager to win this honor that a bitter quarrel seemed likely. To avert it, the gods decided that each deity must produce a gift for the benefit of mankind, and the one that produced the more useful gift

The transformation of Arachne

would have the honor of naming the new city.

Neptune struck the earth with his trident and from it sprang a beautiful horse, struggling with its hind legs to throw off the encumbering earth. As it stood before the gods tossing its proud head and pawing the ground with its hoofs, the gods exclaimed in wonder. Then Pallas Athena struck the earth with her spear, and hardly had the point of

Statue of Athena from the front of the ancient temple of Athena on the
Acropolis—Athens, Greece

the spear left the ground when up from the soil sprang a
noble tree, laden with glossy black fruit, the olive. The
gods, gazing into the future, saw how many uses the tree
and its produce would have for mankind. With one accord
they acclaimed Athena victor, and the city was named
Athens.

On another occasion Athena contested for honors with
a mortal. This mortal was Arachne. Her father was Idmon,
skilled in the art of dyeing in purple, and from infancy the
girl had been taught her father's art, joined with that of
weaving. In all the land there was none that surpassed her.
So conceited did she become that, lifting her head proudly
to the skies, she challenged Athena herself, patron of the
arts of the household, to compete with her.

Pallas Athena had watched the progress that Arachne was making, and when she heard the presumptuous challenge, she assumed the guise of an old woman and came to the spindle at which Arachne was weaving.

"I am," she said, "a woman old in experience, and I have seen much in this wide world. To me has come the knowledge of your challenge to Athena. Let me counsel you to withdraw your words. You surpass and shall surpass all other mortals, but how vain and foolish it is to contend with the immortal gods, from whom comes all skill!"

"Be silent, foolish old woman," replied Arachne scornfully. "I fear not Athena, but shall put her to shame with my skill. Let her appear and put me to the test."

Even as she spoke, Athena threw off her disguise and in solemn majesty stood before the girl.

"Athena is here," she said; and at her words Arachne trembled and realized too late how insane had been her challenge. But she summoned up her courage and began to weave her most skillful web in which she pictured some of the love affairs of the gods. She wove the web in all colors, but mostly in the royal purple of which her father was the master. At last her work was complete.

Then Athena began to weave, and she depicted wondrous scenes in high Olympus, and from her very web floated forth divine fragrance of nectar and ambrosia. An unearthly beauty hovered over the design. In the corner Athena pictured the fate that had come to mortals who had defied the gods, and as she went from one to the other Arachne began to feel doom stealing closer and closer. As the last corner was completed, Athena turned to her, touched her with her magic spindle, and said:

"Punished shall you be for your presumption, but the gods will not let die such skill as you have shown. Change to an insect, that other mortals may take warning from you, but ever weave a web of marvelous design."

At the words of Athena, Arachne began to shrink and shrivel. Shortly she was completely transformed. Where a girl had stood an insect crawled—the spider; and before the eyes of the terrified beholders it scuttled off to a corner and immediately began weaving a web of shimmering threads. So to this day the Greeks call the spider "arachne."

PRACTICAL APPLICATIONS

Myths in Literature

Of all the stories related in this chapter, the most profound effect has been made by that of Œdipus. Both the ancients and the moderns have found in it a powerful illustration of the doctrine that it is impossible to escape one's fate, and that to run away from a dreaded event often helps to bring it on. The greatest of ancient dramatists, Sophocles, followed the strange fortunes of Œdipus in three plays, all of which have fortunately come down to us. The Sphinx who appears in the story has become identified with the mysterious object in the Egyptian desert, although archæologists now believe that the latter is intended as an allegorical portrait of an Egyptian king.

Europa may have been an actual princess carried off by ancient Hellenes or Greeks to their own land; and a long tradition which ascribes the introduction of the alphabet into Greece by the Phœnician Cadmus may be based on fact. Byron refers to this tradition when, in a poem addressed to the Greek still enslaved by the Turk, he exclaims:

> You have the letters Cadmus gave—
> Think you he meant them for a slave?

Europa's abduction has been treated by Walter Savage Landor, Edward Dowden, and other poets. Tennyson, in *The Palace of Art*, paints a series of pictures, among which is one of the Phœnician princess:

> Or sweet Europa's mantle blew unclasp'd—
> From off her shoulder backward borne:
> From one hand droop'd a crocus; one hand grasp'd
> The mild bull's golden horn.

46

Swift has taken the tale of Baucis and Philemon, transposed it to modern times, and furnished it with modern details, in a poem which burlesques the old story. References to the contest between Arachne and Minerva and between the latter and Neptune have been made by poets, who have not, however, been inspired to any long flights of fancy on these subjects.

Specific Literary References

What do the following references mean? Where a word or phrase is italicized, explain only the word or phrase.

1. And there, they say, two bright and aged snakes,
   Who once were Cadmus and Harmonia,
   Bask in the glens or on the warm seashore.—*Arnold*
2. Fear is the fire that melts *Icarian* wings.—*Coates*
3. Your *Icarian* flight melts into a groveling existence.—*Disraeli*
4. And angry Juno's unrelenting hate.—*Dryden*
5. Cadmus by sowing dragon's teeth, we read,
   Raised a vast army from the poisonous seed.—*Gay*
6. For in the charge of Zeus all strangers and beggars stand.—*Homer.*
7.   By this gloom,
   And by old *Rhadamanthus'* tongue of doom.—*Keats*
8.   Heeding Zeus,
   Who holds the guest-right sacred.—*Ledoux*
9. Next she placed on the board some olives, green and ripe, truthful Minerva's berries.—*Ovid.*
10. Play unto this riddle the Œdipus.—*Poe*

Suggestions for Oral or Written Composition

1. The princess Europa relates her adventures to a nymph who becomes her companion on Crete. What would she tell her?

2. Prepare a talk on "Ancient Inventions." What were some early tools? How old is the wheel? How was time measured at the beginning? Who first, like Dædalus, attempted to fly?

3. Put the story of Baucis and Philemon into the form of a brief drama. Only two scenes will be necessary: one in the homely cottage, in which the travelers relate their experiences; and one on the summit of the hill.

4. When Neptune produced the horse, and Pallas Athena produced the olive, each addressed the assembly of citizens and predicted to them the future of the horse and of the tree, praising the value of the gifts. What might each of them have said? Have two sections in your sketch: the first, Neptune's speech, the second, Athena's speech. At the close the assemblage hails Athena and cries out, "Name the city Athens!"

Word Study

1. Explain the origin of the following geographical and astronomical terms:

   Europe—one of the continents
   Icarian Sea—part of the Ægean Sea
   Europa—a satellite of the planet Jupiter
   The Great and the Little Bear—also called the Big and Little Dipper
   Athens—the capital of Greece

2. Look up the following words in a mythological dictionary and practice the correct pronunciation. (Check the index in this book also.)
   Europa, Phœnicia, Minos, Dædalus, Icarus, Callisto, Baucis, Philemon, Arachne, Œdipus.
3. Explain the origin of the following words: *labyrinth* and the Greek word for "spider." Why is a library or a learned society sometimes called an "Athenæum"?
4. Repeat the "riddle of the Sphinx."

Questions for Review

1. In what part of the world was the father of Europa a ruler?

48

2. In what guise did Jupiter carry off this princess?
3. To what land did he carry her?
4. Which one of her sons later ruled this land?
5. Which two became judges in the underworld?
6. Who was the forefather of inventors?
7. What was the *labyrinth*?
8. What other device did this inventor prepare?
9. How was it used?
10. What command did the father of Europa lay upon her brother? How did he carry it out?
11. How did he offend Mars?
12. What service to Greece is credited to this brother?
13. What finally became of him and his wife?
14. What oracles did the father of Œdipus and Œdipus himself seek to evade? What were the consequences?
15. What was the riddle of the Sphinx?
16. What caused Juno to become the enemy of Callisto?
17. What fate did she visit on her?
18. What became of Callisto and her son?
19. How did Jupiter test the hospitality of the inhabitants of Phrygia?
20. What couple was successful in the test?
21. What was their reward?
22. In what two contests did Minerva engage?
23. Who was her opponent in each instance?

Reading List

Poems and Plays

Arnold, Matthew: Fragment of an *Antigone*
De Vere, Aubrey: *The Rape of Europa*
Emerson, Ralph Waldo: *The Sphinx*
Garrick, David: *Upon a Lady's Embroidery*
Landor, Walter Savage: *Europa and Her Mother*
Sophocles: *Œdipus the King*
Sophocles: *Œdipus Coloneus*
Sophocles: *Antigone*
Taylor, Bayard: *Icarus*

Venus lamenting the death of Adonis—painting by Benjamin West

4 Stories of Venus

Creator Venus, genial power of love,
The bliss of men below and gods above!
Dryden

Venus and Adonis[1]

Venus had, of course, many love affairs, but the most famous of them is that which took place between her and Adonis. Adonis was a youth of a country in Asia Minor. He was so handsome that even today we call a man of exceptional attractiveness an "Adonis." One day Venus was idly toying with the arrows of her son Cupid and accidentally scratched herself with one

[1]In some versions of this story Venus is given the name of the Assyrian goddess of love—*Astarte* or *Ishtar*.

of them. Before the wound was healed and the dangerous venom out of her veins, she beheld Adonis and immediately fell deeply in love with him.

Then she neglected all her ordinary pursuits and was seen no more in the haunts that she usually visited. Her only joy was to be with Adonis and to accompany him wherever he went. Adonis, despite his beauty, was of a very manly character, and loved hunting above all things. With him, then, in his pursuit of dangerous game of all kinds went Venus, and daily they roamed the woods together. No longer did Venus adorn herself with all her charms, nor did she spend, as she used to, hours in heightening her attractions. Rather she went roughly clad, bearing a bow and quiver like the huntress goddess, Diana. She, too, learned to follow and kill the deer, but she left to Adonis the slaying of wolves and bears, panthers and boars.

Yet Venus warned Adonis and urged him not to be too bold. She feared that sooner or later some ferocious beast would turn against him and harm him. So indeed it happened. For one day Venus left Adonis and flew to Olympus in her chariot drawn by doves. Her last word to Adonis was a caution. But Adonis would not heed any counsel to cultivate cowardice. He was always first in the chase, the first to come up to the animal to be killed; and he scorned the idea of letting others bear the brunt of the danger. On this day a wild boar, huge and ferocious, had been roused by the dogs and had fled before them. With eagerness in his heart, and spear ready for the thrust, Adonis rushed forward. He managed to wound the animal, but the spearpoint went in only a little way, and then the beast rushed headlong at Adonis. He buried his tusks savagely in the sides of the fair youth, who fell dying upon the plain.

Long and bitterly did Venus lament for Adonis, and yearly the inhabitants of that region renewed her mourning for him in a sacred festival. It was said, from his blood sprang the anemone, and it was said, too, that Jupiter, in pity for his daughter, allowed Adonis to ascend from the lower world for six months of every year to dwell with Venus as her husband. During these six months summer dwells on the earth.

What moment in Psyche's life is the sculptor trying to capture?

Cupid and Psyche

One of the most beautiful of ancient stories was told by a Latin writer named Apuleius. There was once a king, he told, who had three daughters, of whom the youngest, Psyche, (which in the Greek means either "soul" or "butterfly"), was the most beautiful. So fair was she that when she walked in the streets, people strewed flowers before her, and so much admiration was paid her that even the altars of Venus were neglected.

The goddess of love was enraged when she saw how Psyche had supplanted her in the affections of the people, and she resolved to punish the maiden whose beauty was so presumptuous. She therefore called her son Cupid and made him prepare the means of her revenge. He was ordered to go to Psyche with certain waters from a fountain in the garden of Venus and inspire her by them with love for a low and mean person. Cupid flew away on his mission, but when he beheld Psyche lying in lovely sleep he almost repented of his mission. Yet he performed his errand. As he bent over her, he accidentally wounded himself with one of his own arrows. Paying no attention to his own hurt, he sought to counteract the effect of the magical waters. From another vial he poured over her a sweet, medicinal draft and flew away.

From that time forth Psyche, despite her beauty, won no favor. Her two sisters were married to powerful princes, but no one came to sue for the hand of Psyche. At last her parents consulted an oracle, which told them that they must send Psyche to the top of a mountain, where in a house appointed for her, a monster, of immortal birth, awaited her as a husband. With lamentations and tears they dressed Psyche as a bride and took her to a lonely cliff whereon stood a mean house. There they abandoned her to her fate.

But suddenly the west wind, Zephyrus, lifted Psyche gently up, and bore her to a fragrant valley, and there, in the midst of flowers, stood a noble palace, its roof supported by pillars of pure gold. Psyche in amazement entered the palace, and at every step new wonders met her eye. As she paced through the high halls a voice of a maiden met her ear, and she learned that she had at her service many invisible servants, ready to do whatever she commanded. A delicious meal was prepared for her, and, as she ate, sweet strains of music fell upon her ears. When she retired it was to a chamber gorgeously decorated with many scenes from the adventures of the gods, and still in deep wonder, she fell asleep.

At midnight a melodious voice awakened her.

"I am your husband," it said. "This house and all that is in it are yours, but on one condition—that you must never attempt to see my face."

So only at night were Psyche and her husband united, and although she heard his voice, never did she catch a glimpse of his face.

For a long time Psyche was very happy, but as the months rolled by she was filled with a desire to see her parents and sisters again. Her desire made her pine away, and at last her husband realized that something was amiss. He questioned her, and reluctantly then she told him how much she longed to visit her home again, if only for a little while. For a time her husband was silent, but at length he agreed to let her go for a short time.

Venus was warned that her son Cupid would remain a child until he had a brother. With the birth of her second son, Anteros, Cupid grew into manhood.

"But do not let them persuade you," he warned her, "into asking to see my face."

Joyfully Psyche prepared for her journey, bearing with her many beautiful gifts. Once more Zephyrus bore her gently along, and carried her again to the cliff on which her parents had left her. She made her way quickly down the mountain and shortly reached the palace. In amazement her parents welcomed her, and they rejoiced that their daughter was still alive. Her sisters, too, were glad to see her. She told them that her husband visited her at night, and that she had never seen his face. She described to them the marvelous palace in which she lived, and recounted to them the unending service which the invisible nymphs of the palace gave her.

As she spoke her sisters were filled with jealousy. They cast suspicion upon Psyche's story, and tried to persuade her that she was indeed married to a monster. They advised her that she must provide herself with a lamp to enable her to see what her husband was really like and with a knife to slay him if he turned out to be a monster.

Psyche at first refused to credit their suspicions, but finally they had their effect upon her, and she made up her mind to do as they counseled. When she went back to the palace she bore with her a lamp and a knife. Her husband returned as usual to the palace. When she knew that he was plunged in slumber, Psyche silently lit the lamp and bent over him. To her wonder and joy she saw before her a most beautiful youth, and immediately her love for him was as great as his for her. But before she could withdraw the lamp, a drop of oil from the vessel fell upon his shoulder and awakened the sleeping god. Cupid saw immediately what had happened, and without a word spread his white wings and flew away.

When Psyche knew that Cupid had left her, she was filled with despair and reproached herself so much for her base suspicions that she cast herself into a river and wished to die. But the river god refused to slay anything so beautiful and cast her up on the shore. Then for a long time Psyche wandered disconsolate over the earth, and took no heed how rough the ways were or how ill she fared. At last she came to a temple of Venus, and resolved to enter the service of the goddess. Venus knew that her son had married Psyche, but she was still filled with anger against the girl. Through the mouth of the priestess she told her that if she wished to deserve love, certain hard tasks would have to be performed by her. (She believed that Psyche would never perform these tasks.) But Psyche accepted the hope eagerly and asked what it was she had to do.

Then Venus gave her the first of the tasks. In an enormous storehouse of the temple lay heaped together seeds of all kinds which were used as food for the guardians of the temple and for the doves of Venus.

"Separate these each in a heap by itself," ordered Venus. "The task must be accomplished by nightfall."

Psyche could not have finished this task in ten days, let alone by nightfall. But Cupid, who still secretly watched over her, stirred up the ants to do the work. The whole nation of them labored eagerly together, and by nightfall each kind of seed was in a heap by itself.

When Venus returned and saw that Psyche had carried out her first command, she was indignant, for she knew that the girl could not have accomplished it by herself. Then she set the second task:

"Gather me from the golden-shining sheep in yonder field three tufts of their wool."

Psyche set out for the field, walking slowly along the side of a river. There the reeds whispered to her and bade her wait, for the sheep were very fierce.

"Wait," they urged, "until midday has passed, and then look at the bushes."

She obeyed this counsel, and in the afternoon found tufts of golden wool hanging upon the bushes against which the sheep had rubbed in passing. Joyfully she returned with these to Venus.

Grimly the next morning Venus assigned the third task.

"Go to Proserpina, the queen of Hades," she bade the girl, "and bring me a box of the ointment wherewith she preserves her divine beauty."

Terrible was this task, but she accomplished it, entering the underworld through a cave, prevailing on Charon to ferry her across the Styx, and convincing Proserpina out of pity to give her the precious ointment. But on the way back Psyche could not resist opening the box. Immediately she fell to the ground in a deadly sleep. Then Cupid could no longer resist flying to her aid. He awakened her from her insensibility and begged the king of heaven to favor his cause. Jove interceded with Venus and persuaded her to accept the girl as Cupid's wife. Mercury then conveyed Psyche to Olympus, and there the girl ate of the divine ambrosia and became immortal. To Love and Soul was born in time a daughter, and her name was Pleasure.

How many lives were touched by the God Mercury?

Atalanta and Hippomenes

A contest of another kind was that of Atalanta, a maiden of Bœotia. While she was still a child, it was prophesied of her that her marriage would be fatal to her. So she made up her mind never to marry. She avoided all communication with men and lived in the woods as a worshiper of Diana, devoted to hunting and other woodland sports. Yet because she was so beautiful and because outdoor life had given her such health and vigor, many men approached her as suitors. They troubled her constantly and would not be denied.

At last Atalanta hit upon a stratagem. She called her suitors together and announced that she would become the bride of the one who could conquer her in a foot race. On those who failed, however, would be imposed the penalty of death. For a time there was silence among the suitors, but then a number of them announced their readiness to engage in the contest. All of them failed, for never was there maiden who ran with such swiftness as Atalanta, and no man could approach her in speed. Upon all those who failed was imposed the cruel penalty.

In one race in which she engaged, a certain youth, Hippomenes, acted as a judge. He had spoken with scorn of those foolish enough to engage in the contest, and had boasted that no maiden was so beautiful or desirable as to be worth the hazard of death.

Yet when he saw the graceful form of Atalanta skimming over the ground as lightly as a bird and when he gazed upon her face as lovely as that of a goddess, he changed his mind, and was as eager as the rest to win her.

She came forward flushed with the contest, and Hippomenes eagerly approached her and challenged her to another race on the morrow.

"These are only laggards," he exclaimed. "It shall be another story with me who am of the divine lineage of Neptune."

Atalanta looked at him and was sorry, for of all the youths who had contended with her none pleased her better than Hippomenes, and she felt a pang in her heart

Atalanta—"Never was there a maiden who could run with such swiftness."

that he must suffer death. But Hippomenes forthwith sought the aid of the goddess most likely to help him. He prayed to Venus, and bade her consider how a victory of Atalanta would be contrary to her rule of love. Venus heard him, and listened to his prayer. Going to the Garden of the Hesperides, far to the west of the world, she gathered three of the wonderful apples that grew on the great tree in the center of the garden, and gave them to Hippomenes with instructions how to act.

The next day the race took place before a great concourse of people. Both contestants flashed from the starting place like arrows from a bow, but shortly, despite his best efforts, Hippomenes saw the girl take the lead. Then from his hand he whirled directly into the path of Atalanta one of the golden apples. Its beauty dazzled her eyes, and without realizing what she was doing she stooped and snatched it from the ground. As she did so, Hippomenes overtook and passed her. But again she hastened and passed him, and again a golden apple fluttered into her path. Again she paused to pick it up and once more gave Hippomenes the advantage. But her speed was so great that even these handicaps were not enough for Hippomenes, and in a few moments she led the way again. Now the end of the course was near, and in desperation Hippomenes threw forward the last of the golden apples. It rolled to the side of the track, and Atalanta hesitated, deciding whether or not to stop to pick it up. But the wonder of the apple was so great that she turned aside and stooped and lifted it from the ground. As she did so, a great shout thundered in the air. Hippomenes had won.

Atalanta was not altogether sorry to become the wife of Hippomenes, but her doom was yet to be fulfilled. Both lovers failed to give due gratitude to Venus, from whom the victory of Hippomenes had come. Angered at their forgetfulness, the goddess changed them to beasts—Hippomenes to a lion, Atalanta to a lioness, and harnessed them to the chariot of Rhea (also called Cybele).

Pygmalion and Galatea

Once there lived a king of the island of Cyprus named Pygmalion, who was not only a wise ruler but also an excellent sculptor. He had, however, one peculiarity: he distrusted women, and announced that he intended forever to remain unmarried.

At one time Pygmalion was working on a statue of ivory, in the semblance of a maiden. Day by day he worked, and ever the statue became more beautiful. Pygmalion wove all his dreams and expressed his sincerest ideals in it. He was himself delighted with the statue, and when nightfall came he continued to give it little touches here and there to add to the beauty, until his eyes ached and deep darkness lay over his studio. He called the statue Galatea.

"My Fair Lady" is a variation of "Pygmalion and Galatea."

At last the statue was completed, and then, to his own surprise, Pygmalion found that he could not rest in quiet away from his masterpiece. Sooner or later he found his way back to the fine chamber in which he had placed it, and constantly his eyes gazed in delight at his work. Only one day did he awake to a realization of the truth—he was in love with the statue.

Not long afterwards a festival of Venus was celebrated in Cyprus. Standing solemnly before the altar of the goddess, Pygmalion addressed her, reminded her of his respect and devotion to her temple, and begged a great favor; namely, that his statue might take flesh and live.

When he returned home that night Pygmalion went with slow steps to the room where the statue stood. To his amazement a garland of fragrant flowers hung around her neck, and he knew that this was a favorable sign, for none was allowed to enter the room except himself. As he stood there in wonder, he saw how a delicate flush of red began to run over the marble whiteness of the statue. Then came a tender pulsing on the forehead and at the wrists, then a slow moving of the knees and of the head. Hesitatingly, Pygmalion moved forward and touched Galatea's hand, and as he did so, her fingers were clasped around his. Slowly her foot moved forward, and she stepped from the pedestal.

"Galatea!" cried Pygmalion, as she moved smilingly to his embrace.

Venus blessed the wedding of Pygmalion and Galatea. From their union was born Paphus, who founded a city sacred to the goddess of love.

Hero and Leander

On the Hellespont, almost directly opposite each other, lived a youth named Leander, whose home was in Abydos, and a maiden named Hero, who dwelt at Sestos. Hero's beauty was such that it was said that both Apollo and Cupid sued for her hand, but in vain.

Now Hero served Venus as a priestess, and one day it happened that Leander came to Sestos to do honor to the goddess. There he beheld Hero, and she at the same moment saw him, and both fell in love at first sight. But Hero's parents would not listen to the suit of Leander, and they even forbade the young people to see each other.

Not so easily were they thwarted, however. They managed to arrange a code of signals, and whenever at night Hero hung a lantern upon the tower of the temple, Leander would swim the Hellespont and join her for a brief hour or two. But one night a storm arose after Leander had set out on his dangerous journey. Shortly the winds blew out the guiding lantern, and Leander instead of swimming to safety directed his course toward a treacherous patch of sea. In vain he struggled; the storm was too much for him, and he perished. Next morning the waves washed his body ashore at the very feet of Hero, who was anxiously looking out to sea, dreading lest harm might have overtaken him. In deep grief she threw herself into the ocean and was drowned.

Is there a parallel between "Pyramus and Thisbe" and "Romeo and Juliet"?

Pyramus and Thisbe

In Babylon lived Pyramus, a youth noted for his handsome appearance, and Thisbe, often regarded as the most beautiful maiden in all the city, in those days when Queen Semiramis reigned. They lived in adjoining houses, and as childhood passed into youth, their friendship deepened into love.

But their parents objected to their marriage. All communication between them was forbidden, and they were able to converse only by signs and glances. One day, however, they discovered a crack in the wall that separated their houses, and through this crack they were able, at times, to whisper their undying devotion.

At length they could endure separation no longer, and they arranged to meet, one evening at dusk, under a white mulberry tree that stood just outside the city walls. Thisbe

"West Side Story" is a more modern version of "Pyramus and Thisbe."

arrived first at the place agreed upon, but as she
approached she saw a terrifying lioness before her. She
screamed and fled in haste, dropping her veil as she ran.
The beast made no attempt to pursue Thisbe, but picked up
the veil in her blood-streaked mouth and then dropped it.
Not long afterward she turned away to the nearby woods.

At this very moment Pyramus came to the rendezvous.
He saw the veil on the ground, and marked the spots of
blood upon it; deadly fear seized him.

"Thisbe has been slain!" he exclaimed. "But she does
not die alone!" With these words he plunged his sword
into his side. As he lay dying upon the ground, Thisbe came
back. She had conquered her dread, and wished to warn
Pyramus of the danger that awaited him. But she was too
late, and when she saw what had happened, she too sought
an escape from a life that no longer held any joy for her.
The same sword that had slain her lover was the means of
her death. The commingled blood from the youth and
maiden mounted up the trunk of the mulberry tree and
stained its fruit a deep purple. So it has remained ever
since, in memory of the hapless lovers.

PRACTICAL APPLICATIONS

Myths in Literature

The love stories narrated in this chapter have offered an inexhaustible mine of material to poets and writers.

Naturally Cupid has been a favorite subject. Every good poet apparently considers it a duty to write at least one poem about the little god of love. Many poets have endeavored, moreover, to retell what has been called "the last great myth"—that of Cupid and Psyche, originally told by the Latin writer Apuleius, in his novel, *The Golden Ass*. The best English version of this story is to be found in Walter Pater's *Marius the Epicurean*.

Musæus wrote about Hero and Leander in ancient times, and his poem was ably rendered into English by two contemporaries of Shakespeare—Marlowe and Chapman. The story of Pygmalion has been told excellently by William Morris (teller of so many ancient tales), and made into an effective play by William S. Gilbert; Morris wrote, too, on Atalanta's race. Shakespeare wrote a long, languorous poem on *Venus and Adonis,* and there are many other references to this love story in English poetry. Shakespeare also made use of the story of Pyramus and Thisbe, in an amusing burlesque form, in *A Midsummer Night's Dream*. Thisbe laments:

> Asleep, my love?
> What, dead, my dove?
> O Pyramus, arise!
> Speak, speak! Quite dumb?
> Dead, dead? A tomb
> Must cover thy sweet eyes.
> Those lily lips,
> This cherry nose,

These yellow cowslip cheeks,
Are gone, are gone!
Lovers, make moan.
His eyes were green as leeks.

Specific Literary References

What do the following references mean? Where a word or phrase is italicized, explain only the word or phrase.

1. Woe, woe for *Adonis*, he hath perished, the lovely Adonis!—*Bion*
2. I found the *god of love*, his bow and arrows cast aside.—*Gosse*
3. From his hand now dropt
A golden apple.—*Landor*
4. O Aphrodite, kind and fair,
That what thou wilt canst give,
O listen to a sculptor's prayer,
And bid mine image live!—*Lang*
5. Sinking bewilder'd 'mid the dreary sea:
'Tis young Leander toiling to his death.—*Keats*
6. At Sestos *Hero* dwelt, Hero the fair,
Whom young Apollo courted for her hair.
　　　　　—*Marlowe*
7. 　　　　　With these in troop
Came Astoreth, whom the Phœnicians called
Astarte, Queen of Heav'n, with crescent horn.
　　　　　—*Milton*
8. 　　　　　Set at naught
The frivolous bolt of *Cupid*.—*Milton*
9. And let fair Venus, that is queen of love,
With her *heart-quelling son* upon you smile.
　　　　　—*Spenser*
10. A hoarse voice spoke through the letter-box
"Has he gone, laddie?"
I put my mouth to the slit, and we talked together
like *Pyramus and Thisbe*.—*Wodehouse*
11. Rose-cheek'd *Adonis* hied him to the chase.
　　　　　—*Shakespeare*

Suggestions for Oral or Written Composition

1. Write a supposed dialogue between Venus and Adonis. Venus, just before she sets out for a visit to Mount Olympus, warns Adonis against being too reckless and bold in the chase. Adonis replies.

2. When Cupid awakens and sees that Psyche has disregarded his warning, he prepares to fly away. But Psyche holds him back by the hand and tries to apologize and explain. Naturally she would speak in broken phrases and before she can say very much, Cupid disengages her hand and leaves her—without a word. Describe the scene and plea of Psyche.

3. Can you think of any other stories in which someone is set a task that no one, apparently, can fulfill? Remember, for example, some of the fairy stories you have read. Retell one of these stories.

4. Which of the stories in this chapter would be best suited to a motion-picture production? Describe the way the story would be given in motion-picture form.

5. With the help of several other students, give to your class a presentation of Shakespeare's burlesque of the Pyramus and Thisbe story (see *A Midsummer Night's Dream*, act v, scene 1).

6. Compare the love story of Pyramus and Thisbe with that of Romeo and Juliet, as you find it in Shakespeare's play or in Lamb's *Tales from Shakespeare*.

Word Study

1. Look up the following words in a mythological dictionary and practice the correct pronunciation. Astarte, Psyche, Proserpina, Hippomenes, Hesperides, Pygmalion, Cyprus, Thisbe.
2. What does "an Adonis" mean? What does "psyche" mean in Greek? Give an English derivative from this word. What does "zephyr" mean? What is its origin?
3. Give the Greek forms for *Venus, Jupiter, Jove, Diana, Cupid, Neptune*.

Questions for Review

1. Who was Adonis?
2. How did Venus's love for him change her?
3. What was the cause of his death?
4. How did Venus show her devotion to him?
5. Why was Venus angry with Psyche?
6. What command did she give Cupid concerning Psyche?
7. What effect did Psyche have on Cupid?
8. By what means did she become his wife?
9. What warning did he give her?
10. What caused her to disregard it?
11. What was the result?
12. What penances were laid on Psyche?
13. How did she carry them out?
14. Was Venus finally reconciled to her?
15. Why did Atalanta of Bœotia wish to avoid marriage?
16. What condition did she impose on her suitors?
17. What means did Hippomenes devise to win her?
18. Why were both punished?
19. What was the attitude of Pygmalion toward women?
20. How did he fall in love?
21. What prayer did he address to Venus?
22. How was the prayer granted?
23. What obstacle did Hero and Leander meet?
24. What obstacle did Pyramus and Thisbe meet?
25. How did the first pair evade opposition?
26. What was the result?
27. What happened to Pyramus and Thisbe?
28. Who was Semiramis?
29. What was the origin of the purple fruit of the mulberry tree?

Reading List

Poems and Plays

Browning, Elizabeth Barrett: *Psyche*
Browning, Robert: *Pheidippides*

Bunner, H. C.: *A Lost Child*
Byron, George: *Stanzas Written after Swimming from Sestos to Abydos*
Chapman, George: *Sequel to Marlowe's "Hero and Leander"*
Doolittle, Hilda ("H. D."): *Pygmalion*
Herrick, Robert: *The Cheat of Cupid*
Hunt, Leigh: *Cupid Drowned*
Jonson, Ben: *Venus' Runaway*
Keats, John: *Ode to Psyche*
Kilmer, Aline: *To Aphrodite, with a Mirror*
Landor, Walter Savage: *Hippomenes and Atalanta*
Lang, Andrew: Bion's *Lament for Adonis*
Lazarus, Emma: *Venus of the Louvre*
Lyly, John: *Cupid and My Campaspe Played*
Marlowe, Christopher: Musæus's *Hero and Leander*
Moore, Thomas: *Cupid and Psyche*
Morris, William: *Atalanta's Race—Pygmalion and the Image—The Story of Cupid*
Noyes, Alfred: *The Venus of Milo*
Ovid: *Leander to Hero* (in *Heroines*)—*Hero to Leander* (in *Heroines*)
Sappho: *Hymn to Aphrodite*
Shakespeare, William: *A Midsummer Night's Dream*
Tennyson, Alfred: *Hero to Leander*
Wilde, Oscar: *The Garden of Eros*

Apollo with his lyre

5 Stories of Apollo

God of the golden bow,
And of the golden lyre,
And of the golden hair,
And of the golden fire.

Keats

Latona

Among the daughters of the Titans was Latona, goddess of darkness. Her beauty was very great, and Jupiter fell in love with her and thereby incurred the anger of Juno. Juno, indeed, never forgave her, and whenever she had an opportunity she visited some form of punishment upon Latona.

Latona bore twin children to Jupiter, the sun god Apollo and the moon goddess Diana. With her infants in her arms she wandered from land to land, followed everywhere by the jealousy of Juno, who foresaw the future greatness of Latona's two children and was enraged that the offspring of her rival should attain such splendor.

In her wanderings Latona endured many hardships. Once, in Lycia, she saw ahead of her a pleasant, tree-shaded pool. Joyfully she hastened toward it with her children, for she was weary and thirsty. But as she approached and stooped down to the cool waters, a number of rude country folk jostled her out of the way and forbade her to drink. In vain she implored them. She pointed to the infants who were with her, and reminded them in the name of Jove that hospitality was sacred to the gods. But they merely jeered at her and would not allow her to come near the pool. Some of them even waded through the water so as to make it too muddy to drink.

Then at last Latona lost her patience and remembered that she, too, was a goddess. Pointing her hand in wrath she cried: "Never leave the pool! Let it be your place of habitation forever!" Even as she spoke, the rustics were strangely transformed. Their hands and bodies turned green, their heads became flat, their voices became harsh. Their descendants the frogs still live today in many a muddy pool.

For a time Latona and her children dwelt in the mountain glens of Pieria, a favorite haunt of the Muses. There the nine sisters taught Apollo the art of music and song, until in time, instead of being their pupil, he became their master. But he did not as yet have the lyre, which Mercury later presented to him. Diana was brought up in a cave of Mount Cynthus (she was therefore sometimes called *Cynthia*), and her guardian was Hecate, queen of witches. In the glades of Cynthus, Diana roamed freely and fearlessly, and there she learned to know and understand the wild creatures. When both Apollo and Diana were full-grown they went to Mount Olympus, and took their places among the high gods.

Apollo Belvedere—The shiny god of poetry and light has inspired
writers, painters and sculptors down through the ages.

Hyacinthus

Apollo was the god most beloved by
the Greeks and they wove many legends around him. He
was a protector of men—especially when in the vigor of
their youth they engaged in sports and contests. It was told
of him, among other stories, that he gave his friendship to a
fair lad named Hyacinthus, son of the king of Sparta. The
boy loved all kinds of games, and Apollo accompanied him
on his fishing expeditions and hunting trips, and
participated in all the sports in which Hyacinthus took part.
Zephyrus, god of the west wind, was equally fond of

Hyacinthus and tried to win his favor, but the lad cared only for Apollo.

One day Apollo and Hyacinthus began a game of quoits. Both were skillful players, and now one, now the other made the farther throw. Unnoticed by either of them, Zephyrus crept up and observed them. He was filled with jealous anger that Hyacinthus preferred Apollo to him. Suddenly he could endure it no longer. Apollo was casting a quoit, and as it whizzed through the air the West Wind seized it in his invisible grasp, changed its course, and sent it with deadly force toward Hyacinthus. The heavy missile struck the boy on the head, and he fell senseless to the ground. Not all the efforts of Apollo could revive him, and the god mourned for him bitterly, as he lay dying. But taking the boy's lifeless body in his arms, Apollo gave him promise of immortal life.

"You die," he exclaimed to the boy, "but from your blood shall spring a flower that all shall love."

As he spoke a delicate blossom, in shape like the lily, but of a delicate purple hue, sprang from the ground. On its petals were marked the letters, "Ai, Ai," meaning "Woe, Woe." The Greeks called this flower the hyacinth, but today it is called the iris, in honor of the goddess of the rainbow.

Apollo and Marpessa

Marpessa was a mortal maiden who rejected the love of Apollo. She was the daughter of a king, named Evenus, who selfishly thought he could keep her with him forever and wanted her never to marry. But she was very beautiful, and had many suitors. Among them the contest narrowed down finally to two—Idas, a brave and handsome nobleman, and the great god Apollo. Of these Marpessa favored Idas, who urged her father to let him marry her. But Evenus angrily denied his request, ordered him out of his sight, and threatened to kill him if he ever returned.

Idas was in despair, but at this moment Neptune came to his rescue. The sea god presented Idas with a wonderful chariot, to which were attached not only some of the swiftest horses that ever lived, but also a pair of wings that still further hastened the progress of the chariot. With this chariot Idas waited for Marpessa at a well where she was accustomed to draw water for her household. He persuaded her to elope with him, and hardly had she mounted to his side, when the chariot sped away, fast as the wind. Word came to Evenus as to what had happened. In great anger he mounted his own chariot and set off in immediate pursuit. But all was in vain. Marpessa and Idas were beyond his reach.

Apollo was not willing that Idas should so easily win Marpessa in marriage. Suddenly he appeared in front of the speeding chariot, and seized the horses by the bridles. Haughtily he commanded Idas to give up the maiden to him. Although Idas knew that his doom was certain, he prepared to fight till death. Again, however, Neptune came to his aid. Sitting on high Olympus beside Jupiter, he pleaded with the king of gods and men to do justice in the unequal contest. So, even as Apollo spoke, there was heard in the air the great rumble of thunder.

Apollo heard and bowed to the ground and trembled, for he knew the sign of Jupiter. Then came the voice of Jupiter himself, commanding: "Let the maiden decide whom she will wed."

So the two lovers, the mortal and the god, pleaded before the maiden in her chariot. Apollo promised her endless felicity, a knowledge of all things past and to come. He told her that she should have it within her power to bring bliss or bane to men, to lift up and to cast down. Then Idas spoke, in deep humility. He could offer her nothing but love, he could appeal to nothing but her pity for one to whom her beauty was the light of the world.

As he spoke she stretched out her hand to Idas and said:

"Idas is my choice. For he and I shall grow old together, and even old shall I still love him and he, me. But Apollo in time would tire of me, faded and mortal."

Apollo bowed his head to her decree and returned to the haunts of Olympus, without anger but grieving, while Idas and Marpessa wandered off happily together.

Phaëthon and Æsculapius

Apollo had two sons, Phaëthon and Æsculapius, who perished by the thunderbolts of Jove. Phaëthon was the son of Apollo and the nymph Clymene. He was brought up as a mortal, but often his mother would point to the sky and tell him that the sun god was his father. When Phaëthon told this story to his playmates, they scoffed at him and refused to believe that he was of divine parentage. He came to his mother in tears and she consoled him. She told him that if he visited the sun god, Apollo would accept him as his son and prove to all the world that he was divine.

So Phaëthon set off for the palace of Apollo. Far off, where the stream Oceanus winds its way around the edge of the earth, he came upon the house of his father. There stood the god, in his shining and fragrant garments, and around him hovered the Days and the Hours, the Seasons and the Years. Awed by the splendor he saw before him, the youth could not speak. But the sun god, in kindly tones, asked him to tell what was on his mind.

"Am I truly your son?" stammered the boy.

Then Apollo gazed more closely upon him and recognized his son. He kissed him and made much of him.

"But what brings you on such a far journey?" he asked Phaëthon.

Phaëthon told him then what had occurred, and asked a favor of him.

"Let me have the fulfillment of one wish," he pleaded, "and all shall be well with me. Just grant me one wish."

At the sight of the tears and distress of his son, Apollo at once granted his request.

"By the head of Jupiter, you shall have whatever you ask," he swore.

Phaëthon was overjoyed. Quickly he cried out:

"Let me drive your sun chariot over the sky for a single day."

When he heard the lad's words, Apollo was terrified at his boldness. In vain he warned the boy of the dangers through which he must pass, of the dreadful perils of such a journey, of the fierceness of the steeds which he must drive, and of the overpowering heat that would surround him. Phaëthon insisted, however, and since his father's word had been given, nothing could be done to save him.

So the next morning the great steeds of the sun, blowing flame from their nostrils and champing fiercely at their bits, were brought forth and harnessed. Sorrowfully Apollo bade farewell to his son and helped him seat himself in the chariot. Scarcely were the reins in the boy's hands when the steeds leaped out across the sky. Almost at once the sun horses recognized an unfamiliar and weak hand on the reins, and in a short time they were uncontrollable. Amazing were the antics of the sun that day. Sometimes the chariot swung too high in the sky, and bitter cold assailed the human beings below. In Africa, however, it came too close, and everybody was scorched.

At last it looked as if the whole earth would be shriveled with heat and destroyed. All mankind prayed for aid to Jupiter. Reluctantly he laid his hand on a thunderbolt and hurled it forth, and Phaëthon, blazing like a falling star, fell headlong to the earth. The steeds of the sun, left riderless, returned panting to their stables. Apollo was so filled with grief at the death of his son that for days he refused to come forth, and left the sky covered with black clouds. The sisters of Phaëthon mourned bitterly for him, and they were changed into poplars.

The doom of Æsculapius came about in a different way. He was the son of Apollo and of the Thessalian princess Coronis. His mother died at his birth, and Apollo intrusted his education to Chiron, one of an odd race of divinities, called *centaurs*. They were represented as half horses and half men, and were said to have been the offspring of a mortal named Ixion and a cloud. On one occasion the centaurs were invited to a wedding feast by a tribe called the Lapiths, but became so disorderly that the other guests attacked them and they were driven out of their home in Thessaly. Ancient artists loved to represent this battle.

Chiron was the wisest and noblest of all the centaurs, and had received instruction from Apollo and Diana in hunting, medicine, music, gymnastics, and the art of prophecy. He was the teacher of many of the great heroes

The centaurs were an odd race of divinities represented as half horse and half man. They were said to be offsprings of a human and a cloud.

of Greece. Even in later ages Leonardo da Vinci, one of the greatest geniuses that ever lived, had at times a most vivid hallucination—that he saw and spoke with Chiron.

Chiron did more for Æsculapius than for anyone. The child grew wiser and wiser; and when he reached maturity, he became a great physician. He not only cured the sick, but in one instance, so wondrous was his skill, that he recalled a dead man to life. Then Jove feared that if Æsculapius continued to grow in his command of the healing art, he would help men to escape death altogether. So he hurled a bolt at him and slew him, but placed him afterward among the stars. Æsculapius had two sons who became physicians too, but they were never so great as their father, who became the god of medicine. He is usually represented as carrying a serpent-entwined staff.

The Shepherd of King Admetus

The death of Phaëthon had filled Apollo with great displeasure toward Jupiter, and the slaying of Æsculapius increased his anger still more. This time he was not content with mere thoughts and words of anger. In a most ungodlike fashion he resolved to wreak his wrath on the innocent forgers of the thunderbolts of Jove—the one-eyed Cyclopes who worked in Vulcan's forge underneath the volcano of Mount Etna. So he shot his potent shafts at them and slew them. Jupiter was furious at this unjust act and determined to banish Apollo to the darkness of the underworld. But the mother of Apollo interceded for him, and finally Jupiter decreed that as punishment for his wicked deed Apollo must serve a mortal for the space of a year.

Admetus, king of Pheræ in Thessaly, was selected for the honor of being the master of the sun god. Apollo was placed in charge of the flocks of Admetus, and for one year he wandered with the sheep along the river shore and across the meadows of the king. Then it was, according to the legend, that Apollo, to amuse himself, learned to play the lyre, and with it charmed all who heard its sweet music.

So honorably and kindly was Apollo treated by King Admetus that he conceived a great fondness for his mortal master, and tried to aid him in all things. While Apollo tended the flocks of Admetus, they were extraordinarily fruitful and increased in number beyond all measure. Apollo also aided Admetus in another way. Admetus wished

78

Head of Apollo by Praxiteles, a 4th century B.C. Athenian sculptor

to have as his bride a beautiful maiden named Alcestis, the daughter of Pelias, who was a son of Neptune. But Pelias announced that he would give his daughter in marriage only to the man who should come for her in a chariot drawn by lions and boars. Admetus despaired of ever being able to perform this task. Apollo, when he heard what conditions Pelias had imposed, came to his aid. With Apollo's help Admetus harnessed both lions and boars to his chariot, and drove triumphantly to the palace of Pelias. Pelias was then obliged to carry out his promise, and Alcestis became the happy bride of Admetus.

Admetus and Alcestis

One of the most beautiful of Greek legends concerns the later life of this pair.

After several years of wedded happiness, Admetus became seriously ill. Soon it was evident that his death hour was approaching and all the skill of his physicians availed him nothing. Not even Apollo, who was anxious to repay him for his justice and kindness to him when he had been his herdsman, could help him. But Apollo approached Jupiter and obtained one favor for Admetus.

"If there be any one," declared Jupiter, "who is willing to die in place of Admetus, then his life will be accepted in place of that of the king, and the years of Admetus will be prolonged by as many years as his savior still had to live."

Joyously Apollo returned to the palace of Admetus with the tidings of this decree of the king of gods and men. As he came within the palace he found his family and friends, his retainers and soldiers clustered in tears around the king. Silence fell upon them as Apollo approached and raised his hand. Eagerly the sun god announced in what fashion the life of Admetus might yet be spared, and he thought, "Surely all these mourners will be glad to die for the king."

But as Apollo concluded not a voice answered him. He turned to the aged parents of Admetus, and implored them to give their lives for Admetus. But they refused, saying that they wished to enjoy what few days remained to them. He turned then to his followers, whom Admetus had often led into battle; to the courtiers who had often assured the king in flattering tones that they would willingly die for his slightest whim. All remained deaf to his pleading.

But even as he argued with them, there broke in upon him a clear and brave voice. It was that of Alcestis, the wife of the king.

"I will glady die for my husband," she said.

Apollo was horrified.

"What!" he cried. "You will give your young life for his! Think too of your little children and how they will be left motherless without you—left to the care of an unpitying world. Better that Admetus should die than that your life should be offered in place of his."

And Apollo turned to go. But Alcestis ran to him and held him and told him he must fulfill the command of Jupiter. So in sorrow he agreed, and Alcestis reclined on a couch. Slowly, then, her face grew pale, strength left her limbs, her breath faltered. But as life ebbed from her body, it returned in increasing strength to Admetus. The blood returned to his visage, he felt the vigor of renewed vitality course through him from head to foot, and in a few minutes he sprang from the bed on which he had been lying—as well and healthy as he had ever been.

But on her couch Alcestis lay dying.

Just at this moment a strange diversion occurred. A great hero named Hercules (about whom many stories will be told in a later chapter) happened to be passing through Thessaly, and had stopped at the palace of Admetus to pay his respects to the monarch. As he approached the palace gates he wondered at the strange silence that prevailed, and was amazed that no gateman sprang up to bid him halt, that no attendant came to greet him. As he came nearer, he heard the wails and lamentations that issued from the chamber in which Admetus lay. He turned towards this chamber, stood at the portal unnoticed and heard all that took place within.

As he listened to the magnanimous offer of Alcestis and as he watched the pallor of death steal over her, he was filled with pity that so brave a woman must die. Just then he heard a rustle. He turned around and there, at his very side, was Death—a shadowy, black-robed figure. Stealthily Death stole forward, ready to bear Alcestis away in his grasp. But Hercules, who was daunted by no terrors of either heaven or earth, made a sudden resolve.

"Never," he cried to himself, "shall Death take this noble soul!"

So saying he rushed forward and seized Death. Almost impalpable was the substance of the Ill-Omened One, but Hercules used every cunning of the wrestler's art, and try as Death would, he could not escape from the hero's grasp. Finally Death gave up the struggle and resigned Alcestis to Hercules. The hero placed her again in the arms of her husband. The great mourning of the Thessalians and the bitter wails of the little children of Alcestis were changed to rejoicing and thanksgiving. Alcestis, so miraculously restored to life, lived with her husband in happiness and prosperity for many years. Both men and gods were glad to do honor to her noble spirit. When, at last she died, a very old woman, Admetus did not long survive her.

Athletic Games

A fierce monster was slain by Apollo, and because of his deed men venerated him and paid him great honor.

On the sides of Mount Parnassus there dwelt a terrible dragon, named the Python, which not only molested human beings who came by, but even opposed the passage of the gods. Once it lifted its head in wrath against Latona, mother of Apollo and Diana, and she called on her son for assistance. Apollo sped to the mountain and sought out the dragon. A great battle took place, but soon the snake lay dead on the ground, pierced by the arrows of the god.

The Greeks were very fond of contests and greatly admired athletic prowess. After Apollo had slain the Python, therefore, they established the Pythian Games, which took place at regular intervals at Delphi in honor of Apollo's victory. Even more important were the Olympic Games, held in honor of Jupiter every four years. The Greeks thought so highly of these games that they reckoned their calendar by them, speaking of an event as taking place in the seventh or the seventy-ninth Olympiad—that is, in the four-year space between the games. The Nemean Games also were celebrated in honor of Jupiter.

At these and other games the Greeks, who might otherwise be engaged in war with one another, came together in friendly rivalry and paid homage to the gods in common. One day would be given up to sacrifices and processions. Then would come three days of contests—foot races, varying in length from two hundred yards to three miles; the pentathlon, which included five kinds of skill—throwing the discus, throwing the spear, running, jumping, and wrestling. There were also chariot races, boxing and wrestling matches. Besides these, there were usually contests in poetry and music. On the last day of the festival the prizes would be awarded—beautiful wreaths that varied in appearance according to the god. At the Olympic Games the wreaths were of olive leaves, at the Pythian Games of laurel, at the Nemean Games of parsley.

Representations of ancient and modern discus throwers

Following the games would come new sacrifices and much feasting. Great honors would be paid to the victors in the various contests, not only then but also after the crowds had dispersed. Poets wrote odes about them, sculptors designed their forms in bronze and marble, and their native cities received them on their return home with delegations of welcome and choral songs. An athlete who won three victories at Olympia was allowed the honor of having his statue erected outside the temple of Jupiter.

PRACTICAL APPLICATIONS

Myths in Literature

Apollo has inspired many poets to sing his praise. All the adventures of Apollo have been told again and again in rhyme and story.

Perhaps the most beautiful of all treatments of the Apollo legends is Stephen Phillip's narrative poem called *Marpessa*. Unforgettably the poet has told the story of a mortal's rejection of an immortal in favor of another mortal. He pictures the scene when the three met, the god and the man each ready to plead his cause:

> They three together met; on the one side,
> Fresh from diffusing light on all the world
> Apollo; on the other without sleep
> Idas, and in the midst Marpessa stood.
> Just as a flower after drenching rain,
> So from the falling of felicity
> Her human beauty glowed, and it was new;
> The bee too near her bosom drowsed and dropped.

Many poets have been won by the nobility of the Admetus-Alcestis story. One of the most moving of ancient plays is the *Alcestis* of Euripides. Browning turned this play into a narrative of his own, *Balaustion's Adventure;* and the story has been excellently treated by poets as diverse as Emma Lazarus, James Russell Lowell, Walter Savage Landor, and William Morris.

Among the Greeks a fruitful theme for poetry was the victor in an athletic contest. Pindar was the greatest of the poets who celebrated such contests and their heroes. In his poems he introduced many mythological references and connected the family history of the winner with ancient gods and demigods.

84

Specific Literary References

What do the following references mean? Where a word or phrase is italicized, explain only the word or phrase.

1. Who drives the horses of the sun,
   Shall lord it but a day.—*Cheney*
2.   Pitying the sad death,
   Of Hyacinthus, when the cruel breath
   Of Zephyr slew him.—*Keats*
3. Methought I saw my late espouséd saint
   Brought to me like *Alcestis* from the grave.—*Milton*
4. How charming is divine philosophy!
   Not harsh and crabbed, as dull fools suppose,
   But musical as is *Apollo's* lute.—*Milton*
5. As when those hinds that were transformed to frogs
   Railed at Latona's twinborn progeny.—*Milton*
6. Why, Phaëthon,
   Wilt thou aspire to guide the heavenly car,
   And with thy daring folly burn the
   world?—*Shakespeare*
7. I will go lie in wait for Death, black-stoled
   King of the corpses. I shall find him sure. . . .
   Confident I shall bring Alcestis back.—*Browning*
8. Who fears nor Fate, nor Time, nor what Time brings,
   May drive Apollo's steeds, or wield the
   thunderbolt.—*Coates*

Suggestions for Oral or Written Composition

1. Imagine that you, like Latona, were a wayfarer in ancient times and were approaching the pool—just behind her and her children. Describe the scene you witnessed.
2. In a gentle breeze that moves its petals, the iris speaks. It relates how once it was a mortal youth, beloved of Apollo, and goes on to tell of its sudden death and strange transformation. Give the words of the flower.
3. Prepare a pantomime in two scenes, showing the story of Marpessa. In one Idas appears before King Evenus and is angrily ordered away. In the second Apollo confronts Marpessa and Idas, and the two suitors make their plea to

the maiden, who chooses the mortal. Write stage directions describing actions and gestures.

4. Describe a scene in the schoolhouse of Chiron, as he gives a lesson in hunting or gymnastics to Æsculapius.

5. Give an account of the modern Olympic Games. How do they resemble and how do they differ from those of ancient times? Do you know personally some participant in the Olympic Games? If so, interview him or her, and obtain details as to how the games are conducted.

Word Study

1. Explain the origin, according to the Greeks, of the word *hyacinth*. What modern flower corresponds to it?
2. What does the word *phaëton* mean in English? Explain its origin. How is it pronounced? What is a *python* in modern usage? What is meant by "the Æsculapian art"?
3. How are the following words pronounced? Æsculapius, Phaëthon, centaur, Chiron, Alcestis, Cyclopes, Pelias, Python, Nemean, pentathlon.
4. The *centaury* (by some believed to be the cornflower) was an herb the usefulness of which in medicine was discovered by Chiron. What was his connection with the art of healing?
5. Give the Greek names of the following deities: *Latona, Juno, Diana, Neptune, Jupiter.*

Questions for Review

1. Who was Latona?
2. Over what realms did her two children rule?
3. Who was jealous of her?
4. How did Latona punish the boors of Lycia?
5. What youth was the friend of Apollo?
6. By whose jealousy did this youth die?
7. For the favor of what maiden were Apollo and a mortal rivals?

86

8. Who was successful?
9. What were the names of two sons of Apollo?
10. What ambition did one of them cherish?
11. How was it gratified, and what was his fate?
12. By whom was the other educated?
13. In what art did he attain great skill?
14. How did he die?
15. What revenge did Apollo take?
16. How did Jupiter punish him?
17. What master did Apollo serve?
18. What doom threatened this master?
19. What sacrifice did Alcestis make?
20. How was she saved?
21. What monster did Apollo slay?
22. What games were established in commemoration of his deed?
23. What other athletic contests were held in ancient Greece?

Reading List

Poems, Plays and Novels

Doolittle, Hilda ("H. D."): *Centaur Song*
Drummond, William: *Song to Phœbus*
Hood, Thomas: *Lycus the Centaur*
Keats, John: *Hymn to Apollo*
Landor, Walter Savage: *Hercules, Pluto, Alcestis and Admetus*
Lazarus, Emma: *Admetus*
Lowell, James Russell: *The Shepherd of King Admetus*
Morris, William: *The Love of Alcestis*
Noyes, Alfred: *The Inn of Apollo*
Phillips, Stephen: *Marpessa*
Saxe, John G.: *Phaëthon*
Shelley, Percy Bysshe: *Homer's Hymn to Apollo—Hymn of Apollo*
Snedeker, Caroline D.: *The Perilous Seat*
Wordsworth, William: *The Power of Music*

Diana (Greek: Artemis), goddess of the moon and hunting

6 Stories of Diana

Queen and huntress, chaste and fair.
Ben Jonson

Endymion

Diana, goddess of the moon, was usually as cold and withdrawn as the orb over which she ruled; and she was regarded as the particular patron of unyielding maidenhood. Sometimes she was pursued by lovers, but she would never surrender to them, and for some she prepared a cruel fate. But once she really fell in love—with Endymion.

Endymion was a young shepherd who tended his flocks on the green slopes of Mount Latmos. So beautiful a youth was he and so noble in his demeanor that the people of the vicinity regarded him with awe, and said of him that he must surely be the son of Jupiter. One summer night Endymion, after he had taken care of his flocks, lay down to sleep under an oak. When he fell asleep it was still deep night, unlighted save by the stars, but in a little while Diana came riding over the skies in her silver chariot and illuminated both mountain and valley. Slowly Diana drove her milky steeds, and as she drove she gazed upon the earth beneath. Suddenly she caught sight of Endymion, and fell deeply in love with the handsome shepherd lad.

She gazed on him with ecstasy, and would gladly have awakened him to tell him of her love, but she dared not do so. For she had often reproached other gods for their admiration of mortals, and had often boasted that she herself was immune to such weakness, that she was the goddess of unvarying maidenhood.

So she stole softly from her chariot, and seated herself beside Endymion, and gently kissed him, but took care not to awaken him. Upon his sleep she cast lovely dreams, in the midst of which often moved the figure of the goddess of the moon, and Endymion sighed happily in his slumbers. So Diana passed night after night.

But the other gods began to remark that Diana was often absent from the skies, and that her chariot moved with no regular speed over the heavens. They began to spy on her, and shortly her secret was revealed to all on high Olympus. The others, particularly Venus, would have mocked Diana, but Jupiter checked them. The father of gods and men feared that in time Diana, because of the shepherd lad, would entirely neglect her duties as luminary of the sky at night.

He resolved therefore, that Endymion must be given a difficult choice. He called the youth to him and had him elect which he would take: a death in any manner he chose, or perpetual youth plunged in perpetual sleep. Endymion chose the latter fate, and he still sleeps in a cave on Mount Latmos, where, when her course leads her to a certain point in the sky, Diana may see him.

Orion

The magnificent constellation called Orion was supposed by the Greeks to have been originally the body of the great giant, a son of Neptune. He was a handsome man and an eager hunter, and very vain of his personal appearance and of his skill in the chase. He was a great favorite of Diana, and some even suspected the moon goddess of being in love with him. Apollo sometimes scolded her for her attentions to Orion, but to no avail.

Once Apollo pointed out to his sister a black spot far off in the waters and challenged her to hit it with her arrow. She did so, and too late discovered that she had killed Orion. But she placed him in the stars, where his dog Sirius follows him, the Hare flies before him, and the Pleiades are frightened at his coming.

The Pleiades, according to the Greeks, were seven maidens, daughters of Atlas, who had been pursued by Orion until in desperation they called on Jupiter for help. He changed them first into doves, then into stars.

Niobe

That vindictiveness which Apollo shows in some episodes appears again in the story of Niobe. Niobe was the daughter of King Tantalus. She was married to Amphion, a son of Jupiter, and in the course of time became so proud of her descent, her husband, and her fine family of seven brave sons and seven beautiful daughters, that she boasted unduly about them.

Once in particular she went too far. It was on the occasion of a feast day of Latona, the mother of Apollo and Diana. In her overbearing conceit, Niobe urged the people to stop worshiping Latona, who had only two children, and to pay reverence to her instead, with seven times as many.

Latona heard about this, and addressed her son and daughter reproachfully. They were just as indignant as she

Niobe and daughter

was at Niobe's irreverent boastfulness; and both resolved to punish the foolish woman at once.

Swiftly they approached the city in which Niobe dwelt. They surveyed the scene before them and saw the seven sons of Niobe among the youths who exercised proudly on the plain, engaging in athletic sports of various kinds. Swiftly the two children of Latona drew their bows to their shoulders and the arrows flew. All seven sons of Niobe fell.

Yet even so Niobe's pride was not humbled, and still she defied Latona.

"My daughters still are better and greater than your two children!" she exclaimed; and scarcely had the words left her lips, when the daughters, too, dropped to the ground even as they mourned their brothers. At the sight Niobe was turned to stone with grief. But her tears continued to flow; and the gods, in pity, changed her into a fountain.

Meleager and Atalanta - painting by Rubens

Meleager

A maiden named Atalanta (but not the one who raced with Hippomenes) was renowned for her skill in hunting and in games. Her father had abandoned her in the woods of Arcadia as an infant, and she had been found by a she-bear, which brought her up as it might have done a cub. Under the special protection of Diana she grew up into a bold huntress.

Now it happened in the region called Calydon that the ruler, Œneus, failed to pay certain honors to Diana, and she in anger sent an enormous boar to punish him. The beast laid waste all the land and spread terror among the inhabitants. The wife of Œneus was named Althæa, and among their children was a son named Meleager. At his birth his mother had dreamed that she saw the three Fates spinning the web of his life, and that she heard snatches of their conversation.

"As soon," said one of them, "as the wood now burning on the hearth of his mother shall be consumed, so soon shall the span of his life be ended."

Hastily awakening from her dream, Althæa ran to the hearth and snatched from it the burning piece of wood. She quenched it in water, and laid it aside carefully among her most precious possessions.

Meleager grew up into a manly and courageous young man, liked by all who knew him. When word of the boar came to him, he resolved that he would make the slaying of it a great festival. So he sent messengers into every part of Greece and summoned all the heroes of the land to take part in the hunting of the boar. They willingly responded to his call. Among others came Atalanta, eager to be the one to slay the monster. As she approached, she and Meleager came face to face, and immediately the young hero fell in love with her.

As the hunt progressed he was ever at her side. To win her approval he performed deeds of great valor, and when at last the boar was driven to bay, it was Meleager who delivered the fatal blow that stretched the monster out dead before them.

Now the monster was skinned, and his huge hide, a marvelous trophy of the chase, was handed to Meleager. But he gave it to Atalanta—as a gift from him. At this act of chivalry two brothers of Althæa, men of low minds, began to murmur.

"What!" they cried. "Shall it be said that this great prize went to a mere girl? It ought to hang forever in the king's halls."

With the words they strode angrily towards Atalanta and rudely snatched the hide from her hands. When Meleager saw what was happening, he did not pause for reflection, but drawing in bow to his shoulder, dispatched two shafts at his uncles. They fell to the ground, mortally wounded.

In horror the others gazed on their bodies, and immediately messengers, bearers of evil tidings, hastened back to the court, filling the air with their lamentations. Althæa heard them, and came to meet them. When she heard what had happened, a senseless anger fell upon her.

She hurried to the place where she kept her treasures, seized the wood that she had hidden at Meleager's birth, and without allowing herself time for thought, cast it into the blazing hearth. Eagerly the flames seized it and shortly it was consumed.

Meanwhile on the hunting ground Meleager stood talking sorrowfully to Atalanta. Suddenly burning pains seized him. He fell to the ground, and in a few minutes lay dead.

When Althæa heard how her dream had been fulfilled, and that the piece of wood had truly concealed the life of her son, she killed herself.

PRACTICAL APPLICATIONS

Myths in Literature

Most magnificent of all the works which the myths included in this chapter have evoked is Algernon Charles Swinburne's *Atalanta in Calydon*. This great English poet was saturated in the spirit of the Greeks, and in this drama he produced his masterpiece. The Greeks themselves never wrote finer poetry about their gods and the stories associated with their gods than did Swinburne in *Atalanta in Calydon*. The greatest passage in the poem is the chorus addressed to Diana, of which part reads:

> Come with bows bent and with emptying of quivers,
> Maiden most perfect, lady of light,
> With a noise of winds and many rivers,
> With a clamor of waters, and with might;
> Bind on thy sandals, O thou most fleet,
> Over the splendor and speed of thy feet;
> For the faint east quickens, the wan west shivers,
> Round the feet of the day and the feet of the night.

Endymion, too, has been a favorite subject; and John Keats made his entrance into English poetry with a long poem called by the name of the beloved of Diana, of whom he says:

> Therefore 'tis with full happiness that I
> Will trace the story of Endymion.
> The very music of the name has gone
> Into my being.

Byron made splendid use of the Niobe story when, in his *Childe Harold,* he referred to the then desolate and ruined city of Rome as:

> The Niobe of nations! there she stands,
> Childless and crownless, in her voiceless woe.

Specific Literary References

What do the following references mean? When a word or phrase is italicized, explain only the word or phrase.

1. Alas, no charm
   Could lift *Endymion's* head.—*Keats*
2. Poor, lonely Niobe! when her lovely young
   Were dead and gone.—*Keats*
3. On such a tranquil night as this,
   She woke Endymion with a kiss.—*Longfellow*
4. Amid her daughters slain by Artemis
   Stood Niobe.—*Ovid*
5. Like Niobe, all tears.—*Shakespeare*
6. Then all abode save one,
   The Arcadian *Atalanta:* from her side
   Sprang her hounds.—*Swinburne*
7. Many a night, from yonder ivied casement, ere I went to rest,
   Did I look on Great *Orion,* sloping slowly to the West.—*Tennyson*
8. *Endymion* would have passed across the mead
   Moonstruck with love.—*Wilde*

Suggestions for Oral or Written Composition

1. Write a brief play, giving the dialogue between Jupiter and Endymion, when the latter is summoned before the ruler of gods and men to make a choice of dooms.

2. Were the children of Latona justified in taking such extreme vengeance on Niobe? Give reasons for your answer.

3. When Althæa hears how Meleager has slain her brothers, she is faced with a terrible dilemma—whether or not to end the life of her son. What arguments would she address to herself? Tell what she might say.

Word Study

1. How are the following words pronounced?
   Endymion, Orion, Pleiades, Niobe, Meleager.

2. Give the Greek names of the following deities:
   Diana, Vulcan, Venus, Jupiter, Jove, Latona.

3. Explain the following phrases: "a mighty hunter, like Orion"; "melting away in tears, like Niobe."

Questions for Review

1. Did Diana ever fall in love?
2. What choice of fates was offered to Endymion?
3. Which did he choose?
4. What was the character of Orion?
5. How did he come to his death?
6. Where may he still be seen?
7. Who were the Pleiades?
8. In what way did Niobe incur the wrath of Latona?
9. On whom did Latona call for help?
10. What doom overtook the sons of Niobe?
11. Why were her daughters slain?
12. What was the fate of Niobe herself?
13. Who was Atalanta of Arcadia?
14. Why did a monster ravage the fields of Calydon?
15. Who was Meleager?

96

16. What strange dream did his mother have when he was born?
17. What action did Meleager take to get rid of the monster?
18. Who came to the Calydonian hunt?
19. Why did Meleager's uncles quarrel with him?
20. What was the outcome?
21. How did his mother punish Meleager?
22. What was her own fate?

Reading List

Poems and Plays

Catallus: *A Hymn to Diana*
Gosse, Edmund: *The Praise of Artemis*
Jonson, Ben: *Hymn to Diana*
Keats, John: *Endymion*
Lang, Andrew: *To Artemis*
Longfellow, Henry Wadsworth: *Endymion—The Occultation of Orion*
Lowell, James Russell: *Endymion*
Lyly, John: *Endymion*
Noyes, Alfred: *Niobe*
Procter, B. Y.: *The Worship of Diana*
Swinburne, Algernon Charles: *Atalanta in Calydon*
Wilde, Oscar: *Endymion*

Which of Pan's varied characteristics is shown in this sculpture?

7 Gods of Nature

*Now Aurora forsakes the ocean and
crimsons the orient sky.*

Catullus

The Earth

The Greeks believed for many ages
that the earth was flat, with Greece at the very center.
Across the center of the disk of the earth flowed the
Mediterranean Sea—the middle sea, as its name indicates.
Around the edges flowed the River Oceanus. Toward the
north dwelt the Hyperboreans, in a land of eternal
spring—far beyond the mountains from whose slopes and

hollows came the bitter north winds of winter. Toward the south dwelt the Ethiopians, whom the gods, and particularly Neptune, held in great favor. Toward the west lay the Elysian Islands, a kind of paradise.

Out of the River Oceanus and back into it moved the luminaries of the skies. Each day the sun and later the moon traveled chariotwise across the heavens; so too did the stars. From the west, where the sun set, the sun god was conveyed in a winged boat back to his starting point.

Gods of the Earth

The sister of Jupiter, *Ceres* (Greek: *Demeter*), was the goddess of the earth and of its crops and fruits. Hidden in her worship was the veneration of the seed of life in all its manifestations. She was the protectress of farmers. She was represented with a garland of corn ears or of simple ribbons; in her hand she held a scepter or a poppy; sometimes also a *cornucopia,* or horn of plenty, grains and fruits tumbling out of it. Her daughter was *Proserpina,* the goddess of springtime.

Chief among the other deities especially associated with the earth were *Bacchus* (Greek: *Dionysus*) and *Pan.*

Bacchus was the son of Jupiter and Semele. Jupiter placed the education of Bacchus in charge of Silenus, a jovial old drunkard, who had a pug nose and goat feet. Bacchus became the god of wine and, in general, of the fertility and bounty of vegetation. He was a joyous god and with his worship was associated constant merrymaking. His chief festival was celebrated in March of each year, when the wine was ready for drinking. At such times in ancient Greece it was customary to give dramatic performances, so Bacchus also became the god of drama and of the theater. By the Romans he was given the name *Liber.*

Usually Bacchus is shown in a chariot drawn by leopards, his head crowned with vine leaves or with wreaths of ivy and in his hand a *thyrsus,* a staff entwined with ivy and a pine cone at the top. Sacred to him were the

(upper) One of the Nereids riding on a sea horse *(lower)* How did the word "maenad" come to mean a "wild, frenzied woman"?

grapevine, the ivy, and the panther. He had special groups of followers. His female followers were called bacchantes or mænads, and were represented as wild with enthusiasm, their heads thrown backward, their hair disheveled. In their hands they carried thyrsi.

Pan, whose name means "all," has always fascinated persons of imagination. He was the son of Mercury and a wood nymph. God of flocks, shepherds, and of nature, he was described as wandering among the mountains and valleys of Arcadia, either amusing himself with hunting or leading the dances of the nymphs. To him is ascribed the invention of the shepherd's flute. He was usually represented as a bearded man, who had a large hooked nose, the ears and hoofs of a goat, and a body covered with hair. In his hand was his shepherd's flute or a shepherd's crook. Inasmuch as Pan was the god of lonely and desolate scenes, especially in mountain countries, he was associated with the sudden and causeless fear that comes on travelers. Since such sudden and causeless fear, first in the outdoor world, later in the midst of battles, was attributed to Pan, it was called a Panic fear. His followers, the *satyrs*, had goatlike ears, short tails, and budding horns. Silenus was the chief of the satyrs.

Minor deities associated with nature were the nymphs. There were many kinds of nymphs, but five groups were more important than the others—the *dryads* or *hamadryads*, each of whom lived in a tree and was supposed to die when the tree died; the *Oceanids* and the *Nereids*, who dwelt in the waters of the ocean; the *naiads*, who were the presiding spirts of fresh water—of springs, rivers, brooks, lakes, etc.; and the *oreads*, the nymphs of mountains and grottoes.

Gods of the Dawn, Dusk, and Air

Over the coming of the dawn presided each day *Aurora* (Greek: *Eos*), "the rosy-fingered child of the morning." Every morning she left her couch

and in a chariot drawn by swift horses ascended to heaven
from the River Oceanus, to announce the coming of the
sun. She put to flight the morning star; and as she passed,
a fresh wind sprang up; while behind her flamed brighter
and brighter the flush of approaching day. Her special favor
was bestowed upon the splendid dawn of life; and young
people were under her care, especially as they went forth
in the morning to hunt or to fight.

Phosphor, the Morning Star, was the son of Aurora and
the hunter Cephalus. Hesper, the Evening Star, was
according to some legends the father of the Hesperides,
three maidens who guarded the Tree of the Golden Apples
in a wonderful garden far to the west of the known world.
Other legends call them the daughters of the Titan Atlas.

The king of the winds was Æolus, who dwelt on the
steep islands later known as the Æolian Islands. There he
confined the winds in a mountain cavern, letting them out
only as they were needed. The four wind gods were Boreas,
the North Wind; Zephyrus, the West Wind; Notus, the
South Wind; and Eurus, the East Wind.

Gods of the Waters

Just as in the skies there were elder
and younger gods, so in the ocean an older dynasty was
displaced—in part at least—by a younger group.

During the reign of Cronus *Oceanus* and *Tethys* ruled
the waters, with the help of innumerable ocean nymphs.
This monarch and his wife dwelt in a wonderful palace,
surrounded by gardens. One of their daughters, Doris,
married another ocean-dweller, *Nereus,* a wise old man
who had the gift of prophecy and the additional gift of
being able to assume various forms. Like the other
inhabitants of the deep Nereus is often represented with
seaweed instead of hair. Nereus and Doris had fifty
daughters, known as the *Nereids,* who made up one of the
kinds of sea nymphs. They were all renowned for their
loveliness and are sometimes pictured as half maidens and
half fish—like mermaids. Among the most famous of them

Neptune (Greek: Poseidon), god of the sea, horses and earthquakes

were Thetis, Galatea, and Amphitrite. Amphitrite married Neptune, and so formed a friendly bond between the old dynasty of the ocean and the new. Oceanus and Tethys dwelt undisturbed in their palace, though their power had passed to Neptune.

Neptune dwelt sometimes in his palace in the sea and sometimes on Mount Olympus. In the waters he had many attendants—among whom were the water nymphs. His son, *Triton,* was his trumpeter and carried a sea shell on which he blew blasts that raised or calmed the waves. Another attendant was *Proteus,* who in many ways—in the power to prophesy and to change his form—resembled Nereus. He had special charge of the seals of Neptune. At midday he rose from the sea and slept in the shade of the rocks on one of his favorite islands, with the monsters of the deep reposing around him. Anyone could seize him while he slept, and could compel him then to reveal what the future would bring. But even after he had been grasped Proteus still had his tricks. He assumed every possible form, wriggling suddenly from one shape into another. Only after he saw that his efforts were of no avail did he resume his

"In gulfs enchanted where the siren sings . . ." Holmes

usual form and make answer to his captor's questions.

Among others who inhabited the waves were the *sirens*. They were sea nymphs, half bird and half woman, who had the power of charming by their songs all who heard them. Many a luckless mariner, his judgment and caution put to sleep by their wondrous melodies, allowed his ship to drift on the rocks. Too late he saw the wrecks of ships and bones of men lying around the reef where the sirens sang.

Scylla and *Charybdis* were two monsters who dwelt on neighboring rocks. Scylla, once a beautiful maiden, had been transformed into a creature with six necks and heads, each armed with three rows of sharp teeth and each barking like a dog. When she could reach toward a ship, she seized men for food. Nearby lay Charybdis, an immense shapeless mass, under a huge fig tree. Thrice each day she swallowed the waters of the sea and thrice she belched them forth again. Only those especially favored of the gods were able to pass in safety between these terrors of the sea.

PRACTICAL APPLICATIONS

References to Mythology in Literature

1. There came a noise of revelers: the rills
   Into the wide stream came of purple hue—
   'Twas *Bacchus* and his crew!—*Keats*
2. I prayed to *Pan*, half god, half goat;
   He played his pipes.—*Keller*
3. And with his *trident Neptune* smites the earth.
   —*Ovid*
4. *Ceres*, most bounteous lady.—*Shakespeare*
5. *Demeter*, rich in fruit and rich in grain.—*Theocritus*
6. With lucid lilies in her golden hair,
   Eos, sweet Goddess of the Morning, stood.—*Horne*
7. The moss-lain *dryads* shall be lulled to sleep.
   —*Keats*
8. And here is manna, pick'd from Syrian trees,
   In starlight, by the three *Hesperides*.—*Keats*
9. An arch face peep'd—an *oread* as I guess'd.—*Keats*
10. Old *Silenus*, bloated, drunken,
    Led by his inebriate satyrs.—*Longfellow*
11. Seldom has a winter not extremely cold been so
    hard on the furnace-tender. *Boreas* was usually
    looking in at him through the cellar-window.
    —*New York Times*
12. His usual company, *satyrs* and *bacchanals*,
    thronged around him.—*Ovid*
13. *Æolus*, to whom the father of gods and men has
    granted the power with winds to soothe and lift up
    the waves.—*Virgil*
14. Cold streamlets trickle, and at *Zephyr's* breath
    Crumbles and cracks the clod.—*Virgil*
15. Have sight of *Proteus* rising from the sea,
    Or hear old *Triton* blow his wreathéd horn.
    —*Wordsworth*

Suggestions for Oral or Written Composition

1. An artist is about to draw a colored picture of Ceres. Give complete directions.

2. Imagine that one of each of the five kinds of nymphs will appear in a play. As each appears on stage, she explains briefly who she is and what she does. Giving details from your imagination, tell what each would say.

3. Prepare a talk, accompanied by a chart, showing how Neptune is related to Oceanus and Tethys. Introduce Triton also.

Word Study

1. Explain the origin of the following words:

   panic—extreme or sudden fear
   cereal—grain
   boreal—northern, cold
   auroral—rosy
   aurora borealis—northern lights
   zephyr—a gentle breeze
   protean—changeable, very variable
   Bacchic—jovial or riotous
   siren—a steam whistle or fog signal

2. Give the Greek names of the following deities: *Jupiter, Ceres, Neptune, Bacchus, Aurora*. What was the name of the staff that Bacchus carried?

3. What does the expression, "between Scylla and Charybdis," mean? What is meant when a man is called a "Silenus"? or a woman a "siren"? What is an "æolian harp"?

4. Some think that "satire" is connected with "satyr." Do you see any connection?

5. One species of butterfly is called *Nymphalidæ*. Is the name appropriate to these bright-winged insects? Why or why not?

Questions for Review

1. What was the Greek notion of the earth?
2. What was the realm of Ceres?
3. Who was her daughter?
4. What was the character of Bacchus?
5. Over what realms did he rule?
6. How is he generally represented?
7. Who was Pan? Give his characteristics.
8. Who were his followers?
9. Who was the chief of them?
10. Name the principal five kinds of nymphs.
11. Who was the goddess of the dawn?
12. Who was Phosphor? Hesper? the Hesperides?
13. Who was the king of the winds? Name the North Wind and the West Wind.
14. Who were the first rulers of the ocean?
15. How were they related to Neptune, the later ruler?
16. Who was Nereus?
17. What were his daughters called?
18. Who was Triton? Proteus?
19. Who were the sirens? Scylla and Charybdis?

Reading List

Poems and Plays

Beddoes, T.L.: *Song of the Stygian Naiades*
Browning, Elizabeth Barrett: *The Dead Pan—The Musical Instrument*
Buchanan, Robert: *Pan*
Campion, Thomas: *A Hymn in Praise of Neptune*
Doolittle, Hilda ("H.D."): *Oread*
Emerson, Ralph Waldo: *Bacchus*
Fletcher, John: *Song of Pan—Song of the Priest of Pan*
Gosse, Edmund: *The Praise of Dionysus*
Longfellow, Henry Wadsworth: *Drinking Song*
Milton, John: *Comus*
Shelley, Percy Bysshe: *Hymn of Pan*
Swinburne, Algernon Charles: *The Palace of Pan*
Tietjens, Eunice: *The Bacchante to Her Babe*

Mosaic from Pompeii of Ceres (Greek: Demeter), goddess of agriculture

8 Stories of the Gods of Nature

As frighted Proserpine let fall
Her flowers at the sight of Dis.

Hood

Ceres, Proserpina, and Pluto

When Jupiter at the beginning of his reign divided the sovereignty of the world, he assigned to his brother Pluto (sometimes called *Dis* and sometimes *Hades*) control of the underworld and the shades of the dead. In later days the land of the dead was itself called Hades.

Pluto was not very well pleased at having been given so gloomy a realm over which to rule, but he protested in vain.

"Be content," urged Jupiter. "Though now you have no people in your kingdom, in time to come it shall be well peopled. All that live shall in the end come under your sway. You have, moreover, in your keeping all the vast wealth that lies hidden in the earth. You shall be the god of wealth, you shall be Pluto the wealthy one."

So Pluto perforce submitted and in time grew contented with his lot. But he craved a wife to share his destiny, and Jupiter promised him *Proserpina,* the beautiful daughter of Ceres. But he feared to tell the girl's mother his plan, and not all the urging of Pluto that he fulfill his promise, sufficed to make him announce his decision. Pluto then resolved to take the matter into his own hands.

One day Proserpina and her maidens were gathering flowers in the sunny fields of Sicily. As they chattered of the joyous days to come, the earth suddenly trembled, a rift opened at their very feet, and out of it sprang a chariot, driven by a man of dark and forbidding visage. He leaped from the seat, and without a word seized Proserpina and carried her to the chariot. Her screams and struggles were of no avail. The chariot disappeared again into the earth.

When Ceres missed her child, she was frantic with despair. No one could tell her who it was that had snatched Proserpina away. She searched all over the earth for her in vain. In her sorrow she neglected her duties. The crops withered and died, and famine threatened the race of men. Jupiter tried to persuade the goddess of harvests to resume her care of the fruits of the earth, but Ceres sent back word that she would not set foot in the house of Jupiter again nor allow the fields to bear their harvests until her daughter had been returned to her.

Then Jupiter said, "If the maiden Proserpina has not tasted food during the days she has spent in the abode of Hades, she shall be free again, and shall not be his spouse."

So he sent Mercury, the fleet-footed messenger, to the dark palace of the underworld and had him command Pluto to release the maiden. Pluto obeyed, but before Proserpina

The abduction of Proserpina

left he set before her food and drink. Now up to this time Proserpina had refused to let a morsel of food pass her lips, for she knew that whoever eats of the fare of Hades becomes his henchman. But in her joy she relaxed the vow she had placed upon herself, and cut a pomegranate in half and ate six of the seeds.

Then she departed with Mercury, and returned to her dear mother. But because she had broken her fast she was destined to return to Hades six months of every year. So Proserpina, goddess of the spring, disappears when the summertime is over, Ceres in her sorrow once more neglects her duties, and winter reigns over the earth until Proserpina returns.

Bacchus

As a child the character of Bacchus was innocent and happy, and he was tended by the nymphs and herdsmen of Nysa. When he grew up, the legends say, he was pursued by Juno, who was jealous of him, and he wandered through many parts of the world establishing the culture of the vine and teaching its use. But he taught, too, the arts of peace and of justice and honorable dealing. He had many adventures and punished severely those who interfered with his rites. One of his most celebrated feats was performed when he hired a ship to carry him from Icaria to Naxos. The mariners were in reality pirates, and they resolved to sell into slavery the beautiful youth whom they were carrying as a passenger. So they turned their vessel toward Asia. Thereupon the god changed the mast and oars into serpents and himself into a lion; ivy grew around the vessel, and the sweet sound of flutes was heard on every side. The mariners, beholding in amazement these miraculous events, were seized with madness, leaped into the sea, and were transformed into dolphins.

Midas

Pan was so proud of his knowledge of music that once he challenged Apollo to a contest. Apollo agreed to compete with him, and Midas, the king of Phrygia, was selected as the judge. Apollo played beautiful harmonies on the lyre, Pan replied with sweet notes on his flute, and Midas, without much pondering, decided in favor of Pan. Apollo was greatly incensed and, in a most unsportsmanlike way, resolved to punish Midas for showing such bad taste—bad in Apollo's opinion. So he changed the ears of Midas to those of an ass. Midas was very much ashamed at this odd transformation. He contrived, however, to conceal his ass's ears under his Phrygian cap. According to the story, however, his barber discovered the secret when he cut Midas's hair. Midas threatened him with severe punishment if he told anyone about the king's deformity, and for a long time the barber managed to keep quiet. But one day he could hold the secret no longer. He went out into the fields, dug a hole, and whispered into the cavity, "Midas has the ears of an ass!"

Later reeds grew up at the very spot, and by their whisperings betrayed the secret to the whole world.

It was this same Midas to whom another misfortune happened. He once performed a service to Silenus, who was the teacher of Bacchus. The latter told Midas he would grant him any favor he wanted. In his folly Midas begged, "Let all I touch be changed to gold!" He was already fabulously rich, but he wanted still more. The consequences can be imagined. Everything Midas touched was indeed changed—including his food and water and even his beloved child. Finally in desperation Midas prayed to Bacchus and begged him to take his gift back again. Bacchus commanded him to bathe in the sources of the River Pactolus, and when Midas did so, the curse was removed. But ever since that time the Pactolus has had an abundance of gold in its sands.

"... Aloft, young Bacchus stood"—Keats

Io

Many stories are told of the beautiful nymphs, and often the gods of Olympus strayed on the earth because of the attractions of some lovely earth-goddess. Jupiter himself fell in love with Io, daughter of the river god Inachus, who was himself a son of the mighty Oceanus. Once, as Jove was talking to the nymph, he suddenly noticed that he had attracted the attention of Juno. So he promptly spread a cloud around himself and Io. But Juno, suspicious and jealous, brushed away the cloud, and saw Jupiter—with a beautiful heifer standing beside him. For Jupiter had changed Io into that form in order to escape the reproaches of Juno.

Juno praised the heifer and asked Jupiter to give it to her. Reluctantly the god acceded to her request, and then Juno turned the heifer over to her servant Argus to watch. Argus was a good watchman, for he had a hundred eyes, which took turns sleeping. It seemed that nothing could

Does this picture hint at the meaning of "Junoesque"?

throw him off his guard or distract his attention. The poor
heifer suffered greatly in her new form, and could not even
express her distress except in a way that nobody
understood. But Jupiter remembered her and sent Mercury
to put Argus out of the way.

Mercury approached the hundred-eyed watchman in
the guise of a shepherd. He sat down beside him, told
stories, and played upon his pipes. Argus was pleased at
the shepherd's attention and often seemed on the point of
dropping off to sleep, but always some of his eyes remained
watchful. At length Mercury told him the tale of the
invention of the syrinx, the pipes on which he was playing.

"Once, ages ago," he said softly, "the god Pan fell in
love with the nymph Syrinx. But she was a faithful follower
of Diana and would have nothing to do with him. 'I shall
never marry,' she told him. He paid no attention to her
words, but sought to embrace her. She escaped from his
arms and fled swiftly toward a nearby river. Closer and
closer came Pan, and now seemed on the very point of
seizing her. She called for help to the god of the stream,
and as Pan threw his arms around her, he found himself

embracing not a nymph but a clump of tall reeds. Pan sighed with regret, and as he sighed his breath moved musically through the reeds. The air, as it touched the hollow stems, made a gentle, soothing melody. Pan, pleased with the music, broke off the reeds and fashioned a pipe for himself. Then he sat down on the bank of the river and for a long time played sad, sweet songs, to which the shepherds listened with delight. So was born the syrinx."

As Mercury concluded his story he saw that all of the eyes of Argus were closed in sleep. At once he leaped up softly and slew him, and set Io free. In reward for the faithfulness of her servant, Juno took the eyes of Argus and scattered them in the tail of the peacock, where they may still be seen.

But she continued to pursue Io. She sent a gadfly to torture the poor heifer, who in torment fled into the sea and swam across. It is still called, after her, the Ionian Sea. After many wanderings she reached Egypt, and when Jupiter promised Juno that he would pay her no more attentions, Juno agreed to release her from the bondage of her heifer form.

Apollo and Daphne

The name of the glorious and beautiful god Apollo is, of course, associated with the names of many nymphs. As handsome as Apollo was, however, the nymphs did not always favor him.

There was Daphne, for example. She was the daughter of the river god Peneus in Thessaly. Apollo fell in love with her because of a trick of Cupid. One day Apollo saw the son of Venus playing with his bow and arrows. He taunted the little god and suggested that he leave such weapons to those that were able to understand and use them.

"You shall see," promised Cupid, "how well I understand my bow and arrows."

Shortly afterward Apollo was straying with the beautiful nymph Daphne. Cupid saw them and let fly two arrows—a leaden shaft at her to excite dislike, and a golden shaft at him to produce love.

Apollo's life became one of endless torment. The more skillfully and persuasively he pleaded his cause, the colder Daphne grew. She told him that she abhorred all thoughts of love, that her delight was in hunting and in woodland sports. Desperate at last, Apollo resolved to carry her off and make her his wife in spite of her coldness. He seized her, but she escaped from his grasp and fled through the thickets and forest. The more rapidly she fled, the more beautiful she seemed to the god. His pursuit became faster. She had more and more difficulty in escaping him. At last her strength failed her, and she sank to the ground, but as she fell she breathed a prayer to her father.

"Help me, O father!" she cried. "Save me from Apollo!"

Peneus heard her, and resorted to a desperate device to save his daughter. Even as Daphne spoke her form began to change, and Apollo cast his arms about her only to find that he was embracing a beautiful laurel tree instead of the nymph. Even so he still loved her; and the laurel became his favorite tree. Since that time those who win the favor of Apollo are crowned with the laurel. Poets in particular have always regarded the laurel wreath as a mark of special honor.

Apollo and Clytie

In the case of Clytie, however, the tables were turned, and it was Apollo who proved cold to the advances of the nymph, who was one of the daughters of Oceanus. Timidly she showed her affection to the god, but he became more and more indifferent. So she began to pine away. All her thought was for the sun god and her gaze was ever upon him. She gave no care to herself, taking neither food nor drink, giving no heed to her clothing, her hair or her appearance. In time she died, but even in death, she remained constant to her idol. Her limbs became

Apollo and Daphne—Why could this be entitled "Cupid's revenge"?

Stories of the Gods of Nature   117

rooted in the ground, her body changed to a slender trunk, and her head became a flower. But, unlike other flowers, Clytie's head moved on the stalk. She always turned her gaze toward the sun, looking at the east in the morning and at the west in the evening. For Clytie became the sunflower, who

> turns on her god when he sets
> The same look that she gave when he rose.

Echo and Narcissus

Most celebrated of the nymphs was Echo, a beautiful oread who was the special favorite of Diana. Juno, too, was fond of her, but one day she discovered that Echo had purposely delayed her with interesting conversation while Jupiter was being entertained by other nymphs. Juno in anger punished Echo by taking from her all power to begin a conversation—Echo could only repeat what someone else said to her.

This was merely an annoying punishment until a beautiful youth named Narcissus happened to wander into the woods that Echo haunted. Echo immediately fell in love with him, but when Narcissus spoke to her, all she could do was repeat his last words. Narcissus thought she was making fun of him and did all he could to avoid her. But everywhere that he went Echo followed him; and to all the reproaches of Narcissus she could merely reply by repeating to him what he had just said. In despair Echo faded away until she was no more than a voice—a voice that still haunts caves, cliffs and desolate places, and repeats what you say.

Narcissus, however, not only repelled Echo—he also repelled all the other nymphs, for he was very conceited and believed nobody quite good enough for him. One maiden finally prayed that he might have the experience of knowing what it was to love and not to be loved in return; and the prayer was granted—in a most curious way.

118

Narcissus pines away for love of his own reflection.

Narcissus, bending one day over a mountain pool to drink its cooling waters, caught a glimpse of his own image in the waves. He thought it was some coy water nymph hiding from his advances. He talked to it, spoke of love, and finally reached over to embrace it—but all in vain. So, like Echo, he too pined away and died. But from his body sprang a flower that still bears his name.

Aurora and Tithonus

Many legends are associated with Aurora, but the best known is the story of Tithonus. He was the son of the king of Troy, and when Aurora beheld him, she fell in love with him. She stole him away and made him her husband. So deeply in love was she with him that she desired to keep him with her forever. She went to Jupiter, therefore, and begged a special favor from him.

"Grant Tithonus eternal life," she prayed.

Jupiter smiled as he answered that her request was granted; for Aurora had forgotten to add to her prayer that he be granted, at the same time, eternal youth. Slowly, then, Tithonus grew old. White hairs began to show, the wrinkles in his face grew deeper and deeper, and he became completely decrepit. Finally, Aurora shut him up in a chamber, from which only his feeble voice could be heard in endless petition. Then, at last, she changed him into an insect—the grasshopper.

Ceyx and Halcyone

A descendant of Aurora named Ceyx, king of Trachis in Thessaly, married Halcyone, the daughter of King Æolus, ruler of the winds. For many years they reigned happily, until the brother of Ceyx died. Many strange events accompanied his death—long-lasting tempests, darkenings of the sun and moon, and the appearance of terrifying monsters. Ceyx thought he had better consult the gods, and therefore announced that he intended to sail to Claros in Ionia, to ask help of the oracle of Apollo there. His wife tried to dissuade him, for it was a season of storms, but he insisted on setting forth. He was almost at his goal when his ship was wrecked and he was drowned. But as he sank beneath the waves, he prayed to Neptune that the waves might carry his body until it reached his native land, and that Halcyone might see it and bury it.

Month after month passed and Halcyone, full of anxiety, awaited her husband's return. She offered prayers, incense and sacrifices to the gods and most of all to Juno; and she implored of them that her husband might return safely. Juno finally was moved at her entreaties; and inasmuch as she could do nothing for a man already dead, she resolved to let Halcyone know that there was no further hope.

She therefore called her messenger Iris to bid her carry

Apollo - Roman mosaic

a command to Somnus, the god of sleep. Over her bow of
many colors Iris hastened to the land of darkness, where
dwelt the drowsy god of slumbers. She found him in a cave
from which all light was excluded, and to which all sounds
and noises of the world penetrated either not at all or dully
muffled. Around the gloomy chamber fluttered innumerable
dreams; and some sat on the very head of Somnus, who lay
on a feathery couch plunged deep in sleep. Iris had much
trouble in arousing him, but at last she was able to make
her message clear to the heavy-lidded god. He called his
son Morpheus and bade him send a dream to Halcyone.
Hardly were the words out of his mouth when he fell back
on his couch fast asleep. Iris hastened out of the cave,
brushing dreams away from her face and keeping herself
awake with difficulty.

Meanwhile Morpheus himself flew to the palace of
Ceyx, and there, assuming the very form of its master,
appeared to Halcyone. But how changed was that form in
the dream! He had on him the pallor of death, and the
water dripped from his bedraggled robes. He told his wife
that a storm on the Ægean had sunk his ship, and that he
was dead.

Stories of the Gods of Nature   121

As her dream vanished, Halcyone awoke, and tears rolled down her cheeks. Early the next morning Halcyone went down to the sea, and as she paced the beach, she saw floating toward her an indistinct object. Nearer and nearer it came, and as it touched the shore she saw that it was the body of her husband. She could not endure the sight of the corpse and threw herself into the water. But Jupiter in pity changed her even as she leaped into the waves; and she became a bird that sang dolefully as it flew over the water. Ceyx was likewise transformed, and joined his wife again. From them descend the kingfishers.

Their devotion so moved King Æolus, that because of them he granted a special favor to all mariners. Seven days before the winter solstice begins and seven days after it, no winds blow. It is a season of calm and peace; and then Halcyone, whose nest floats over the sea, sits on her nest in quiet. Sailors call this period "the halcyon days," for then the ruler of the winds forbids all storms to blow that his grandchildren may be born in peace.

PRACTICAL APPLICATIONS

Myths in Literature

Of all the material included in this chapter the story of Pluto and Proserpina has proved most fascinating. Interesting in itself, the story has also the attraction of an allegory and typifies the passing of summer and the coming of spring as no other story does. A whole galaxy of poets has celebrated the divine maiden snatched away to dwell in the underworld—Swinburne, George Edward Woodberry, Lewis Morris, Aubrey De Vere, R. H. Stoddard, Tennyson, and others.

Nowhere did the Greek imagination work more lovingly than on the forces and appearances of nature—as may be seen when Greek myths are compared with those of most other nations.

Poets of all times have therefore regarded these ancient Greek legends with joy and have adopted them as their own in many poems and stories.

To different types of mind, however, different types appeal. The wild revels of Bacchus have often been sung, as by Dryden, Catullus, Longfellow, Edmund Gosse, Thomas Love Peacock, and B. W. Procter.

Pan, as a symbol of nature in its wilder forms, has also fascinated many writers. Milton called him "Universal Pan." Shelley wrote a *Hymn of Pan* full of ecstatic melody. Elizabeth Barrett Browning in one of the most musical of her poems, *The Musical Instrument,* tells how Pan made the first flute:

> **Sweet, sweet, sweet, O Pan!**
> **Piercing sweet by the river!**
> **Blinding sweet, O great god Pan!**
> **The sun on the hill forgot to die,**
> **And the lilies revived, and the dragon-fly**
> **Came back to dream on the river.**

She also lamented *The Dead Pan,* while Edmund Clarence Stedman quizzically pictured *Pan in Wall Street.*

The water deities have been less fortunate than the land or air gods in winning poets to celebrate them. But the sirens have always had their bards—beginning with Homer and Virgil. Often a poet has tried to imagine what song the sirens sang. William Morris thus repeats what they sang to Jason and the Argonauts. Rossetti, Andrew Lang, and Lowell have, likewise, written of the sirens. A remarkable story of them, in a modern setting, is Edward Lucas White's, *The Song of the Sirens.*

Triton and Proteus appear in Wordsworth's famous sonnet, *The World Is Too Much with Us:*

> **Have sight of Proteus rising from the sea,**
> **Or hear old Triton blow his wreathéd horn.**

Stories of the Gods of Nature   **123**

James Russell Lowell, at the beginning of his *Fable for Critics*, makes a burlesque use of the story of Daphne:

Phœbus, sitting one day in a laurel tree's shade,
Was reminded of Daphne, of whom it was made,
For the god being one day too warm in his wooing,
She took to the tree to escape his pursuing. . . .
"My case is like Dido's," he sometimes remarked,
"When I last saw my love, she was fairly embarked
In a laurel, as she thought—but (ah, how Fate mocks!)
She has found it by this time a very bad box!
Let hunters from me take this saw when they need it—
You're not always sure of your game when you've treed it.
Just conceive such a change taking place in one's mistress!
What romance would be left? Who can flatter or kiss trees?
And, for mercy's sake, how could one keep up a dialogue
With a dull wooden thing that will live and will die a log—
Not to say that the thought would forever intrude
That you've less chance to win her the more she is wood?
Ah! it went to my heart, and the memory still grieves,
To see those loved graces all taking their leaves;
Those charms beyond speech, so enchanting but now,
As they left me forever, each making its bough:
If her tongue had tang sometimes more than was right,
Her new bark is worse than ten times her old bite."

Specific Literary References

What do the following references mean? Where a word or phrase is italicized, explain only the word or phrase.

1. No sane man would demand from the gods the gift of Midas.—*Blackwood's Magazine*
2. *Dawn* rose from her couch by high *Tithonus,* to bring light to immortals and to mankind.—*Homer*
3. As frighted *Proserpine* let fall
   Her flowers at the sight of *Dis.*—*Hood*
4. Sweet *Echo,* sweetest nymph, that liv'st unseen
   Within thy airy shell.—*Milton*
5. Even when he had been received into the infernal abodes, he kept on gazing his image in the Stygian pool.—*Ovid*

6. The halcyon days of American shipping—*Peattie*
7. And I will sing how sad Proserpina
   Unto a grave and glowing lord was wed.—*Wilde*

Suggestions for Oral or Written Composition

1. In the introduction it is stated that a myth is often an attempt to explain some phenomenon of nature. Give a talk on the myths in this chapter, showing how they illustrate this definition.

2. One of the maidens who were gathering flowers with Proserpina in the Sicilian field tells her mother just what occurred when Pluto appeared. Write down the conversation.

3. Imagine a conversation between Narcissus and Echo, in which Echo can do more than repeat the last word or syllable of what Narcissus says.

4. You are a courtier in the service of King Midas. Describe the scene on the day when Midas is given his gift of changing all he touches to gold.

5. Invent a myth to account for some object in the world around us—the rose, for example, or the first automobile, or the coming of twilight. Introduce into your myth the figures of some of the gods about whom you have learned.

Word Study

1. Give the Greek names of these deities: *Pluto, Bacchus, Juno, Mercury, Cupid, Diana, Aurora.*

2. What is a heifer? a Phrygian cap? a syrinx? a pomegranate?

3. Explain the title, "poet laureate," given to the official poet of the court of England.

4. What is meant by the expression, "the touch of Midas"? by "halcyon days"? by "plutocrat"?

5. How did the Greeks explain the origin of the word *echo?* of the name of the Ionian Sea?

Questions for Review

1. What other names has Pluto?
2. Over what realm did he rule?
3. Who was promised him as his wife?
4. What means did he use to obtain her?
5. What happened when Ceres missed her child?
6. What did Jupiter promise her?
7. What, meanwhile, had happened in Hades?
8. What does the story explain?
9. What punishment did Bacchus visit on pirates who treated him disrespectfully?
10. What two gods once competed in musical ability?
11. Who was the judge, and what was his decision?
12. What revenge did the defeated god take?
13. What other misfortune happened to Midas?
14. Who was Io?
15. How did she incur the wrath of Juno?
16. Into what form did Jupiter change her?
17. Whom did Juno set to guard her?
18. How did Mercury outwit the watchman?
19. What nymph rejected Apollo's advances?
20. How did she manage to escape him?
21. Whose love did Apollo reject?
22. What was her fate?
23. How did Echo originate?
24. With whom did she fall in love?
25. What fate overtook him?
26. What favor did Aurora ask for Tithonus?
27. What did she forget to ask?
28. Why did Ceyx set forth on his journey?
29. What happened to him?
30. Why did Juno intervene?
31. What was the final fate of the husband and wife?

Reading List

Poems and Plays

Bridges, Robert: *Demeter*
Doolittle, Hilda ("H.D."): *Demeter*
Frank, Florence Kiper: *The Return of Proserpine* (in *Three Plays for a Children's Theater*)
Ingelow, Jean: *Demeter and Persephone*
Ledoux, Louis V.: *The Story of Eleusis*
Rossetti, Dante Gabriel: *Proserpine*
Shelley, Percy Bysshe: *Song of Proserpine*
Stoddard, R. H.: *The Search of Proserpine*
Story, W. W.: *Clytie*
Swinburne, Algernon Charles: *The Garden of Proserpine—Song to Proserpine*
Taylor, Bayard: *An Epistle from Mount Tmolus*
Tennyson, Frederick: *Daphne*
Tennyson, Alfred: *Tithonus*

Attic black-figure amphora showing Hercules and Cerberus

9 Stories of the Underworld

*Easy is the descent to Avernus, but to
retrace one's steps and escape to
the upper air, that is difficult, that is
toilsome.*

Virgil

Regions of the Underworld

The realm of the underworld which
Pluto ruled stretched in many directions and the regions
that it embraced were varied. The entrance was called
Avernus. Through it flowed five rivers. The first to which
the shades of the dead came was called the *Styx*. So
dreadful in color and appearance was this river that the
gods swore by it, and an oath taken "by the Styx" was

never broken. The dead waited on the shore until the ferryman Charon, an old man with a bedraggled beard and a mean dress, approached to carry them to the other side. His pay was an obolus—a Greek coin placed on the mouth of every corpse previous to burial. Once on the other side the ghosts wandered on until they came to the River *Lethe*, the river of forgetfulness. Kneeling on its shore they cupped their hands, and drank of its water. Immediately all memory of their past lives disappeared from their minds. To and fro, like hurried clouds, the bands of ghosts wandered on in the lampless regions of Hades. The other rivers were *Acheron*, river of woe, with its tributaries—*Phlegethon*, the river between whose banks flowed fire instead of water, and *Cocytus*, the river of wailing. These rivers were the boundaries of the underworld, which lay "beneath the secret places of the earth."

At the gate of Hades stood a terrifying guardian—*Cerberus*, a monstrous dog, with three heads and the tail of a dragon. He never attempted to molest the shades that entered Hades, but he was ferocious to those who attempted to leave. When Æneas visited Hades, as the great Latin poet Virgil tells, he made up a cunning pill that contained a sleeping potion, and threw this sop to Cerberus, who ate it and immediately fell unconscious. But this hero and a few others especially favored by the gods were the only ones that ever thwarted Cerberus.

The palace of Pluto himself, where he sat with his cap of darkness, with the key to the underworld in one hand and a magic staff in the other, was dark and gloomy.

Hades, which sometimes was called *Erebus*, was divided into several regions. The greater part of it was called *Acheron*, after the river, and here, with troubled and vacant faces, moved aimlessly to and fro the majority of those that had died. Far to the west lay *Elysium*, a realm somewhat like our idea of Paradise. To this place came certain favorites of the gods—noted poets, minstrels, and great heroes. Over them reigned Cronus, exiled after his overthrow by Jupiter; and here they lived again a new Golden Age. Quite other was the dire region of *Tartarus*, to which were consigned those whom the gods desired to punish. Such persons lived in misery and torture.

Charon prepares to escort a lady across the River Styx.

Chief Figures of Hades

Besides Pluto, Proserpina, Charon and Cerberus, there were other inhabitants of the underworld. When the souls of the dead had to be submitted to trial and judgment, the king of Hades and his queen acted as judges. Terror-inspiring figures of Hades were the *Furies*, three creatures that attended Proserpina. They were winged maidens, with serpents twined in their hair and blood dripping from their eyes. They pursued those who had escaped punishment for crimes they had committed, and afflicted them with all the horrors of a guilty conscience. The Greeks called the Furies *Eumenides*.

Hecate was a mysterious goddess, a Titaness who retained her power after Jupiter had seized the rule of the world, and who was honored by all the gods. She helped Ceres search for Proserpina, and she remained with the queen of Hades. It was she who sent forth at night all kinds of demons and terrifying phantoms from the underworld to the land of the living. She was the goddess of witchcraft and sorcery; her approach was announced by the weird howling and whining of dogs. She was the personification of the terror of night, just as Diana was the goddess of its bright and beautiful moonlight.

Somnus (Greek: *Hypnos*), whose palace was described in the last chapter, was the god of sleep. He held in his hand a poppy of forgetfulness or else a horn; from the horn trickled the drops of slumber. His twin brother was *Mors* (Greek: *Thanatos*), or Death, often represented as a quiet, pensive youth, with wings, who stood beside a funeral urn decorated with a funeral wreath. Sometimes he held in his hand an extinguished torch. *Morpheus* was the guardian of dreams, which he kept confined in his palace. Idle and deceptive dreams he sent forth from the ivory gate of his palace, prophetic and meaningful dreams he sent forth from the horn gate.

Dwellers in Tartarus

Far down in the uttermost gulfs of Tartarus dwelt those Titans who had made war against Jupiter and had been conquered. Here, too, lived in torment others whom the gods punished—among them Tantalus, Ixion, Sisyphus, and the Danaïdes.

Tantalus had been a monarch while alive, and the gods had bestowed on him many favors. But in spite of this he committed many grave crimes, even killing his own son. When he died he was condemned to suffer a never-ending punishment. He found himself standing in clear water that barely touched his chin; and right above his head there hung branches of all manner of fruit trees, weighed down with the ripe and tempting fruit. Tantalus, constantly tortured with hunger and thirst, sought ever to sip the water and to grasp the fruit. But it was always in vain—always the water receded from his panting lips and the branches moved away from his grasping hands.

Ixion had murdered his father-in-law that he might avoid making the bridal gifts, customary in those days; and later he showed deep disrespect for the gods. In Tartarus he was chained perpetually to a wheel that rolled forever down an endless road.

Sisyphus, the king of Corinth, had promoted trade and navigation, but was a man of avarice and fraud. On his death he was condemned to roll uphill a huge marble block. When, after endless and bitter toil, he reached the top with it, the stone immediately rolled back to the bottom of the hill, and Sisyphus had to begin all over again.

The Danaïdes were the daughters of Danaüs, king of Argos. All were guilty of the crime of murdering their husbands, at the instigation of Danaüs. When the women died they were punished in Hades by being compelled to carry water in a sieve, their labor being in vain and going on forever.

Islands of the Blest

Elysium was a kind of Paradise, to which came certain favored mortals. It was a land of perpetual and soothing sunshine. "Here fell not hail or rain or any snow, nor ever winds blew loudly." Upon its eternally blossoming and fragrant meadows heroes and minstrels reclined in endless bliss, or roamed about in everlasting happiness.

When Æneas, in his journey through Hades as described by Virgil, came to the Happy Isles, he found that its inhabitants breathed a freer air than that of the world above, and saw all things clothed in a purple light. Their land had a sun and stars of its own. Some of the inhabitants indulged in sports on the grassy turf, others engaged in

Pluto and Proserpina - chief inhabitants of the underworld

dancing and singing. Sublime bards struck the chords of their lyres; and elsewhere the great warriors whom Æneas had known rested in peace, their armor rusting, their chariots unused. Here, too, were all the poets and artists and those who in any other way had rendered their memories blessed by serving mankind.

Orpheus and Eurydice

One of the bards who might be seen in Elysium was a son of Apollo himself, and he had a singular experience with Death, being one of the few persons who visited Hades while still in the flesh.

This was Orpheus, whom the Muse Calliope bore to the sun god. He was presented with a lyre by Apollo and given instruction in its use, and soon won renown as one of the greatest bards of Greece. He enchanted with his music not only people, but even the wild beasts of the field, whose savage breasts were soothed by the tunes he played. It was said of his playing that the very trees and rocks were affected and tried to move and follow his music.

In Thrace lived Eurydice, a lovely maiden with whom Orpheus fell in love. Their marriage was approved by all, and for a year or two they lived in great happiness. Then, one day, as they were wandering through a flowery meadow, Eurydice was stung by a serpent, and before aid could be summoned, she died in the arms of her husband. He was heartbroken. In constant lamentations and elegies he recounted his grief, and at last made up his mind that he would follow his wife into the dread regions of Pluto. He found a cave in the side of a volcano, and passing through many dark passages and uncanny pits he came at last to the realm of Hades. There he took up again his divine lyre, and began to play. As the strains of wonderful music sounded through Tartarus, Sisyphus and Ixion paused in their endless torments, and for a moment the torturing thirst and hunger of Tantalus were allayed.

Orpheus passed on through the clouds of ghosts, who followed after him in enchanted silence. As he came to the throne of Pluto and Proserpina, Orpheus bowed before them, and with magic skill pleaded his cause to the music of his lyre. Tears rolled down the iron cheeks of Pluto, and Proserpina remembered the blossom-strewn fields of Sicily as she wept.

"Grant me my wife again," Orpheus begged; and the fullness of his sorrow made the tears roll down his own cheeks.

Pluto could not resist such pleading, and he granted the prayer of Orpheus. But to the favorable answer was attached one condition, announced as Eurydice was called before Pluto and restored to the arms of Orpheus.

"As you leave Hades," commanded Pluto, "do not cast a look behind. If you break this commandment, Eurydice shall be snatched from you again, and shall once more become my subject."

Orpheus charming the animals—mosaic from a villa near Palermo, Italy

They promised that they would obey, and the pair set out on their happy journey back to the land of the living. Lovingly Orpheus guided his wife on the dangerous path, guided her through gloomy caverns and endless roads, beside dangerous abysses and waters. The hazardous journey was almost ended when they came to a long passageway through which they could go only in single file. Orpheus led the way, stumbling over crags as he went. Now the end was in sight, and before them they could see the blessed light of the sun.

Then, at that fateful moment, anxiety overcame Orpheus. He was seized with terror lest in some way Eurydice might have fallen, or lest some of the terrible creatures of the underworld might have seized and held her. So he gave a swift glance backward. There, quite safe, followed Eurydice; but, even as he gazed, she disappeared from his view and with a terrified scream was drawn back into the realm of Pluto. Orpheus, too, tried to turn back,

"Black Orpheus," a movie set in Brazil during Carnival, is a modern adaptation of "Orpheus and Eurydice."

but he found that his way was barred with solid rock. Never again could he find a way into the underworld.

Thereafter life meant less than nothing to Orpheus. He wandered in deepest gloom from country to country, waiting only to die. Once a band of mænads, followers of Bacchus, sought to entice him to take part in their drunken orgies. He refused, and in rage they hurled rocks at his head. But the music of his lyre charmed the stones, and they fell harmless at his side. Then the mænads yelled so dreadfully and loudly that the noise of his playing was drowned, and the stones struck him from all sides. Mortally wounded he fell, and for a second time passed to Hades and joined Eurydice again. His lyre was placed by Jupiter among the stars.

PRACTICAL APPLICATIONS

Myths in Literature

The regions of darkness and their drear inhabitants have enthralled poets. Undoubtedly the most wonderful description of that region occurs in Dante's *Inferno,* the first part of the great Italian poet's *Divine Comedy.* A very vivid description may also be found in Stephen Phillip's *Christ in Hades.* Swinburne, in *The Garden of Proserpine,* thus pictures the land of the dead:

> No growth of moor or coppice,
> No heather-flower or vine,
> But bloomless buds of poppies,
> Green grapes of Proserpine,
> Pale beds of glowing rushes,
> Where no leaf blooms or blushes
> Save this whereout she crushes
> For dead men deadly wine.

Naturally the story of Orpheus and Eurydice has attracted the poets. Milton reaches the climax of his *L'Allegro* with a detailed reference to Orpheus, and in *Il Penseroso* he uses the same story, thinking in the one case of music so sweet

> That Orpheus' self may heave his head
> From golden slumber on a bed
> Of heaped Elysian flowers, and hear
> Such strains as would have won the ear
> Of Pluto to have quite set free
> His half-regained Eurydice.

In the other poem he regrets that inspiration is unable to bring back the ancient poet Musæus,

> Or bid the soul of Orpheus sing
> Such notes as, warbled to the string,
> Drew iron tears down Pluto's cheek,
> And made Hell grant what love did seek.

Shakespeare similarly introduces Orpheus into one of his most famous passages—a hymn on the power of music in *The Merchant of Venice:*

> Therefore the poet
> Did feign that Orpheus drew trees, stones, and floods:
> Since naught so stockish, hard, and full of rage,
> But music for the time doth change his nature.
> The man that hath no music in himself,
> Nor is not mov'd with concord of sweet sounds,
> Is fit for treasons, stratagems, and spoils.
> The motions of his spirit are dull as night,
> And his affections dark as Erebus.
> Let no such man be trusted.

Specific Literary References

What do the following references mean? Where a word or phrase is italicized, explain only the word or phrase.

1.   Like one who dream'd
   Of idleness in groves *Elysian.—Keats*
2.   On the verge
   Of light he stood, and on Eurydice
   (Mindless of fate, alas! and soul-subdued)
   Looked back.—*Landor*
3. With useless endeavor,
   Forever, forever,
   Is Sisyphus rolling
   His stone up the mountain!—*Longfellow*
4.   Hence, loathéd Melancholy,
   Of *Cerberus* and blackest Midnight born.—*Milton*
5. Lethe, the river or oblivion.—*Milton*
6. Gloomy Pluto, king of terrors.—*Pope*

7.   Of itself the water flies
    All taste of living wight, as once it fled
    The lip of *Tantalus.*—*Milton*
8. It may be we shall touch the *Happy Isles.*
    —*Tennyson*
9. In melancholy moonless *Acheron.*—*Wilde*
10. By reedy *Styx* old *Charon,* leaning on his oar,
    Waits for my coin.—*Wilde*

Suggestions for Oral or Written Composition

1. The torments of Tantalus, Ixion, Sisyphus, and the Danaïdes have a certain grim humor in them. Can you invent some mild torment that would be an appropriate punishment for a minor offense?

2. Characters of many ages meet down in Hades. Imagine a meeting between two such characters of different eras. What would Homer, for example, say to Shakespeare, or Alexander the Great to Napoleon, or Cæsar to George Washington? Write the dialogue, as you think it took place.

3. In a dream you visit the Elysian Fields, and there behold many famous men—great writers, great warriors, great rulers. Give an account of your visit.

4. Orpheus, on his return to earth after losing Eurydice the second time, tells his friend Menander what happened and expresses his own despair. Repeat what he said.

Word Study

1. Explain how the following words came to have their present meaning:

Lethean—producing forgetfulness
Elysian—like heaven or paradise
hypnotic—causing sleep
morphine—a drug producing sleep or relief from pain
tantalize—to tease by keeping something desired in view, but just out of reach

Orphic—mystic, used of poetry or prophetic utterances

Cerberus—a vigilant but surly custodian or guardian

2. Look up the following words in a mythological dictionary and practice the correct pronunciation. Charon, Lethe, Cerberus, Æneas, Eurydice, Elysium, Morpheus, Sisyphus, Orpheus, Calliope.
3. Give the Greek names of the following deities: *Pluto, Ceres, Somnus, Mors, Bacchus.*
4. What is an obolus? asphodel? a lyre?
5. What is meant by the expressions, "to swear by the Styx," "dreams through the ivory gate," "to carry water in a sieve," "a sop to Cerberus," "Stygian darkness," "lethargy"?

Questions for Review

1. What was the region of the underworld called?
2. Who ruled over it?
3. What five rivers flowed through it? Describe two of them.
4. Who was the ferryman of the underworld?
5. Who was its guardian?
6. Into what three parts was it divided?
7. What were the Furies?
8. Who was Hecate?
9. Who was the god of sleep? of death? of dreams?
10. How and why was Tantalus punished? Ixion? Sisyphus? the Danaïdes?
11. What were the characteristics of Elysium?
12. Who was Orpheus?
13. What happened to his wife?
14. What plea did he make to Pluto?
15. What was Pluto's reply?
16. What happened on the journey to the upper world?
17. How did Orpheus die?

Reading List

Poems and Plays

Dante: *Inferno*
Dowden, Edward: *Eurydice*
Gosse, Edmund: *The Island of the Blest—The Waking of Eurydice*
Landor, Walter Savage: *Orpheus and Eurydice*
Lang, Andrew: *The Fortunate Islands*
Lowell, James Russell: *Eurydice*
Morris, Lewis: *Epic of Hades*
Noyes, Alfred: *Orpheus and Eurydice*
Phillips, Stephen: *Christ in Hades*

Humorous Novels

Bangs, John Kendrick: *The House-Boat on the Styx—The Pursuit of the House-Boat*

Acrisius encloses Danaë and the infant Perseus in a wooden chest.

10 Stories of Heroes and Friends

What was that snaky-headed Gorgon shield
That wise Minerva wore,
unconquered virgin?

—Milton

Trials of Perseus

Danaë was a beautiful maiden and her father, King Acrisius of Argos, was very proud of her. But one day he consulted an oracle of the gods, and was told that the son of his daughter would one day kill him. So, in an attempt to avoid his doom, Acrisius shut Danaë up in a tower and forbade anyone, except her chosen attendants, to have access to her. But not so could Acrisius escape what the gods had in store for him. Jupiter himself, beholding the maiden, fell in love with her and, according to the legend, appeared to her first in a shower of golden rain. In time a son, named Perseus, was born to Danaë.

When Acrisius learned what had happened, he was furiously angry. He had mother and child shut up in a great wooden chest, closed the top, and set it afloat on the sea. The chest did not sink, but as if guided by some unseen steersman, moved steadily over the waves.

In the course of time the strange boat came to rest on the shore of an island. A fisherman saw it and when he forced open the lid, to his astonishment found within the chest a sleeping mother and child, both of surpassing beauty. He brought them to Polydectes, the king of the land, who received them kindly and gave them every care.

But their troubles were by no means over. Polydectes fell in love with Danaë and urged her to marry him. Year after year she refused, for her only thought was to take care of her son. At last, when Perseus was approaching manhood, Polydectes resolved to get rid of him, hoping that if he were gone, his mother would change her mind. So he commanded the lad to bring him the head of the Gorgon Medusa.

Now Medusa was a fearful creature—one of three sisters whose locks were hissing serpents, who had wings, brazen claws, and enormous teeth, and whose glance turned any beholder to stone. Perseus knew that by himself he could do nothing to conquer Medusa, so he sought the help of Minerva and Mercury. Minerva counseled him to seek out the Three Gray Sisters, who could not only reveal where the Gorgons lived, but could also supply him with three things without which it was useless for him to attempt the quest. She also told him how to get the Three Sisters into his power, since of their own accord they would tell him nothing.

Perseus journeyed far until he came to the lonely land where the Three Sisters dwelt. Quietly he stole up to the cavern where they came at noon when the sun was hot. Now these Three Sisters, who had been gray since they were born, had a remarkable peculiarity—they had only a single eye among them, and this they passed from one to the other. While the eye was being passed they were all quite blind.

As Perseus lay in wait, one of the three said:

"Come, sister, your time has passed. Let me now have the eye."

The sister in whose head the eye was took it out. At that very moment Perseus stretched out his hand and snatched the eye from her.

"Where is the eye?" cried the second of the Three Sisters.

Thereupon Perseus spoke: "I have it."

At the sound of his voice the Three Sisters trembled. They pleaded with Perseus and begged him to return the eye. He told them that he would gladly return vision to them, if they would grant him a favor. They would not at first grant him his wish. But when he threatened to go away and leave them blind forever, they realized that they had no choice. So they revealed to Perseus the hiding place of the Gorgons, and they told him where the sea nymphs lived who gave him the three things he needed—the helmet of Pluto, which rendered him invisible; a pair of winged sandals, which enabled him to fly with the speed of the wind; and a pouch in which to place Medusa's head after he had severed it. The friendly sea nymphs gave him other helpful counsel.

Then Mercury gave him additional assistance. He provided him with a sickle of exceeding sharpness to use in cutting off Medusa's head, and Perseus was equipped for his battle. He flew quickly until he came to a rocky island in the midst of the stream Oceanus. The ground was thick with evil-smelling and noxious weeds, and everywhere deadly snakes squirmed over the ground. In a cavern at the center of the island lived the Gorgons. When Perseus reached them they were asleep. He did not dare look at them directly, but gazed at their reflection in a highly polished shield that he carried. He was able to recognize Medusa by the fact that she was smaller than the others. Holding the shield in front of her Perseus severed her head with one sweep of his sickle. He thrust it in his pouch and flew away. Hardly had he done so when the two other

Ancient representation of Perseus beheading Medusa

Gorgons awoke and realized that their sister was dead. Shrieking with wrath they darted out of the cavern and looked for her slayer. The magic helmet of Pluto, however, rendered him invisible, and he escaped in safety.

Rescue of Andromeda

After flying for many days Perseus at length reached a country in Ethiopia of which Cepheus was king. Now it happened that at the time the whole land was plunged in lamentation. A little before this, Cassiopeia, the queen of Cepheus, had become so proud of her great beauty that she boasted that she was more beautiful than the Nereids. They were very angry and begged Neptune to punish her. He did so by sending a huge sea monster, which laid waste the land and devoured both people and cattle.

The king in despair consulted an oracle and asked what he should do. He was told that nothing would mollify the offended sea deities except the sacrifice of the king's daughter, Andromeda, to the monster.

Now Andromeda was even lovelier than her mother, and her parents were in despair. Yet day by day the monster ascended the shores of the land and did frightful damage. At last the inhabitants came in great mobs and stormed the gates of the palace.

"Sacrifice Andromeda!" they cried. "She must atone for your impiety!"

So at last a day was set on which Andromeda, chained to a rock, was to await the coming of the monster and by her death free the land from devastation. Weeping and yet brave, she was led to her doom; and her parents and attendants sadly left her to her fate.

As she lay on the rock Andromeda prayed that her doom might come quickly. Yet at that very moment her salvation was approaching. For Perseus, flying over Africa, saw below him the great commotion, and sweeping closer, he perceived the beautiful maiden chained to the rock. He landed from the sky at her feet and removed the helmet of Pluto that rendered him invisible to her gaze. At first she was frightened at the sudden apparition, but Perseus reassured her and asked her to tell him why she was chained to the rock. When he heard her story, he determined to rescue her. In silence both awaited the coming of the monster.

Suddenly the water was lashed into mountains of foam, and the monster, huge as a whale, approached. He plunged his way straight toward the rock on which Andromeda reclined. But a youth with a shining weapon stood in his way. The monster turned aside to destroy Perseus with one crunch of his massive jaws. Instead, he received a fierce thrust that brought his heart blood spouting to the surface in great fountains and dyed the water crimson in every direction. As the monster looked again for Perseus, he had disappeared, and even then a blow struck him from above. In vain the beast contended against the winged hero. Blow after blow rendered him powerless, until at last his tremendous bulk floated dead on the waves.

146

Perseus frees Andromeda from the rock.

From afar the Ethiopians had witnessed the combat, and now they came with rejoicing and freed Andromeda from the rock. Perseus claimed the maiden as his wife, and her parents were glad to give her to him in marriage. But her uncle Phineus, to whom she had been promised at an earlier time, now claimed her also, although he had made no effort to save her from her deadly peril. Her parents would not heed him. At the marriage feast, however, he suddenly appeared with a great host of followers, and sought to carry her off. When it looked as if Perseus would be overcome, he suddenly brought forth the Gorgon's head, and instantly Phineus and his followers were changed to stone.

Minerva (Greek: Pallas Athena), goddess of war, wisdom, and weaving

Return of Perseus

Cepheus provided Perseus and his bride with a handsome ship, and they set off for the island in which Danaë dwelt. She, he found, had been obliged to take refuge in a temple of the gods to escape the attentions of Polydectes, and the king was now trying to starve her into submission. When Polydectes heard that Perseus had returned, he raised an army and attacked him. But once more Perseus showed the Gorgon's head and turned his foes to stone. Thus he freed his mother. He made the brother of Polydectes king in his stead, and he returned to the Three Gray Sisters the objects he had borrowed from them. To Minerva he presented the head of Medusa, and ever after the goddess wore it on her breastplate.

There remains to be told in the story of Perseus only that event by which was fulfilled the doom of King Acrisius. Danaë, despite the way in which he had treated her, still loved her father, and as Perseus, too, wished to see his grandfather, both set out to pay him a visit in that ship which Cepheus had given his son-in-law.

Now when word was brought to Acrisius that his daughter and his grandson had not perished, and that they were actually coming to see him, he was filled with fear lest the oracle be fulfilled. So he hurriedly left the country, and when Perseus reached Argos, no one knew where the king had gone.

To while away the time Perseus resolved to attend an athletic contest that was taking place in a neighboring country. He himself took part in the games and carried off many prizes. Nobody knew who he was, and all marveled at his prowess. Toward the end of the games there was a discus-throwing contest. Perseus stepped forward to try his skill, but as he lifted up the heavy stone plate, it slipped out of his hand, flew sideways, and killed an old man who was watching the games. From the dead man's attendants it then became known that the spectator thus unfortunately slain was Acrisius, king of Argos, who had fulfilled his doom by running away from it.

Perseus was deeply grieved at the accident and conveyed the body to Argos for a splendid burial. Then he assumed the crown of Argos and for many years lived in happiness and ruled wisely.

Early Adventures of Theseus

Weary with the care of state, Ægeus, king of Athens, once retired for a time to the court of his friend, King Pittheus of Trœzen. There he met and fell in love with King Pittheus's daughter, the princess Æthra. Ægeus wooed and won Æthra, and when a son named Theseus was born to them, King Ægeus rejoiced that he had an heir to the throne of Athens.

At length, however, Ægeus felt it incumbent on him to return to Athens and resume his responsibilities. But he decided that it would be much better to let Theseus remain in his grandfather's pleasant home than to take him to the too busy city of Athens; and he would be safer, moreover, from the king's many enemies.

"When the lad can lift up the great stone at the entrance to the wood," he said to Æthra, "and find the sword which lies underneath, send him to me."

Impatiently Theseus waited for the time when he could satisfy this test of strength. At last came a day when, as he fiercely matched his muscles against the rock, he moved the obstacle a little. Once more he tried—and the stone rolled slowly away. Underneath it lay a beautifully ornamented sword and a pair of fine sandals.

"These were left to you by your father," explained Æthra. "He is king of Athens, but his brother is his enemy, and he feared that you would be killed if you came to him before you were strong enough to hold your own. Now go to him, and may the gods protect you."

His grandfather advised him to take a short and safe way to Athens, but the boy was eager to prove his manhood, and he deliberately chose a road that was infested by many perils. He ran into these perils almost as soon as he set out. First he encountered a lame but very strong bandit, named Periphetes, who was supposed to be a son of Vulcan. This bandit sprang out at Theseus savagely, and aimed a great iron bludgeon at him. But Theseus evaded the blow, and in a short time managed to kill the fellow.

Another robber was called Procrustes, or the Stretcher. He, too, was of gigantic size, and he had a grim sense of humor. When he captured a hapless traveler, he slung him over his shoulder and strode off to his den in the woods. There he had an iron bedstead upon which he threw the traveler. If the bed was too short, he lopped off the traveler's limbs until he fitted. If the bed was too long, he stretched the traveler's limbs to equal the bed. But Theseus proved more than a match for him, and when the hero had vanquished the giant, he punished him by making him fit his own bedstead.

150

Theseus and the Minotaur

When Theseus reached Athens and came into the king's presence, the latter at once recognized the sword he had left for his son and welcomed him joyfully. He immediately declared him heir to his throne.

At this time there was deep sorrow in Athens. Each year the city was obliged to send as a tribute to Crete seven youths and seven maidens, all selected for their beauty and strength, to be devoured by the Minotaur, a strange monster half bull and half man.

He lived at the center of a maze called the labyrinth, from which no one who went in without knowing the secret of its construction, could make his way out again.

When Theseus heard about this tribute, he demanded that he be selected as one of the seven youths. Ægeus in vain implored him to change his mind. Theseus was resolved either to slay the Minotaur or to die in the attempt. Ægeus demanded one favor.

"If you return safely," he begged, "change these black sails that your vessel carries to white ones, that I may know you have triumphed over the Minotaur."

Theseus promised to do this, and set out for Crete. There the young men and maidens were brought before King Minos. He marveled at the boldness of Theseus, whose rank he knew, in asking to be included in the tribute, but told him that no more mercy would be shown him than was shown those who were with him.

"Tomorrow you must meet your fate," he said.

Now it happened that beside King Minos sat his daughter Ariadne. She was filled with pity as she gazed on the handsome young hero, and she made up her mind to save him, despite her father's decree. That evening she managed to gain access to the room in which the Athenian prisoners were confined. She made known her identity to Theseus. Secretly she passed to him two objects—a sword and a ball of thread. She urged him be of good courage.

The next morning the guards took Theseus and his companions to the labyrinth. They left the Athenian victims

Theseus slaying the Minotaur

at the entrance and did not notice that Theseus fastened one end of the thread to the outward gate. Slowly and tearfully the Athenians made their way into the maze, hoping that somehow the monster would not find them. Only Theseus remained cheerful. At last they heard the fierce bellowings of the monster, which had caught the scent of human blood. Nearer and nearer it came, until it finally plunged into the room in which the Athenian prisoners stood cowering and lamenting.

But Theseus awaited it with drawn sword, prepared to fight to the death. The monster rushed full at him, seeking to impale Theseus on its horns, but Theseus evaded the blow and severed one of the beast's legs. Then as it lay on the ground, he plunged his sword into its heart.

Quickly then Theseus, attended by the still trembling prisoners, followed the clue of the thread back to the starting point. There Ariadne stood waiting to welcome him, pale with suspense. With a glad cry she hailed his approach, and hurried him and his companions to the ship that had brought them and was still waiting. They hoisted sail immediately and escaped from the Cretan coast before Minos and his men realized what had occurred.

Later Adventures of Theseus

Theseus, unfortunately, was not very grateful to Ariadne, whom he abandoned on the way home upon the island of Naxos. It is said he did this by command of the god Bacchus, who shortly appeared on the island and took Ariadne to be his wife. Moreover, as he approached Athens, Theseus quite forgot the injunction of his father as to the sails. The aged king had watched the horizon day by day, hoping against hope that Theseus might somehow have vanquished the Minotaur. Then at last he caught sight of the sails on the horizon—still black. The sight so grieved him that he threw himself into the sea.

Theseus bitterly regretted his oversight. He was hailed as king of Athens and ruled for many years. His life was rich in adventures. Once, for example, he seized one of the Amazons, who were a nation of women warriors, and made her his queen. The other women then made war on him. When they saw the wife of Theseus helping her husband in battle, they became so angry that they slew her. Later Theseus married the sister of Ariadne, named Phædra.

Bellerophon

The Chimera was a terrible monster. It was a strange and awe-inspiring mixture of many beasts—its body part lion and part goat, its hind legs those of a dragon, and its breath of fire. It lived in Lycia and caused great damage. The king of the land, Iobates, had sought all over Greece for a hero able to destroy this monster, when Bellerophon, whose father was the king of Corinth, came to visit him. When he heard about the Chimera, he volunteered to try to conquer it. Iobates accepted his offer, and Bellerophon prepared for the battle.

Before he set out, however, he consulted an oracle of the gods, and was advised to secure as a help in the combat a winged horse named Pegasus, which had sprung from the blood of the Gorgon Medusa. This horse had later been captured by Minerva who presented it to the Muses. Bellerophon sought the aid of Minerva who presented him with a golden bridle and led him to the spring at which Pegasus was accustomed to drink each morning. With the help of the bridle Bellerophon captured and mastered the steed. On his back the hero mounted into the air, and when he found the Chimera he was able to send his arrows into the monster from every side and to avoid its burning breath. Thus he overcame it.

It is said that later Bellerophon became overproud of his mastery of the winged steed and even attempted to fly to Olympus. But Jupiter sent a gadfly that stung the horse in mid-flight. He started violently and threw Bellerophon from the saddle. The young hero was killed, and the horse returned to the service of the Muses.

154

Bellerophon killing the Chimera

Damon and Pythias

Among the most admired heroes of ancient times were the two friends, Damon and Pythias, who became models of loyalty.

It is likely that these men actually existed. According to the story, they were subjects of the tyrant Dionysius, who ruled over Syracuse in Sicily during the fifth century. Both Damon and Pythias were renowned for their wisdom and goodness, but in some manner of which there is no record, Pythias incurred the anger of the tyrant and was condemned by him to death. He bore the sentence bravely, but he asked Dionysius to grant him one favor—permission to go home and settle his affairs. Damon offered to be a hostage for the safe return of his friend.

The tyrant agreed to let Pythias go.

"But you must be here by such and such an hour," he warned him, "or your friend will die for you."

Pythias set out for his home, which was a considerable distance away. He settled his affairs, divided his goods among his kinsfolk, and set out on his way back to Syracuse. Unfortunately, however, he was delayed at every turn. First it was a river swollen with floods that he had to ford, and then a tremendous storm made the road impassable. He struggled on desperately, and reached Syracuse in the very nick of time, for the executioner was already lifting up his sword to behead Damon. Pythias forced his way through the spectators, and cried out:

"Hold your sword! Here I am!" and knelt down to receive the blow. But Dionysius was so filled with astonishment and admiration at the loyalty of the friends that he pardoned Pythias, and even asked that he might be admitted to his and Damon's friendship.

PRACTICAL APPLICATIONS

Myths in Literature

Various phases and portions of the story of Perseus have been treated in literature. Undoubtedly the finest poem on the subject is Charles Kingsley's *Andromeda*, in which the meter employed—dactylic hexameter—is the same as that which Homer employed in the *Iliad* and the *Odyssey*, and which Virgil employed in the *Æneid*. As the title indicates, Kingsley has concentrated on that part of the adventures of Perseus in which Andromeda is concerned. Thus he pictures the sea beast:

Onward it came from the south, as bulky and black as a galley.
Lazily coasting along, as the fish fled leaping before it;
Lazily breasting the ripple, and watching by sand bar and headland,
Listening for laughter of maidens at bleaching or song of the fisher,
Children at play on the pebbles, or cattle that passed on the sand hills.

Bryant has rendered the *Lament of Danaë,* by Simonides, a famous Greek poet. Dowden has written of Andromeda; and William Drummond, Thomas Gordon Hake, and Dante Gabriel Rossetti of the Medusa—to whom there are innumerable references in literature. The story of Perseus has been well told by William Morris in one section of *The Earthly Paradise—The Doom of King Acrisius.*

Theseus and the Amazon queen are important characters in one of Shakespeare's plays—*A Midsummer Night's Dream,* in which the poet has curiously mingled classical mythology with the fairy lore of his own land.

Specific Literary References

What do the following references mean? Where a word or phrase is italicized, explain only the word or phrase.

1. So was the *Cretan bull* by *Theseus* done to destruction.—*Catullus*
2. What was that snaky-headed *Gorgon shield* That wise *Minerva* wore?—*Milton*
3. Then whoso will with virtuous wing assay To mount to heaven on *Pegasus* must ride.—*Milton*
4. There sat the crones that had the single eye.
   —*Morris*
5. The star-bright shower That came to *Danaë* in her brazen tower.
   —*Edith Sitwell*
6. Damon and Pythias, whom death could not sever.
   —*Spenser*
7. Now lies the Earth all *Danaë* to the stars, And all thy heart lies open unto me.—*Tennyson*
8. The *labyrinthine* ways of my own mind.—*Thompson*
9. *Pallas,* resplendent with her storm-cloud and grim with her *Gorgon.*—*Virgil*
10. Of lonely *Ariadne* on the wharf At Naxos, when she saw the treacherous crew Far out at sea.—*Wilde*

Suggestions for Oral or Written Composition

1. After Perseus has slain the monster, Andromeda

expresses her gratitude to the hero. She asks his name and then thanks him fervently. What would she say?

2. The Athenian captives appear before King Minos and his court. They are questioned, and the identity of Theseus is revealed. Put the scene into play form.

3. If newspapers had existed in the time of the ancients, one of them (the *Syracuse Herald,* let us say) might have given an account of the Damon and Pythias episode. Write the story in newspaper style, beginning with the scene when Damon was on the point of execution. What headline would you use. What byline?

Word Study

1. Explain the derivation of the following words:

    chimera—an absurd creation of the imagination
    labyrinth—a complicated or confused situation

2. Look up the following names in a mythological dictionary and practice the correct pronunciation.
    Perseus, Polydectes, Andromeda, Cassiopeia, Phineus, Theseus, Minotaur, Ariadne, Chimera, Pegasus, Damon, Pythias.
3. Give the Greek equivalents of the following names: *Jupiter, Neptune, Mercury, Minerva.*
4. What is meant by the following expressions?—"To stretch on a bed of Procrustes," "to mount Pegasus," "to fight a chimera," "as true as Damon and Pythias or David and Jonathan."

Questions for Review

1. What oracle concerning Danaë terrified her father, King Acrisius?
2. How did he try to avert his doom? What happened?
3. When Perseus was born, how did King Acrisius again try to outwit fate? What happened?
4. Why did Polydectes want to get rid of Perseus?
5. On what mission did he send him?
6. Who was Medusa?

7. Whose help did Perseus win?
8. How did he overcome the Gorgon?
9. What maiden did he rescue on his way home?
10. On what two occasions did he have to employ the Gorgon's head?
11. How did he employ it when he returned home?
12. What did Acrisius do when he heard that Perseus was coming?
13. How did Acrisius meet his doom?
14. Of what monarch was Theseus the son?
15. What injunctions did his father give his mother?
16. When did he set out for Athens?
17. What adventures did he meet on the road?
18. What mission did he undertake on his arrival?
19. What was the Minotaur?
20. With whose help and how did Theseus overcome him? Was he grateful?
21. What forgetfulness killed the father of Theseus?
22. What was the Chimera?
23. How did Bellerophon conquer it?
24. How did the hero later meet his death?
25. What two men were devoted friends?
26. How did they prove their friendship?

Reading List

Poems and Plays

Bryant, William Cullen: Simonides' *Lament of Danaë*
Corneille, Pierre: *Andromeda*
Dowden, Edward: *Andromeda*
Kingsley, Charles: *Andromeda*
Landor, Walter Savage: *Theseus and Hippolyta*
Longfellow, Henry Wadsworth: *Pegasus in Pound*
Morris, William: *Bellerophon at Argos—Bellerophon in Lycia—The Doom of King Acrisius*
Ovid: *Ariadne to Theseus* (in *Heroines*)
Rossetti, Dante Gabriel: *Aspecta Medusa*
Shakespeare, William: *A Midsummer Night's Dream*
Shelley, Percy: *On the Medusa of Leonardo da Vinci*
Tennyson, Alfred: *Parnassus*

An Etruscan vase painting of Hercules and Minerva

11 Adventures of Hercules

Do you seek Hercules' equal?
None is, except himself.

—Seneca

Birth and Early Life

No more celebrated hero lived in ancient times than Hercules (Greek: Herakles). He was the son of Jupiter by Alcmene of Thebes. Juno was always unfriendly to the children of Jupiter by other wives, but against Hercules she cherished a particular hatred. She managed before his birth to arrange matters so that he was deprived of the rulership of a kingdom. As he lay in his cradle she sent two serpents to strangle him, but the infant prodigy, already strong far beyond the ordinary, seized the snakes in his hands and strangled them.

As a young man Hercules received instruction in all the manly arts, and training in character from the best teachers in Greece. Amphitryon, king of Thebes, son of Alcæus[1] and grandson of Perseus, who was his reputed father, gave him lessons in the art of driving a chariot. Autolycus, a son of Mercury, taught him wrestling. Eurytus, himself a king, was his master in archery. Castor, another son of Jupiter and a great warrior, showed him how to bear himself in heavy fighting. Linus, a son of Apollo, gave him lessons in singing and playing the lyre. Rhadamanthus, who became one of the judges of the underworld because of his fine character, trained him in wisdom and virtue. But Hercules as a youth and as a man lacked self-control, and in a fit of sudden rage killed Linus.

For this offense Amphitryon banished him to the country and made him a herdsman. He grew up in the open air, and daily became more powerful. It was at this time that he first began to perform astonishing deeds of strength and courage. He slew the Thespian lion, which had long caused great damage to the flocks nearby. He ever afterwards wore the skin of this lion as his ordinary garment, and carried a huge club, which he cut for himself from a tree in the neighborhood of Nemea.

Marriage and Madness

The career of Hercules was, on the whole, one of service to his fellow men. It is related of him that, early in his life, there appeared to him in a vision two women who stood at a crossroad.

"I am Pleasure," said one, "and I have many gifts for you. Here are ease, luxury and wealth; grateful friends, a

---

[1]Hercules is therefore sometimes called "Alcides"—"of the family of Alcæus."

happy home and children that will remember you. You shall want for nothing, you shall endure no toils, you shall never know sorrow. Come with me."

"I am Duty," spoke the other. "Choose me and you shall be ever acquainted with hardship. Rest shall be a stranger to you. Often shall you suffer pain, and grief will often rend your heart. But mankind will remember you with gratitude. You shall become a hero to your people. Your name shall live forever. Come with me."

Unhesitatingly, in his vision, Hercules chose the path of duty; and duty is still sometimes called "Hercules' choice."

What Duty promised all came true.

When he returned from his exile as a herdsman, he helped his half brother Iphicles and his foster father Amphitryon in a war which they were waging for the freedom of their city, and although Amphitryon was killed, the enemy, by the prowess of Hercules, was overthrown. As a reward he was given the hand of the princess Megara, and for a time lived happily with her and the children that were born to them.

But Juno, looking down from Olympus, could no longer endure the spectacle of the good fortune that had come to Hercules and so sent madness upon him. In his insanity he slew his own children and two of his brother's. Only the intervention of Minerva, who in her pity caused a deep sleep to fall upon him, saved him from further crimes. When he awoke from this sleep, he was in his right mind again, and bitterly grieved over what had occurred.

The First Six Labors

Hercules knew that mere grief over his act was not enough, and sought to purify himself in other ways. He consulted wise and holy men and the oracles of the gods. At last he imposed a sentence on himself. He bound himself to serve his cousin, King Eurystheus, and carry out his commands, no matter what

The infant Hercules strangling the serpents

they might be, for the space of twelve years. Eurystheus, meanwhile, inspired by Juno, set himself to devise tasks for Hercules that would cause him the greatest suffering and humiliation.

First, he ordered him to slay the Nemean lion and bring him the skin. In the valley of Nemea lived a huge and monstrous lion, against whom all attacks had been in vain. Dreadful was the combat between Hercules and this beast. The hero found that his mighty arrows and his tremendous club were of no avail against the lion. At last he seized the monster in his hands and strangled it to death.

Second, Hercules was commanded to kill the Lernæan Hydra. When Hercules came to close quarters with it, he found that it had nine heads. If he struck off one of the heads with a club, two new ones immediately grew in its place; the middle head was immortal and resisted all of his efforts to cut it off. The situation seemed desperate, but with the help of his faithful nephew, Iolaüs, who had accompanied him, he tied up the Hydra, and underneath its mortal heads he built a fire which consumed the new heads as fast as they grew. The ninth head he buried under a huge rock. He even made the Hydra useful, for he dipped his arrows into its blood and made them poisonous.

Third, the capture of the Arcadian stag was imposed upon Hercules. This wonderful animal, of astounding swiftness, had golden antlers and brazen hoofs. For a whole year Hercules pursued it in vain. At last, however, he managed to wound the stag slightly, and then he could seize it, and carry it to Eurystheus upon his shoulders.

Fourth, came the destruction of the Erymanthian boar. Hercules was directed to bring this animal, which had been ravaging the countryside, alive to Eurystheus. He pursued the boar through the deep snow up the mountain where it lived, caught it in a huge net and carried it to his master.

Fifth was the task of cleansing the Augean stables. Augeas, king of Elis, had a herd of three thousand oxen, whose stalls had not been cleansed for thirty years. Hercules managed to dam the rivers Alpheus and Peneus and turn them aside into the stables. As soon as the stalls had been thoroughly washed out, he allowed the rivers to go back to their courses once more.

Sixth of the labors was the destruction of the Stymphalian birds. These birds, which were under the special care of Mars, had brazen claws, wings, and beaks. They used their feathers as arrows, were very greedy, and preferred human flesh to all other food. They lived on a lake near Stymphalus, in Arcadia, and Hercules was ordered by Eurystheus to expel them. Hercules secured the help of Minerva, who provided him with a great rattle. The noise of this rattle startled the birds into flight, and thereupon Hercules slew them with his arrows.

The Last Six Labors

Seventh in the series of the hero's toils was the capture of the Cretan bull. This was a beautiful animal which had been presented by Neptune to Minos, king of Crete. Later it became very ferocious. Hercules was ordered to capture it. He did so, and brought it to Eurystheus on his mighty shoulders.

Eighth of the labors was the capture of the mares of Diomedes. Diomedes was a cruel king who fed his horses on human flesh. With the help of a few friends Hercules seized the horses and set out on his homeward journey. Diomedes and his followers pursued them, and a fight took place in which Hercules was victorious. He killed Diomedes and threw his body to the horses. When they had devoured the flesh of their master, they immediately became tame and thereafter refused human flesh.

Ninth came an unusually difficult task—that of securing the girdle of Hippolyte, the queen of the Amazons. The Amazons were a race of women warriors, who had founded a city in Asia Minor. Hippolyte had received from Mars a girdle of wonderful beauty. Admeta, the daughter of Eurystheus, longed to possess this girdle. She persuaded her father to command Hercules to get it. After various adventures he at last reached the kingdom of the Amazons. There he was received with friendship by Hippolyte, who even promised to give him the girdle as a gift. But Juno took the form of an Amazon and persuaded the followers of Hippolyte that Hercules was carrying off their queen as a captive. They attacked Hercules, and because he thought Hippolyte had been guilty of treachery, he killed her, seized the girdle, and set out for home.

Tenth of the labors was the capture of the oxen of Geryon. Geryon was a three-headed monster who lived on the little-known island of Erythea. He was gigantic, enormously powerful, and armed with mighty weapons. To assist him in guarding his immense herds of cattle, he had another giant named Eurytion and a two-headed dog. It took Hercules a long time to find Erythea. Among the places he passed was the frontier of Europe. To mark his progress he put up two mountains as pillars, called by the ancients, the Pillars of Hercules, and by moderns, the Strait of Gibraltar. Annoyed by the heat of the sun in this region, Hercules shot some of his arrows against the Sun, who so much admired his boldness that he gave him a golden boat that guided itself to Erythea. There Hercules slew Geryon, Eurytion, and the two-headed dog, loaded the cattle on his magic boat, and returned to the coast of Greece, where he gave the boat back to the Sun.

Eleventh of the labors imposed upon him was to fetch the golden apples of the Hesperides. Hercules did not know where this divine garden lay, but he knew that the tree on which the apples grew was guarded by a dragon, whose vigilance would allow no one to pass, and who could not be wounded. But Hercules also knew that near the garden lived Atlas, the mighty Titan who bore the weight of the heavens upon his shoulders, and that this Titan's daughters, the Hesperides, danced forever around the tree that bore the wonderful apples. Hercules after long wanderings at last found Atlas and persuaded him to go and bring back some of the apples. In the meantime Hercules consented to bear in his stead the weight of the sky. So Atlas went and shortly returned with several golden apples. Now, however, he refused to take back his ancient burden. He rejoiced in his freedom and was quite content to let Hercules take his place forever.

"I will take back the apples for you," he said, "and I'll tell him you are unable to bring them yourself."

Hercules pretended to be content to do as Atlas wished.

"But the burden of the sky isn't quite easy on my shoulders," he remarked, shifting the weight in pretended discomfort. "Just hold the sky a moment again while I place my lion's skin as a pad on my back."

Unsuspectingly, Atlas took back the load. No sooner had he done so than Hercules snatched up the golden apples and smilingly bade him farewell.

The *twelfth* and last task was by no means least difficult—to bring Cerberus up from the underworld. Here, once more, Hercules had the help of the gods, for Minerva and Mercury accompanied him on his terrifying journey into the realm of Hades. Pluto granted his request that he be allowed to take Cerberus into the upper world, on condition that no weapons be used against his three-headed watchdog. Hercules struggled with the dog and by sheer strength at last subdued him. He carried him up to Eurystheus for inspection and later returned him to his station in the lower regions.

Later Career

Many other stories are told of Hercules, who became the national hero of Greece. Once again his madness returned upon him, and he slew his

Hercules' combat with Neptune's son

friend Iphitus. For a penance he bound himself to serve three years as a slave. This time he placed himself under the orders of a woman, Queen Omphale, and it is related that to show her power over him, she commanded Hercules to put on the garments of a woman and to spin wool, while she wore his lion's skin.

When Prometheus had been chained to the crag in the Caucasus by Jupiter, one consolation cherished by him in secret was that in time a descendant of Jove himself would come to free him. This event destined by the Fates was fulfilled when Hercules, in the course of one of his journeys, beheld Prometheus and was filled with compassion for the Titan who suffered such torments because of his services to mankind. He therefore slew the bird of prey which fed upon Prometheus and freed the Fire-Giver from his chains. On another journey he encountered Antæus, a son of Neptune, who challenged him to combat. Hercules found that every time he threw Antæus to the ground, the latter rose with redoubled strength after contact with Mother Earth. So he lifted him up into the air and strangled him into submission.

Hercules married Deianira, the daughter of Œneus and a sister of Meleager. It was through her that his death came to him. Once Hercules and Deianira came to the ford of a river. Here a centaur, Nessus, carried travelers across for a fee. Hercules himself was able to cross the stream without difficulty, but he placed Deianira upon the back of Nessus to be carried across. Deianira was very beautiful, and instead of bearing her to the other bank of the stream, Nessus turned around and started off with her for the cavern in which he lived. Hercules, from the other shore, drew his bow and launched an arrow into the heart of Nessus. The centaur, in the moment before he died, whispered to Deianira that his blood was a love potion, which would enable her to retain the love of Hercules.

Foolishly she believed him; and when some time later she became jealous of the attentions which Hercules was paying to a captive maiden, she steeped a robe that Hercules was to wear in the supposed love potion. But it was, in reality, a deadly poison, and when the hero put it on, the evil of it tore into his flesh with excruciating agony. Hercules ascended a mountain, raised a pile of wood, placed himself on this as a funeral pyre, and ordered it to be set on fire. But Jupiter at the last moment intervened, and snatched him up to Olympus.

PRACTICAL APPLICATIONS

Myths in Literature

Hercules was accorded the admiration not only of the Greeks but of all the ancient world—for his manliness, his strength, his willingness to serve, his achievements in ridding the world of evil monsters, and his athletic prowess. He appears in the tales of poets and the representations of painters and sculptors.

Among those in ancient times who told the story of this great hero in dramatic form were Euripides and Sophocles among the Greeks, and Seneca among the Latins. Later George Cabot Lodge's *Herakles* makes striking use of the old story. Perhaps the most effective dramatic use of Hercules is that of Euripides in his drama, *Alcestis,* when the hero enters at a crucial moment to save Alcestis from Death.

The name *Hercules* has become a synonym for great physical strength and courage. Shakespeare, for example, often uses the name in this way. Thus he says:

> How many cowards, whose hearts are all as false
> As stairs of sand, wear yet upon their chins
> The beards of Hercules and frowning Mars.

The Amazons who appear in the story of Hercules are familiar in reference and allusion. Romances and even scientific treatises have played with the idea of a race of women who rule powerfully without the help of men. Poets and others have often turned in thought to the Amazons; Shakespeare, for example:

> For your own ladies and pale-visag'd maids
> Like Amazons come tripping after drums,
> Their thimbles into armed gauntlets changed,
> Their needles to lances, and their gentle hearts
> To fierce and bloody inclination.

Specific Literary References

What do the following references mean? Where a word or phrase is italicized, explain only the word or phrase.
1. Though comparatively weak, opposed to Johnson's *Herculean* vigor, let us not call his style positively feeble.—*Boswell*
2. By her in stature the tall *Amazon*
   Had stood a pigmy's height.—*Keats*
3. He seemed earth-born, an *Antæus,* sucking in fresh vigor from the soil which he neighbored.—*Lamb*
4. Suddenly he sprouts out an entirely new set of features, like *Hydra.—Lamb*

5.   As when *Alcides* . . .
Felt th' envenom'd robe, and tore
Through pain up by the root Thessalian pines.
                    —*Milton*
6. Of Hesperus and his *daughters three*
That sing about the Golden Tree.—*Milton*
7. Voyage over dreamful seas
To lost *Hesperides.*—*Peabody*
8.   My fate cries out,
And makes each pretty artery in this body
As hardy as the *Nemean lion's* nerve.—*Shakespeare*

Suggestions for Oral or Written Composition

1. Select a scene from the twelve labors of Hercules and present it in tableau form. See if your classmates can recognize the scene as you give it.

2. On his return from one of his labors, Hercules is interviewed by a reporter from the *Theban Courier.* He gives an account of his adventure.

3. Compare the career of Hercules with that of Samson in the Bible. How did these heroes resemble each other?

4. Hercules, let us suppose, suddenly finds himself in a city of today. What would he say about the sights and sounds around him?

Word Study

1. Explain how the following words came to have their present meaning:
Herculean—of great strength
Amazonian—warlike or masculine, as applied to women
Hesperian—western
atlas—(1) a globe of the earth; (2) a collection of maps; (3) the first vertebra, sustaining the head.

2. How does the story of Hercules account for the ancient name for Gibraltar? Where, according to your map of Africa, did Atlas probably live?

170

3. Explain the meaning of the following phrases: "great as a labor of Hercules," "a Herculean task," "as bad as cleansing the Augean stables," "the choice of Hercules," "to gain renewed strength from Mother Earth," "an infant Hercules," "hydra-headed evils."
4. Some Spanish explorers, moving up a great river of South America, encountered a race of female warriors. What river was it?

Questions for Review

1. Who was the constant enemy of Hercules?
2. How did she show her hatred of him as a child?
3. Why is Hercules sometimes called "Alcides"?
4. Who were some of his teachers?
5. What was the great fault of Hercules?
6. The skin of what lion did he wear as his garment?
7. What was "the choice of Hercules"?
8. Who was his first wife?
9. Why did he impose a sentence of penance on himself? What was it?
10. How many tasks did Eurystheus set him? Name them and describe each in a sentence.
11. When, later in his life, did madness return on him?
12. What penance did he set himself?
13. What great martyr did Hercules free?
14. Who was Antæus, and what remarkable faculty did he have?
15. How did Hercules overcome him?
16. Who was Deianira?
17. How did Hercules come to his death?

Reading List

Plays and Poems

Euripides: *The Mad Hercules*
Lang, Andrew: *Theocritus' Idyl XIII*
Lodge, George Cabot: *Herakles*
Morris, William: *The Golden Apples*
Ovid: *Deianira to Hercules* (in *Heroines*)

Thessaly, Greece - the land of Jason

12 Jason and the Golden Fleece

And her sunny locks
Hung on her temples like a golden fleece.
—Shakespeare

Capturing His Kingdom

There lived in Iolcus in Thessaly a king named Æson, who grew tired of ruling. His son Jason was still too young to wear the crown and so Æson appointed his half brother Pelias as regent, with the understanding that when Jason came of age, Pelias would surrender the reins of government into his hands. Meanwhile, Æson intrusted the education of Jason to the centaur Chiron; and he himself retired to a distant village.

The years went by, and Pelias grew ever more secure in his power. He thought but carelessly of his promise to Æson and of the lad Jason, and to himself and his powerful army of followers, he was the king of Iolcus. Nor was his rule a kindly one. Yet at moments there came doubts into his mind. To still his half-formed misgivings, Pelias resolved to consult an oracle. This strange answer was given to him:

"Fear a man wearing only one sandal!"

Pelias was mystified by this reply, but resolved to wait and see what time brought forth. Now it happened that on the occasion of a great feast to Neptune, Pelias sent out invitations far and wide, urging everyone to participate. At the very time when preparations for the feast were being made, Jason, grown into a strong and clever young man, had made up his mind to seek out his uncle and claim the throne that was his due. He traveled many days, and just before he came to Iolcus, he saw before him a swift and dangerous stream.

Undaunted, he started to cross it and had almost reached the other side when his foot caught in a projecting rock. He managed to free himself, but when he reached dry land, he saw that one of his sandals was missing. Shrugging his shoulders, he made the rest of the journey toward the city without stopping to obtain another sandal.

It was thus he came into the presence of King Pelias, who sat on his throne in the public square in the midst of revelers. Jason walked toward him and bowed respectfully.

"Hail, king!" he cried. As he spoke he stretched toward Pelias his right hand, on one finger of which blazed a magnificent ruby ring that Æson had bidden Chiron keep for his son as a sign of his kingly authority.

Pelias started as he recognized the king's jewel, but his mind was even more troubled as he glanced downward and saw that Jason wore but a single sandal. Yet he dissembled his fears and pretended to welcome his nephew with joy. Day after day went by, however, and Pelias made no attempt to surrender his crown to Jason. At last Jason boldly reminded him that by right of inheritance he, not Pelias, was the ruler of Iolcus.

"When will you give up your authority, good uncle?" he asked.

Jason and the Golden Fleece

For a time Pelias was silent, pondering what means he could use to get rid of this dangerous youth. He dared not slay him, for already the citizens of the city welcomed the idea of having the son of the kindly Æson as king, in place of the unscrupulous Pelias.

"Nephew," replied Pelias at length, "it has not seemed fitting to me that a youth without experience, one untested in the ways and wiles of the world, should take over this great rule. Would it not be better, think you, to seek first an apprenticeship in danger and hardship? Then shall you be indeed a wise and noble king."

Now Jason was only too anxious to go forth adventuring before he settled down to the humdrum cares of government. This idea appealed to him very much, and he cried eagerly:

"Set me a task, then, to prove me! I will do whatever you bid!"

Pelias smiled to himself as he saw how Jason, with the

overeagerness of youth, had delivered himself into his hands. He replied smoothly:

"Only one quest is fitting for so bold a youth as you—the quest of the Golden Fleece. Bring me that shining trophy, and I shall know you are destined to rule over lolcus in my stead."

Pelias thought he had rid himself of Jason forever by sending him on this quest. The Golden Fleece was the skin of a wonderful ram which Mercury, many years before, had given to Queen Nephole to carry her two children, Phrixus and Helle, to safety, when they were threatened with death. The two children were placed upon this ram, which, vaulting into the air, immediately began to travel magically through the air toward the east. But while over the strait that separates Europe from Asia, Helle lost his hold and fell off; and for many ages after, this stream was called the Hellespont (now it is the Dardanelles). The ram landed Phrixus safely in Colchis, where he was received kindly by the king. The boy later sacrificed the ram to Jupiter, but he gave the Golden Fleece to the king, who placed it in a sacred grove, under the care of a sleepless dragon.

It was this treasure that Jason now started out to win; and he went ahead with eager joy in his great adventure. He employed Argus, the best shipbuilder of the time, to fashion for him a vessel with places for fifty rowers. Minerva sent Jason a beam made of the wood of a sacred oak; and from it was fashioned a marvelous figurehead that had the power of speech. When the vessel was finished, it was named the *Argo* and those who sailed in it were called *Argonauts*. No common crew would Jason take with him on his voyage. He sent invitations to all the heroes of Greece to join him, and when they learned what hazards he had undertaken to face, they came forward eagerly.

So upon his quest there went with him Castor and Pollux, those twins who later became the gods of boxing and wrestling; Orpheus, divine bard, not yet descended to Hades; Zetes and Calaïs, speedy runners; Hercules; the hunter Arcas and the huntress Atalanta; Nestor, wise in council; Peleus and Telamon, youthful warriors; Admetus, later a king and master of Apollo; Theseus, and many others.

Voyage of the Argo

It was on a fair day that Jason set sail from Iolcus, and on the shore stood many who shouted farewell and good luck to him. Swift as birds they sailed on, and after many days came to Lemnos, where only women dwelt. Leaving this land, they came at length to the nation of the Doliones, who at first received them suspiciously but later treated them as friends.

It is said that in the region of the Black Sea they lost Hercules and another of the crew by a strange chance. Some of the oars of the vessel had in one way or another been broken, and Hercules went ashore to find wood from which to make new oars. With him went a lad named Hylas, who was his squire and whom he loved as if he were his own son. Hercules became thirsty, and he asked Hylas go to the nearest stream and draw water for him.

Hylas came to a little woodland pool, shaded by tall trees and fringed by delicate and fragrant flowers. As he bent down to draw water for his pitcher, the nymphs who lived in the stream saw him, and were at once fascinated by his beauty, for there never lived a boy handsomer than Hylas. Swiftly they rose from the pool, gently took him by the hand, and soothingly invited him to their underwater grottoes. Their voices like waters murmuring and leaves rustling lulled Hylas into a will-less slumber, and slowly pulled him down into the embracing waves, which gave him up no more.

When Hylas failed to return, Hercules searched for him frantically through the woods, and would not cease from his searching for all the remonstrances of the other heroes. At last they had to leave Hercules behind, who after many days of vain questing for Hylas, sorrowfully made his way back to Greece.

Soon the heroes came to another country, the king of which took a cruel delight in his great skill in boxing. He made it a condition of his hospitality that every stranger who came to his land must engage in a boxing bout with him. Usually the match ended in the death of the stranger, for the king was both strong and skillful. Now he imposed

The Argonauts prepare to seek the Golden Fleece

this condition on the Argonauts, and asked them to choose a champion among themselves.

"Perhaps later," he boasted, "you will need to choose still another."

But the Argonauts did not have to debate whom to send against this king. Pollux had skill in boxing that came to him from the gods. The bout between him and the king did not last long, and in a short time the royal bully had suffered the fate he had meted out to so many others. The people of his land, however, did not like the outcome very much, and immediately attacked the Argonauts, who were obliged to slay a great many of them before they could get back to their ship.

Soon the voyagers came to a country where there lived a seer named Phineus. Phineus had been cruel to his own family, and the gods had punished him by blinding him and transporting him to a barren land inhabited by two monsters. These creatures were called Harpies. Their bodies and heads were like those of women, but their feet and wings were like those of ravens; and their names were Storm-Foot and Swift-Wing. These Harpies waited until a meal was spread before Phineus by invisible hands. Then they seized the best part of the food and gobbled it up, and Phineus lived in perpetual hunger. He promised the Argonauts that he would give them counsel for their voyage that would save them many hardships and dangers, if only they would free him from these fierce and noxious Harpies.

Now Zetes and Calaïs of the crew were sons of Boreas, the North Wind, and they could move as swiftly as the wind because they truly had the wind's wings. They promised Phineus their help if he would swear kindness forever after to his own kin. He swore most solemnly. So, when the Harpies next appeared, they attacked them in the air, and after a lengthy battle drove them away. In gratitude Phineus told the Argonauts that they would soon come to two dangerous rocks, called the Symplegades or the Clashing Islands, and he advised them how they might pass them. He gave them other wise counsel also.

In half a day the Argonauts came to the rocks of which Phineus had warned them, and indeed they were both very wonderful and very dangerous. For these rocks were not fastened to the bottom of the sea, but ever moved about and crashed together; and no one could tell when their dread meeting would take place. But Jason, as Phineus had bidden him, released a dove as the rocks began to move toward each other. The dove just barely managed to get through as the rocks crashed. As the rocks rebounded, the heroes swiftly urged the *Argo* onward; and with speed equal to that of the dove the vessel passed between. As the heroes looked back, they saw that the rocks no longer moved apart and no longer sailed over the face of the ocean. For it had been prophesied that if ever a ship should pass in safety between the rocks, the rocks would thereafter become rooted to the bottom of the sea.

Winning the Golden Fleece

Not long after this event the *Argo* reached Colchis. Jason threw out anchors of stone and then landed on the shore among the wondering crowds who had never beheld so great a ship. He commanded that he be taken to the king, Æëtes. The monarch welcomed him, and asked him to state his reason for coming to this land.

"I have come for the Golden Fleece," said Jason, "for without it I cannot become ruler of my own land."

Then he explained to the king how Pelias had made it a condition for the surrender of his power to Jason that the latter must bring him the Golden Fleece.

Æëtes was a man of craft, and he had no wish to bring about an attack on his people by the heroes of the *Argo* by bluntly denying Jason the treasure which he sought. But he had not the slightest intention of giving it to him either. He pondered awhile and replied thus to Jason's story:

"Young hero, do not think the Golden Fleece may be won by anyone for the asking. Indeed, I do not believe that such is your thought, for you know that this trophy of the gods is surrounded by many perils. Listen then to the conditions on which you may win the fleece. Tomorrow you must harness the two bulls which Mars keeps in his temple, and you must then sow the dragon's teeth."

Jason agreed to undertake these two tasks, knowing in his heart that deadly danger probably accompanied both. That night, as he lay sleepless on the *Argo*, there appeared suddenly before him a slim maiden veiled in black. For a startled moment he thought that Minerva or another of the divine inhabitants of Olympus stood before him, but shortly a soft voice reassured him:

"I am Medea," said the veiled maiden, "daughter of King Æëtes. I saw with compassion today how my father led you into a cunning trap, for never, without help, can you harness the bulls or sow the dragon's teeth. Yet I will help you, if you will accept my aid."

"Only help me," cried Jason eagerly, "and then escape with me to my country, and there you shall become my queen."

This thought, indeed had been in the mind of Medea when she approached Jason, and now she assented gladly to his proposal.

"Here," she whispered to him, "is a magic ointment with which you must smear yourself. For a day you shall then be impervious to fire and invulnerable to wounds. The bulls of Mars will, therefore, not be able to scorch you with the flames that they spout from their nostrils, nor will they be able to hurt you with their brazen hoofs. As to the dragon's teeth, know that from them will spring armed men, fierce with the lust of murder, and on them you must practice this stratagem."

And bending over Jason, she told him in low tones just what he must do to avoid the peril of the dragon's teeth.

Next day, then, the king and the people of the land assembled to see Jason undertake his two tasks. To the marvel and bewilderment of Æëtes, the young Greek hero went confidently into the grove of Mars and without difficulty harnessed the terrifying bulls to a plow, nor did he seem to heed the spouts of fire that played upon him from their nostrils.

From the king's trembling hand he took next a helmet full of dragon's teeth, and walking up and down sowed them in the furrows that he had made. Hardly were the teeth upon the earth when they took root, and out of the soil sprang fifty mighty warriors, each completely clad in steel and brandishing a sword. Their violent shouts made both the heavens and the watching throngs tremble.

But, unseen by the warriors and by Æëtes, Jason hurled a stone into their very midst. It fell with a loud clangor on the shield of the tallest warrior. Furious with anger, he turned and glared at his neighbor, and before a word could be said, he went at him with his sword. All the others, eager for the combat, took sides, and in a few moments the earth shook with the blows given and received. But Jason, wherever he saw his opportunity, plunged into the combat with his sword, and it was not long before all the warriors lay dead upon the ground; and a sudden quiet reigned.

The king saw that Jason had defeated him in this first encounter and by some mysterious means had avoided the deadly trap he had planned for him. But he resolved that

Why is this picture entitled "The Departure of Jason"?

rather than see Jason secure the Golden Fleece he would kill him and his followers; and he devised an attack against the *Argo* at early dawn.

Medea guessed what was in her father's mind and had already laid plans to defeat him once more. At the dead of night the pair stole to the sacred grove where the Golden Fleece hung on a tree. Underneath slept the formidable dragon. Go as silently as they might, their light footsteps on the grass awakened him, and in a moment he was on guard, his ferocious head thrust forward with gaping rows of fangs. But when he heard the soothing voice of Medea, who was wont to feed him, he became fiercely attentive.

"Here," she said to him, "is a sop for you," and she threw him some of his usual food, which he ate greedily. Mixed with it was a sleeping potion and hardly had he gulped it down when he fell on the ground asleep.

Jason and Medea bring the Golden Fleece to the Argo.

Hastily then Jason seized the precious fleece, and with Medea fled to the ship, where the heroes already awaited him at the oars. The ship slid over the waves and out of the harbor, and by great efforts escaped the pursuing Æëtes.

It is related of Jason and the Argonauts that on their return voyage they experienced other adventures, in one of which only the wondrous melodies of Orpheus saved them from the enchantments of the sirens.

When Jason returned to Iolcus and displayed the Golden Fleece to Pelias, the latter still, on one pretext or another, refused to give up the throne to his nephew. The daughters of Pelias, knowing the great powers of Medea and deeming her a witch who had command over life and death, begged her to compound a magic potion that would make their father young again. She pretended to agree, but gave them instead a deadly poison which killed Pelias. Jason thereupon became king. He offered up the *Argo* to Neptune as a sacrifice, but the Golden Fleece he hung in a temple of Minerva, that young men might come to gaze upon it and be inspired to adventures as brave as his had been.

PRACTICAL APPLICATIONS

Myths in Literature

The quest of Jason in search of the Golden Fleece has attracted several epic poets. In ancient times Appollonius of Rhodes wrote the *Argonautica*. In the eighteenth century John Dyer wrote *The Fleece*. But best of all the poems on the Golden Fleece is William Morris's *The Life and Death of Jason*.

The figure of Medea, often portrayed as a sort of witch or wonder-worker, has always attracted much attention. Euripides wrote a famous play about her, and Ovid wrote a letter in the *Heroines*, supposedly from her to Jason.

A more modern treatment in prose of the Jason story is that of the Irish writer Padraic Colum in *The Golden Fleece*.

Specific Literary References

What do the following references mean? Where a word or phrase is italicized, explain only the word or phrase.

  1. In such a glen, on such a day,
     On Pelion, on the grassy ground,
      Chiron, the aged centaur, lay.—*Arnold*
  2. He could, perhaps, have passed the *Hellespont*.
      —*Byron*

3. In quest of golden cargo brave Jason and his band
   Upon the good ship *Argo* sailed to the Colchian
   strand.—*Graves*
4. "This boy rows us as well without learning, as if he
   could sing the song of Orpheus to the
   Argonauts."—*Dr. Johnson in Boswell's "Life of Dr.
   Johnson."*
5. The sight of sleek, well-fed blue-coat boys in
   pictures was little consolatory to us, who saw the
   better part of our provisions carried away before our
   eyes by *harpies.—Lamb*
6. And the ram that bore unsafely the burden of
   Helle.—*Longfellow*
7. Never was Hercules apart from *Hylas.—Theocritus*
8. These are the flowers which mourning Herakles
   Strewed on the tomb of *Hylas.—Wilde*

Suggestions for Oral or Written Composition

1. Give a talk on the geography in the story of the
quest of the Golden Fleece. Illustrate your remarks by
pointing out the places mentioned on a map—one drawn
by yourself, if possible.

2. Medea keeps a diary. Write a half dozen brief
passages that she might have written after she met Jason.

3. Invent another adventure that the Argonauts might
have had before reaching Colchis.

4. Have Hercules tell a friend about one of his
interesting experiences.

Word Study

1. The word *Argonaut* has, as one meaning, this
   definition: "one who went gold-seeking in California
   in 1849." Explain how this meaning originated.
2. Why would someone speak of a wise man as a
   "Nestor."

3. Give the correct pronunciation of the following names:
   Pelias, Helle, Colchis, Symplegades, Medea.
4. What is a Hellene? What is the meaning of *Hellenic*? Where is the Hellespont? How did the Greeks explain the origin of these words?

Questions for Review

1. Who was the father of Jason?
2. What trust did his father give to Jason's uncle?
3. What happened when Jason came of age?
4. How did Pelias try to get rid of Jason?
5. What quest did Jason undertake?
6. What preparations did he make?
7. What was the name of his vessel?
8. Who were some of his companions?
9. What mischance removed Hercules from the crew?
10. How did Pollux show his prowess?
11. How did the sons of the North Wind serve Phineus, and what help did he give in return?
12. How did the Argonauts get past the Symplegades?
13. What conditions did King Æëtes impose on Jason?
14. Who offered Jason help?
15. How did Jason escape the danger of the bulls?
16. How did he overcome the armed men that sprang from the dragon's teeth?
17. How did he overcome the guardian of the fleece?
18. What happened to Pelias on the return of Jason?
19. What did Jason do with the *Argo?*

Reading List

Poems and Plays

Colum, Padraic: *The Golden Fleece* (in prose)
Euripides: *Medea*
Morris, William: *The Life and Death of Jason*
Ovid: *Medea to Jason* (in *Heroines*)

The Judgment of Paris by Rubens—Research this painting.

13 The Trojan War

Was this the face that launch'd a
thousand ships,
And burnt the topless
towers of Ilium?

Marlowe

Judgment of Paris

One of the most beautiful of the Nereids was the silvery-footed Thetis, who dwelt with her sisters in the depths of the sea, but was a favorite of Juno and often visited the heights of Olympus. So lovely was she that both Jupiter and Neptune wished to marry her, but the oracles declared that her son would be greater than his father, and neither of the deities dared risk being overthrown. She was therefore given in marriage to a mortal, Peleus, king of the Myrmidons of Thessaly.

To the marriage feast of Peleus and Thetis came all the gods, who brought many rich gifts. But one deity had not been invited to the celebrations—*Eris,* or *Ate,* the goddess of discord. She was greatly enraged at the oversight, and resolved that she would take revenge. While the merrymaking was at its height, therefore, she suddenly appeared in the midst of the revelers and threw upon the ground a wonderful apple, brought from the Garden of the Hesperides, and labeled "For the Fairest."

Immediately a contention arose as to who should have the apple. All the contestants finally withdrew, except three: Juno, Venus, and Minerva. They appealed to Jupiter to settle the dispute and award the apple, but he wisely declined to do so. He agreed, nevertheless, to appoint an arbitrator, and told the three goddesses theat Paris of Troy would make the decision.

So the three goddesses then hastened to Paris. Troy was a city in Asia Minor; it was sometimes called Ilion or Ilium. Priam reigned over Troy. He had been twice married, the second time to Hecuba, and had fifty sons, two of whom were of particular note: Hector, one of the noblest heroes of ancient times, and Paris, who was destined to cause the destruction of his people. At the birth of Paris it had been prophesied that he would bring disaster to Troy, and he had consequently been exposed on a mountain side. But some shepherds had found him and had brought him up, and he was at this time a very handsome and attractive youth.

The three goddesses came to him as he tended his sheep. They told him that he must decide which of them was the fairest and to which of them should go the Golden Apple. Each whispered secretly how she would reward him if he gave her the apple. Juno promised him great power and happiness in his domestic life. Minerva assured him of wisdom and of respect from every one. But Venus promised him the most beautiful woman in the world for his wife, and Paris handed the Golden Apple to Venus. He gained her favor, but won for himself and the Trojans the undying hatred of Juno and Minerva.

There was no doubt as to who was the most beautiful woman then living. She was Helen, daughter of Leda and Jupiter, (who had appeared to Leda in the form of a swan), and sister of the great athletes, Castor and Pollux. Even as a child she had inspired almost awe-struck admiration because of her surpassing loveliness. When she passed into girlhood the foremost chieftains of Greece sought her in marriage, and for a time it seemed as if the rivalry for her hand would bring about a deadly war. Among these chieftains, however, there was one very wise man, Ulysses (Greek: Odysseus).

Ulysses proposed that all the suitors of Helen take a solemn oath, not only pledging themselves to abide peacefully by whatever decision she made, but also agreeing that if ever anyone attempted to molest either Helen or her husband, all the others would help him and punish the aggressor. All the chieftains agreed to this oath, and thereupon Helen chose as her husband Menelaus, king of Sparta, whose brother was Agamemnon, king of Mycenæ and the most powerful ruler in Greece.

For a time matters rested as they were. Then Paris reminded Venus of her promise, and she urged him to go to Greece and visit Sparta. There, with the help of the goddess, Paris induced Helen to elope with him, and the pair returned hastily to Troy. Before this Priam had acknowledged Paris as his son; and now when he returned with Helen, he received them in his home, but reluctantly, for he guessed what troubles were in store for him and his people.

Gathering the Hosts

As soon as the abduction of Helen had taken place, Menelaus sent word to all the heroes who had wooed Helen and called on them for a fulfillment of their pledge. He told them that the Greek army was to

The abduction of Helen of Troy

assemble at Aulis, a port in Bœotia, but it was two years before the hosts were gathered.

Many things delayed them, one of them, strangely enough, being the unwillingness of Ulysses to keep his pledge. For Ulysses was very happy in Ithaca, the little island over which he ruled. He had married Penelope, a cousin of Helen, and a son had been born to him, named Telemachus. He did not in the least want to set forth on a long and dangerous expedition. Finally the Greek leaders sent one of the wisest of their number, Palamedes, to persuade Ulysses. When he arrived at Ithaca, Ulysses pretended to be mad. He harnessed an ox and an ass together to the plow, and began to sow salt along the seashore. But Palamedes contrived to get the better of him. He managed to obtain possession of the little boy Telemachus and placed him right in the path of the plow. Ulysses turned aside, and so proved his sanity. Thereupon he agreed to accompany Palamedes to Aulis, but he never forgave him and later on brought about his death by a trick.

Again the army was delayed by the necessity of obtaining as a leader Achilles, son of Peleus and Thetis. The army already had the services of many great heroes—Menelaus, Agamemnon, the sage Nestor and the still wiser Ulysses, the gigantic but slow-witted Ajax, the valiant Diomedes, the loud-voiced herald Stentor, and others. But it had been prophesied that Troy would never fall unless Achilles fought against it. On the other hand, an oracle had declared to Thetis that her son would fall in the war against Troy, and she was naturally anxious to avert this doom for her son. At his very birth she had tried to save him from all perils of war by dipping him in the River Styx, as a result of which he became invulnerable except at the place on the heel where she held him. In his boyhood he received a manly education from the centaur Chiron.

To keep her son out of the Greek army Thetis sent the young hero to stay with his uncle, who was bidden to disguise him in women's clothes. Ulysses learned where he was hiding, and went to the palace as a peddler. On his trays were many articles such as appeal to women, but mingled with them were a sword and a buckler. As he spread out his wares before the royal maidens, he noticed that one of them disregarded the ribbons and linens and fingered the sword eagerly. So he discovered Achilles, and persuaded him to accompany him back to Aulis.

Finally, the Greek army was delayed by an impiety committed unwittingly by Agamemnon. While out hunting he slew a stag that was sacred to Diana. In revenge she afflicted the Greek army with a plague. Oracles declared the cause of the plague and said that Diana would not be satisfied until Agamemnon's daughter, Iphigenia, was sacrificed upon her altar. Much against his will and in deep sorrow Agamemnon sent for his daughter. He knew that his wife, Clytemnestra, would never let her come to Aulis if she were told that her daughter was to die, and so he ordered the messengers to tell her that Iphigenia was about to be married to Achilles. When Iphigenia arrived, the bitter tidings were told her, but she bore her fate bravely. On the appointed day she was placed on the altar, and the priest of Diana approached to slay her. Without letting anyone see what was happening, however, Diana substituted a hart for

190

Ulysses and companions—Roman mosaic from Bardo Museum, Tunis

the maiden, and transported her swiftly to the land of the Tauri, where she became a priestess of the goddess. Here in later years she saved her brother Orestes from death and fled with him back to Greece.

War Against Troy

Now the army sailed in an endless fleet. The Trojans opposed their landing, but in vain, for the Greek numbers were overwhelming. The Trojans finally withdrew behind the city walls, and prepared to stand siege, a siege that lasted for ten years. For the first nine years the war was indecisive, victory coming sometimes to the Greeks and sometimes to the Trojans. The gods and goddesses were as much interested in the matter as the actual combatants, and some of them espoused the Greek, some the Trojan side. Venus, as we know, favored the Trojans, and so too did Mars. Juno and Minerva of course favored the Greeks, and with them sided Neptune. Apollo sometimes helped one, sometimes the other. Jupiter tried to be neutral, but for various reasons was sometimes obliged to intervene.

In the tenth year the Trojan War approached a climax; and it is a part of this year that the greatest of ancient poets, Homer, describes in the first of his two masterpieces, the *Iliad*. For the most part Homer deals with an episode that caused a great deal of trouble to the Greeks, but ultimately brought about the downfall of the mainstay of the Trojans, the hero Hector.

It all began with a quarrel between Agamemnon and Achilles over a division of the spoils of war. Achilles retired to his tent and sulked, and absolutely refused to come and fight for the Greeks. His mother, meanwhile, went to Jupiter and implored him to allow the Trojans to win for a while, as a punishment for the insult offered to her son. Jupiter consented, despite the anger of Juno; and the Greeks, although Menelaus defeated Paris in personal combat and the Trojan was saved from death only by the intervention of Venus, were soon defeated by the prowess of Hector. For he left his noble wife Andromache and his dearly beloved infant son, Astyanax, and went forth to battle. So hard did he press the Greeks that Agamemnon even proposed that they should all reëmbark and return to Greece. Nestor, however, suggested that an embassy should be sent to Achilles, bearing gifts and imploring him to return to help them. This was done, but Achilles refused to fight.

Now the Greeks were obliged to build ramparts to protect themselves against the onslaughts of the Trojans. Hector, wounded by a huge stone hurled at him by Ajax, was stretched senseless on the field but not even this setback sufficed to stay the Trojans. At this critical moment Nestor was able to persuade Patroclus, the dearest friend of Achilles, to borrow the armor of his friend. Achilles, moved by the defeats that the Greeks were suffering, even consented to let him lead his own Myrmidons into battle.

The Trojan War as pictured on a Corinthian bowl—6th century, B.C.

Patroclus and the Myrmidons at once plunged into the contest. The Trojans, beholding the famous armor of Achilles, thought that the great hero had returned to help the Greeks and fled in terror. The Greek heroes, inspired by the turn of events, performed mighty deeds of valor. Hector himself had to turn and flee.

In the course of the battle Patroclus at last came face to face with Sarpedon, grandson of Bellerophon and son of Jupiter himself. Jupiter could not intervene, and in the combat that ensued Sarpedon was slain, and a furious battle arose for the possession of his body. But Jupiter snatched the body from the field, and conveyed it to the hero's native land, where it was given honorable burial.

And now the tide of battle turned. Patroclus had swept onward in his victorious course, when suddenly Hector confronted him. Both heroes at first fought from their chariots, but shortly they contended on the level ground, giving and taking fierce blows. Not against the greatest of the Trojans, however, could Patroclus contend, and in a little while he fell mortally wounded by the spear of Hector. Even greater than the combat over the body of Sarpedon was that over the body of Patroclus. Hector managed to secure the magnificent armor, and he retired immediately to a little distance and put it on in place of his own. The Greeks fought desperately to retain the body, and at last succeeded in bearing it away to their ships.

When Achilles heard what had happened to Patroclus, he was desperate with grief. His groans reached the ears of Thetis, who came hastily to him and tried to console him. He wished to go at once in search of Hector, but his mother persuaded him that he must have suitable armor, and she promised to bring it to him by the morrow. Hastening to Vulcan, she begged him to make for her son an armor such as no man had ever worn before, and to do it before dawn broke. Vulcan laid aside all his other labors and turned to the fashioning of the armor. When it was completed, it was a miracle of craftsmanship, contrived to serve all purposes of war, yet ornamented with beautiful art.

Arrayed in this armor, Achilles left his tent and called the chiefs to council. He made peace with Agamemnon, and arranged to lead the Greek hosts out to battle immediately. The Trojans fled in fear before him, and even Hector, cautioned by Apollo, avoided an encounter with him. But Æneas, one of the Trojan warriors, son of the goddess of love, was willing to undertake a duel to the death with Achilles, and had already lifted up a huge stone to hurl at him, when Neptune in pity intervened and spread a cloud between the two warriors. All the followers of Priam hastily returned to the gates of the city, barely in time to escape the avenging blows of Achilles.

Hector waited without. His father and mother called to him from the walls, and begged him to seek safety. But he felt that upon him more than upon any other rested the welfare of his people. Yet when Achilles approached, terrible as Mars in his shining armor, even Hector was filled with terror and fled. Round the walls of Troy, Greek pursued Trojan, but at last Hector stayed his flight and hurled a spear at Achilles. It fell harmless from the shield of the Greek hero, and Hector lifted his sword and rushed at Archilles. As he came nearer, Achilles measured with his eye a spot where the armor left Hector's neck uncovered, and there he delivered the fatal blow. Hector fell lifeless on the plains of Trou, before the eyes of his people.

For a time Achilles vented his rage on the body of the

194

Trojan hero. He attached the corpse to his chariot and dragged it in triumph around the walls of Troy. But when Priam approached Achilles in secret embassy and reminded him of his aged father Peleus, he at last consented to allow the body of Hector to be taken to Troy for burial. Meanwhile splendid funeral rites were held for Patroclus, and according to the custom of the Greeks, the funeral was accompanied by games that continued for many days.

Stratagem of the Wooden Horse

Yet not then did Troy fall. For weary weeks the siege of the city continued, and it was not long before Achilles himself was killed. Paris, who somehow had learned of the vulnerable heel of the hero, discharged at him a poisoned arrow, from the effects of which he died. The example having been given, the Greeks now used poisoned arrows against the Trojans, and one of the first victims was Paris himself. Not long after his death Helen married his brother Deiphobus. Among the innumerable prophecies relating to the fall of Troy was one that proclaimed the city invulnerable so long as a certain statue of Minerva remained in Troy. So, one night, Ulysses and Diomedes entered the city in disguise and carried it off.

But still Troy was not captured. Then in desperation the Greeks resolved to adopt a stratagem suggested by the crafty Ulysses. Looking out from the walls of their city one day, the Trojans saw with wonder how the Greeks were busy making preparations to leave. Everywhere the tents were struck, the ships made ready, and supplies gathered together. Shortly not a Greek was left on the plains of Troy.

For a time the Trojans hesitated. Then with cries of joy they ran out of the gates of the city. The foremost paused, however, in bewilderment as they saw before them a great wooden horse. They gazed at it from every side and wondered what its purpose could be. Then a priest of

Neptune, named Laocoön, angrily addressed them and urged them to burn the wooden horse at once.

"It surely is some trick of the foe," he said.

Even as he spoke there came from the sea two immense serpents. The people fled to left and right, but the serpents paid no heed to them. Straight for Laocoön they made, and cast their folds not only around him, but around his two children who stood beside him. Shortly all lay dead upon the ground, and the snakes wound their way back to the sea and disappeared.

Of course the Trojans took this as a significant sign that the gods were punishing Laocoön for impiety. Just then some in the crowd dragged forward a captive—obviously a Greek. He told them that his name was Sinon, that he had been left behind by accident, and that the wooden horse (built, he said, by the artificer Epeus) was an offering to Minerva, and had been made monstrous in size especially to prevent the Trojans from carrying it within the city and so regaining the favor of the goddess.

With a shout the people laid hold of the great wooden horse and dragged it toward the walls of the city. There busy hands already hewed and hacked at the wall, in order to open a space large enough for the wooden horse to enter. Then the horse was dragged toward the center of the city, and toward it turned the eyes of revelers all through that noisy day of celebration.

At last came night and with it quiet. Slowly a cunningly concealed door in the wooden horse opened, and out stole the armed men who had lain hidden within. Quickly they ran to the gates of the city and opened them wide to the Greek hosts, who had returned from the sheltering cliffs of a nearby island. Priam and his people were awakened by the strident yells of warriors, and arose to find their city in the hands of the Greeks.

On that night Priam and many other noble Trojans were slain. By the hand of Menelaus fell Deiphobus; and Helen, who since the death of Paris had aided the Greeks on a number of occasions, was reconciled to her husband, who forgave her disloyalty as really due to the urging of Venus. Many of the Trojan women were carried off as captives to Greece, and the city was left a heap of ruins.

Laocoon and his sons strangled by the sea serpents

PRACTICAL APPLICATIONS

Myths in Literature

Of all the great "matter of Greece and Rome" the deepest and most lasting impression has undoubtedly been made by the story of Helen of Troy, with all the remarkable incidents that followed her abduction by Paris.

In Greek literature itself the greatest of Greek poets, Homer, devoted to the subject his masterpieces, the *Iliad* and the *Odyssey*. The greatest of Latin poets, Virgil, took the Trojan War and its consequences for one man, Æneas, as the theme of his *Æneid,* the Roman national epic. Again and again the other poets of classical antiquity selected one aspect or another of the same war and its aftermath as the subject of their writings.

In the Middle Ages and during the Renaissance period the attention paid to this theme was scarcely less. The references to Helen and her contemporaries are innumerable. Chaucer, the greatest of English poets before Shakespeare, wrote a novel in verse about certain incidents of the Trojan War. The same incidents suggested to Shakespeare himself the plot of a play. Into the translation of Homer, George Chapman, a contemporary of Shakespeare, put energy and ability equal to the production of an original work; and since his time one rendering after another of Homer has appeared.

Helen of Troy has exercised her fascination upon poets of all times. Homer, himself, never directly describes the famous beauty, but he tells how the old men of Troy, watching her walk past them, gazed upon her beauty and declared that it was no wonder that a war had been waged for her. Since Homer the poets and dramatists of all literatures have again and again endeavored to picture her, concretely or by suggestion.

Unquestionably the most magnificent of these pictures occurs in Marlowe's play, *Dr. Faustus.* The magician, by his magic arts, has called up the shade of Helen, and looking

198

upon her beauty he exclaims in ecstasy:

> O thou art fairer than the evening air
> Clad in the beauty of a thousand stars!

and again:

> Was this the face that launch'd a thousand ships,
> And burnt the topless towers of Ilium?
> Sweet Helen, make me immortal with a kiss!

The greatest of German poets, Goethe, in addition to writing a play, one of his finest, about Iphigenia, also made Helen one of the most important figures of the second part of *Faust*.

Edgar Allan Poe, again, reached the very height of his genius in the lyric, *To Helen*. This was addressed to a living person, Mrs. Jane Stanard, but the whole inspiration of the verses is Greek, and the fragrance of the Greek heroine fills the opening stanza:

> Helen, thy beauty is to me
> Like those Nicæan barks of yore
> That gently o'er a perfumed sea
> The weary wayworn wanderer bore
> To his own native shore.

Tennyson, in *A Dream of Fair Women*, thus describes Helen:

> A daughter of the gods, divinely tall,
> And most divinely fair.

To Shakespeare she was

> . . . a theme of honor and renown,
> A spur to valiant and magnanimous deeds;

> . . . a Grecian queen, whose youth and freshness
> Wrinkles Apollo's, and makes stale the morning.

The other figure of the Trojan War to receive great attention is Ulysses. More will be said in the next chapter about what poets and dramatists have done with him. Catullus and "H. D." have written of Thetis; Robert Bridges and George Santayana of Achilles; Euripides of Iphigenia and of Hecuba; Sophocles of Ajax; and Ovid, Landor, and Tennyson of handsome Paris. In French literature Racine wrote two of his finest drams on Andromache and Iphigenia.

Specific Literary References

What do the following references mean? Where a word or phrase is italicized, explain only the word or phrase.

1. *Achilles* ponders in his tent.—*Arnold*
2. And, like another Helen, fires another Troy.—*Dryden*
3. So now he smiled and gazed at his boy silently, and *Andromache* stood by his side and wept.—*Homer*
4. There pleading might you see grave *Nestor* stand.
   —*Shakespeare.*
5. Had doting *Priam* checked his son's desire, Troy had been bright with fame and not with fire.
   —*Shakespeare*
6. Her name was *Ate*, mother of debate
   And all destruction.—*Spenser*
7. By trying, the Greeks got into Troy.—*Theocritus*
8. It was for thee gold-crested *Hector* tried
   With *Thetis' child* that evil race to run.—*Wilde.*

Suggestions for Oral or Written Composition

1. The following is an outline of the Trojan War. Prepare a report on one of the main topics.

   A. Causes of the War
      I. The marriage of Peleus and Thetis
      II. The judgment of Paris
      III. The marriage of Helen
      IV. The elopement of Helen and Paris

    B. Gathering of the Hosts
        I. The summoning of the Greek heroes
        II. Iphigenia at Aulis
        III. Important Greek leaders
        IV. Important Trojan leaders
    C. The War against Troy
        I. Early years of the war
        II. The quarrel of Achilles and Agamemnon
        III. The death of Patroclus
        IV. The death of Hector
        V. The death of Achilles and Paris
    D. The Capture of Troy
        I. The building of the wooden horse
        II. The death of Laocoön
        III. Bringing of the horse into Troy
        IV. The taking of the city

    2. As one of the guests, describe the marriage feast of Peleus and Thetis.

    3. One of the cousins of Achilles was present when Ulysses arrived in disguise as a peddler. She tells her father what happened.

    4. You belong to the Myrmidons of Achilles. Describe the death of Patroclus to a comrade in the Greek camp.

Word Study

    1. Look up the following names in a mythological dictionary and practice the correct pronunciation. Nereid, Thetis, Priam, Menelaus, Agamemnon, Penelope, Telemachus, Achilles, Iphigenia.

    2. In modern English, *hector* has come to mean "to bully" or "to treat insolently." The word is derived from the name of the Trojan hero. Does it do justice to his character?

    3. Explain the origin of *myrmidon*—a faithful adherent; *stentorian*—loud-voiced.

    4. What do the following expressions mean?

        "That is his Achilles' tendon."
        "As wily as Ulysses."

"As wise as Nestor."
"Difficult as the judgment of Paris."
"Sulk like Achilles."
"To work like a Trojan."
"An apple of discord."

Questions for Review

1. Why did Jupiter not marry Thetis?
2. Who became her husband?
3. What deity was not invited to the marriage feast?
4. What was her revenge?
5. How did Paris render judgment?
6. What was the name of his father and of his native city?
7. What woman was promised Paris as a reward?
8. What oath did Ulysses propose to her suitors?
9. Whom did she marry?
10. What happened when Paris visited Sparta?
11. What call for help did Menelaus send out?
12. Who failed to respond and why?
13. How was he forced to come?
14. Who was Achilles?
15. What were the oracles concerning him?
16. Who managed to find him and bring him to the Greek camp?
17. Why was the Greek army delayed at Aulis?
18. How was Diana appeased?
19. What happened during the first nine years of the war?
20. Why did Agamemnon and Achilles quarrel?
21. What was the result?
22. How was Patroclus killed?
23. What was the effect on Achilles?
24. How was Hector killed?
25. How were Paris and Achilles slain?
26. What was the stratagem of the wooden horse?
27. What priest tried to save the Trojans?
28. What was his fate?
29. What was the fate of Troy?

Reading List

Poems, Plays and Stories

Bridges, Robert: *The Tale of Achilles*
Browning, Elizabeth Barrett: *Hector and Andromache*
Doolittle, Hilda ("H. D."): *Thetis*
Euripides: *Iphigenia at Aulis*
Gayley, Charles M.: Catullus's *Wedding of Peleus and Thetis*
Homer: The *Iliad,* translated by Lang, Leaf, and Myers
Landor, Walter Savage: *The Death of Paris*
Lang, Andrew: *Helen of Troy*
MacKaye, A. L.: *The Slave Prince* (a novel)
Marlowe, Christopher: *Dr. Faustus*
Morris, William: *The Death of Paris*
Ovid: *Helen to Paris* (in *Heroines*)
Ovid: *Paris to Helen* (in *Heroines*)
Peele, George: *The Arraignment of Paris*
Plutarch: *Life of Theseus* (in prose)
Poe, Edgar Allan: *To Helen*
Putnam, Emily James: *Candaules' Wife, and Other Old Stories* (in prose)
Racine, Jean: *Andromache*
Teasdale, Sara: *Helen of Troy*
Tennyson, Alfred: *Œnone*
White, Edward Lucas: *Helen* (a novel)
Wilde, Oscar: *Serenade* (to Helen)

What is John Linnell portraying in his painting
"The Return of Ulysses?"

14 After the Trojan War

*But Neptune strove still with Ulysses,
till he reached his native land*

Homer

Return of the Heroes

Menelaus and Helen, after the fall
of Troy, returned to Sparta together, and lived there for
many years in happiness. According to some accounts, their
homeward voyage was delayed by storms and the ill favor
of the gods, and they visited many countries of the

Mediterranean, in most of which they were well received. When Telemachus, some years later, visited Sparta in search of his father Ulysses, he found the royal pair just celebrating the marriage of their daughter Hermione to the son of Achilles, Neoptolemus.

To Agamemnon came a different fate. He, it will be recalled, had incurred the deep anger of his wife Clytemnestra by getting her to send their daughter Iphigenia to Aulis on the pretext that she was to marry Achilles. Instead she had, seemingly, been sacrificed to Diana. Neither of them knew that Iphigenia had been snatched away by the goddess and was still alive among the Tauri.

When Agamemnon sailed for home, he carried with him much spoil, including some Trojan slaves. Among the latter was a daughter of Priam and Hecuba, named Cassandra. Apollo had conferred upon her the gift of prophecy. But Cassandra rejected Apollo's advances, and he punished her by decreeing that although her vision of the future would always be true, no one would believe her. During the Trojan War Cassandra had prophesied many dire events, but her predictions had always been received with scorn. So now, too, she foretold what was going to happen to Agamemnon, but he simply smiled at her prophecies and considered her absurd.

When Agamemnon reached home, he found Clytemnestra in, apparently, a friendly and loving mood, but even before he could partake of the banquet offered him, he was killed by her servants. Clytemnestra then hastily married Ægisthus, who had aided her in the crime. It was the purpose of the conspirators to get rid of all of the family of Agamemnon, that their hold on the throne might be secure, but Electra saved the life of her brother, Orestes; and from these children of the slain king vengeance duly came. For Orestes took refuge in the palace of a kinsman; and when he grew up, he returned to his father's palace and slew his mother and Ægisthus.

Such horrifying crimes, whatever the motives back of them, could not, of course, be justified by the gods, and Orestes was consequently pursued by the Furies, those dreadful creatures who typify the conscience. Accompanied

The abduction of Cassandra by Agamemnon

by his friend Pylades, he fled from land to land in madness,
seeking purification. Finally an oracle declared that he must
seek the temple of Diana in the land of the Tauri. When he
arrived there, still in the company of the faithful Pylades,
the savage inhabitants seized them and prepared to sacrifice
them to the goddess, as was their custom with strangers.
But when Orestes was placed upon the altar, the priestess
of the temple, his own sister Iphigenia, recognized him,
and all three fled from the land, taking with them the statue
of Diana. They returned to Mycenæ, and Orestes, freed of
the Furies, took possession of his father's kingdom. Pylades
married Electra, and Orestes, it is said, married Hermione,
daughter of Menelaus and Helen, after the death of
Neoptolemus.

Adventures of Ulysses

To Ulysses came the most startling adventures, recounted by Homer in the second of his masterpieces, the *Odyssey*.

Ulysses left Ithaca, as we know, most unwillingly, and for ten years he fought at Troy. It was ten more years before he returned to Ithaca and to his wife Penelope and his son Telemachus.

1. *The Land of the Ciconians.* Laden with spoil, Ulysses set sail from Troy with twelve ships. His first landing was made at Ismarus, a city of the Ciconians. He sacked the city and took much additional spoil. Ulysses wished to leave immediately, but his men overruled him and reveled for many hours. While they lay asleep on the shore, the Ciconians attacked them. As a result, the Greeks were driven back to their ships, with the loss of seventy-two men.

2. *The Land of the Lotus-Eaters.* For nine days then they sailed on, and on the tenth day they came to the land of the lotus-eaters, who ate a flower as food. Ulysses and his men landed and partook of their own food, but Ulysses sent three of his crew as an embassy to the inhabitants of the country, to find out what manner of men they were. They mingled with the lotus-eaters, who attempted to do them no harm, but gave them the lotus to eat. Straightway these men lost all their strength, and no longer wished to return home, but desired to remain forever in this pleasant land, where it always seemed like a languid afternoon. Only by force did Ulysses get them back to the ships.

3. *The Country of the Cyclopes.* Swiftly the ships hastened from this dangerous land of languor, and sailing onward they came to the land of the one-eyed monsters called Cyclopes. The land where these favorites of the gods lived yielded them food without effort, and each inhabited his own cave. The ships of Ulysses grounded on an island near this country, and for a time he and his men feasted on the flesh of the goats that they found there. But Ulysses decided to go closer to the mainland. He found a cave near the sea, wherein was a lofty hall. Near by many cattle, both

sheep and goats, were sleeping. Taking a large goatskin
filled with wine and choosing twelve men to accompany
him, Ulysses entered the cave, but failed to find its owner
within. His men begged him to seize some of the cattle and
take some of the rich cheese they found within and escape,
but Ulysses chose to remain, hoping that he would obtain
fine presents from the master of the cave.

Shortly there was a great clamor without, as the
Cyclops returned, throwing down a huge load of firewood
from his shoulders. He drove his flocks within the cave, and
at the entrance he placed a great stone as a door;
two-and-twenty good wagons could not have moved it from
the threshold. Suddenly he saw Ulysses and his men.

"Who are you?" he cried in his giant's voice, and
thereat the hearts of all of them trembled.

Ulysses recounted to him their voyage from Troy and
begged him for the gifts due a stranger. Then the Cyclops
mocked him, and asked where his ship was. Ulysses craftily
told him that it had been wrecked, and even as he spoke
the Cyclops siezed two of his men, dashed them on the
ground, and made a meal from their bodies. Thereupon he
fell asleep, and all night long Ulysses pondered ways by
which he might overcome the monster.

The next morning the Cyclops ate two more of the
Greeks, and then left the cave, fastening the door securely.
But now Minerva inspired Ulysses who ordered his men to
sharpen a huge beam, and told them to be ready at a word
to thrust it into the giant's eye when he lay asleep. That
evening he came again, and again slew two of the men for
food. But to him then came Ulysses bearing a present of
wine, and the giant drank and was pleased. Thrice he took
a huge draught, and he asked the name of Ulysses. Once
more Ulysses replied to him craftily:

"Do you ask my name?" he inquired. "Give me then
the gifts due to hospitality, and I will tell you. No One is
my name; so they all call me."

Polyphemus the Cyclops replied cruelly:

"This shall be your gift: I will eat No One last of all."

Even as he spoke he fell back in a drunken sleep.

Then Ulysses heated the beam, and when it began to
glow and take fire, they all took hold of it, and Ulysses,

Ulysses escaping from the cave of Polyphemus

standing above, whirled it round as they moved. They thrust it swiftly into the eye of Polyphemus, and blinded him. Horribly he roared with pain, so that the other Cyclopes hastened up and asked:

"Polyphemus, who is hurting you?"

And he replied:

"O my friends, No One is hurting me."

At his words they were bewildered and returned to their caves.

The next morning Polyphemus was obliged to open his cave to let the cattle out. He stood there, however, as a guard, seeking to prevent the escape of the Greeks. But Ulysses bound each of his men under the middlemost of three rams, and he himself clung to the wool of the last three; and so they escaped the detection of Polyphemus. They returned to their ship, and once on board Ulysses called to the Cyclops and mocked him. Even in his blindness Polyphemus hurled a huge rock in the direction of his voice, and almost wrecked the ship. Then, at a safer distance, Ulysses once more reproached the Cyclops, and told him that if anyone asked him who had blinded him, he might reply that it was "Ulysses, son of Laertes, of Ithaca."

At his words Polyphemus lifted up his hands to the heavens and prayed to his father Neptune:

"Hear me, O earth-shaking, blue-haired Neptune! If I am indeed your son, keep this Ulysses from his home. But if he is destined to reach his home, may he come late and in evil plight, and find calamities in his house!"

Neptune heard him, and was angered at the wrong done his son; and he answered the prayer of Polyphemus. Many years he kept Ulysses from home, and many troubles he found when he at last reached Ithaca.

4. *The Island of Æolus.* Not many days later they came to the home of Æolus, king of the winds, who received them hospitably. When they were preparing to leave, Æolus gave Ulysses a great bag made of oxhide, and told him that he had confined in it all the winds that might oppose his voyage home. So they set sail, and for nine days a steady breeze behind them propelled them toward Ithaca. They were in sight of the shore, when Ulysses, overcome by watching, lay asleep, and his men, who thought he had some treasure concealed in the bag he guarded so carefully, stole the bag and opened it. Immediately the confined winds rushed out, and drove the ships back to Æolus, who refused to aid them again.

5. *The Land of the Læstrygonians.* Tempted by what seemed a friendly and safe harbor, the ships next entered the land of the Læstrygonians. Ulysses was the only one who kept his ship outside the haven. But, instead of a safe, friendly harbor, this was a land of man-eating giants, even fiercer than the Cyclopes; and they destroyed all the ships within the harbor.

6. *The Island of Circe.* Next Ulysses, with his single ship, came to the island Ææa, where dwelt the enchantress Circe, child of Apollo and of a daughter of Oceanus. For two days Ulysses lay off the shore, but at last he divided his men into two companies. By lot it fell that the company headed by his lieutenant Eurylochus was chosen to explore the island. They walked inland, and came to a beautiful palace, surrounded by wolves, lions and other animals, all of whom seemed tame. Within they heard a woman singing over the spindle. They called, and Circe came out and welcomed them. Yet she did not notice that Eurylochus

Circe offering her magic potion to Ulysses

remained outside. She gave them food, mixed with a potent drug; and when they had eaten, she struck them with her wand, and they were forthwith changed to swine.

Now Eurylochus reported to Ulysses that none of his company had returned to him. Then Ulysses took his sword, and resolved to explore the island. But on the way a beautiful youth, with the first down on his lips and cheeks, met him. It was the god Mercury. He told Ulysses of the enchantments of Circe, and gave him a magic herb, called *moly*, to protect him. Then Ulysses entered the palace, and was welcomed by Circe, who set a banquet before him. But when she struck him with the wand, it had no effect, and Ulysses rushed on her with his sword. At that Circe sought to make peace, for she recognized him as Ulysses, but he refused until she had returned his men to human guise.

This she did, and Ulysses remained at her palace month after month. He seemed to have forgotten his native land. At last the urging of his companions brought him to his senses and he made preparations to set sail.

Ulysses escapes from the seductive songs of the Sirens.

7. *The Visit to Hades.* But first, Circe told him, it was necessary for him to visit the underworld and obtain further instructions. With the help of the goddess he was able to do this, and he obtained advice as to the way to get home, from Tiresias, a blind seer who still retained in the underworld his gift of prophecy. In Hades he also saw the shades of his mother, Agamemnon, Achilles, Ajax and many others.

8. *The Sirens.* First of the perils which Ulysses faced after leaving the pleasant island of Circe was that of the sirens—the dangerous maidens who sang a most sweet song and enticed mariners to their destruction on the cruel rocks which they inhabited. As Ulysses approached the place where the sirens dwelt, he instructed his men to fill their ears with wax and to bind him firmly to the mast of their ship. He ordered them under no circumstances to free him. When the sirens sang their sweetest songs and promised Ulysses all sorts of precious blessings, he struggled madly to free himself and with dire threats commanded his men to release him. But they heard neither the sirens' song nor the words of Ulysses. So he and they passed this peril safely.

9. *Scylla and Charybdis.* Between this rock and whirlpool, each inhabited by a monster, Ulysses likewise

212

passed with the loss of only some of his men, where other mariners and their ships perished utterly. For while Ulysses and his men watched Charybdis on one side, the six heads of Scylla seized six of the crew from the other side.

10. *The Cattle of the Sun.* Greater misfortune came to him when the ship reached Thrinacia, where were pastured the cattle of the Sun. Ulysses had been warned by both Tiresias and Circe not to eat these cattle. The ship was becalmed at the island for several days, and the supply of food gave out. So long as he could, Ulysses kept watch, but at last in utter weariness he dozed. While he slept, his men killed some of the cattle and ate them. When Ulysses awoke and realized what sacrilege they had committed, he was horrified. A breeze sprang up and they set sail, but the sun god, in wrath at their impiety, sent a terrible storm. The ship was wrecked and all were drowned except Ulysses who improvised a raft and floated on it to a nearby shore.

11. *The Island of Ogygia.* He found that he was on Ogygia, an island ruled over by a fair-haired nymph named Calypso. She received him most kindly and kept him on the island for seven years. Indeed, she wished to marry him and offered him immortality if he would become her husband. But he refused, and day by day lamented his lot and prayed constantly to be allowed to return to his wife and child. Yet the gods permitted Neptune to vent his anger on Ulysses for the blinding of Polyphemus. One day, however, Neptune was in Ethiopia. Minerva, who was friendly to Ulysses, used the opportunity to urge the council of the gods to help the Greek hero. Jupiter hearkened to her words, and sent Mercury as a messenger to Calypso, bidding her free Ulysses. Calypso demurred, but dared not disobey. So Ulysses built a raft, received food and wine from Calypso, and bade farewell to the nymph.

For many days he sailed in peace and was almost in sight of Ithaca, when Neptune, returning from his visit to Ethiopia caught sight of him. His wrath was kindled, but he knew that he could not keep Ulysses from his native land much longer. Yet for the last time he sent a storm, and Ulysses just barely managed to save himself from the wreck of his raft and swim to a strange and rocky shore.

12. *The Land of the Phæacians.* From this time on Ulysses was under the fostering care of Minerva, and his path was much smoother. The first one he met in this new land was the Princess Nausicaä, who came with her maidens to wash clothes on the beach where Ulysses had been wrecked. She was impressed by his manly appearance and his wisdom in speech. She took him to her father's palace, and there for several days Ulysses was royally entertained. The king, Alcinoüs, and the queen, Arete, would have been glad to give Nausicaä in marriage to this noble stranger, but he implored their aid in returning to Ithaca. Before he left they held in his honor elaborate games, in which Ulysses displayed his strength and skill, and they heard from his lips the tale of his adventures.

13. *The Slaying of the Suitors.* Ulysses was landed secretly on Ithaca by a ship of the Phæacians, which on its return was changed to stone by the angry Neptune. Once in Ithaca, Ulysses set out to discover the condition of affairs in his kingdom. He was able to make himself known to his son Telemachus who told Ulysses that nobody believed he would ever return, and that Penelope was besieged by a host of suitors, who feasted day and night in his palace and insisted that she must marry one of them.

This was evil news for Ulysses, who saw that even in his home he must continue to endure hardships. Disguising himself as a beggar, he made his way to his palace, where none recognized him except Argus, the old dog that had been his companion in his youth. Argus was now old and feeble, but as Ulysses approached he wagged his tail, lifted his ears and tried to move toward him, but the effort was too much and he died.

In the palace Ulysses suffered all manner of abuse from both the suitors and the servants. At last he discussed with Telemachus the plot that was to lead to the undoing of the evil suitors. To determine who should marry Penelope it was proposed that a contest with a mighty bow owned by Ulysses should be held. The one who shot best at a set mark was to have the hand of Penelope. The suitors agreed, and Telemachus carefully removed all other arms from the great hall where the contest was to be held.

The time for the trial of the bow came. The suitors were in the hall, and near Telemachus stood a beggar who was Ulysses in disguise. Unknown to the suitors the doors leading to the hall had been locked. Now the trial began, and the mighty bow was brought forward. First came the business of stringing it. Telemachus tried to bend the bow; then one after another of the suitors tried, but in vain.

"Let me try," said Ulysses, and the suitors laughed in scorn at the impudent beggar.

But with skilled hands Ulysses took the bow, and without effort strung it. Consternation fell upon the suitors, and their faces grew pale. Just then thunder rumbled in the air, and all knew that Jupiter looked with favor on the strange beggar. He picked up an arrow which lay beside him on the table, laid it upon the arch, drew the bow to his shoulder, and sent the arrow straight through the mark. Thereupon he gave the signal to Telemachus, and his son, clad in shining armor and girt with a sword, took his stand beside him.

Then wise Ulysses threw off his rags and sprang to the broad threshold, his bow in hand and his quiver full of arrows. Out he poured the swift shafts at his feet, and as he stood there Minerva gave him the kingly bearing that was his due.

"Dogs!" he cried. "You said that I would never return, and therefore you destroyed my home, wooed my wife, and insulted my son. You feared neither the wrath of the gods nor the indignation of men. Now you shall all die!"

So shaft after shaft he shot at the insolent suitors, until all but two, less guilty than the rest, were slain. Then Penelope learned that her husband had returned, and all was well again in the palace of Ulysses.

14. *The Death of Ulysses.* The stories vary as to what happened after the slaying of the suitors. Some say that Ulysses lived peacefully and died happily, after many years. But others recount that in time Ulysses grew weary of quiet, and longed again for turmoil and danger. At last he could bear it no longer, and collecting a band of kindred spirits, set out once more, aiming to reach some lands, far to the west, of which he had heard. On that quest he died, and no man knew where.

PRACTICAL APPLICATIONS

Myths in Literature

"The wily Ulysses" has passed into a proverb, and with Helen has become the best-known figure of the Trojan War and its succeeding events. But the tragic fate of the powerful Agamemnon has moved poets hardly less.

It is noteworthy that the stories of both Ulysses and Agamemnon have proved especially attractive to dramatists. Plays about Ulysses have been written by Stephen Phillips, Robert Bridges, and Gerhart Hauptmann. In ancient times plays about the return of Agamemnon were composed by Æschylus, Euripides, and Sophocles; in more modern times by Robinson Jeffers.

In the adventures of Ulysses, the sojourn with Circe, the passing by the dangerous rock of the sirens, and the episodes in Ithaca have most won poets. Among those who have treated these themes are Matthew Arnold, Samuel Daniel, Austin Dobson, "H. D.," Walter Savage Landor, James Russell Lowell, Ovid, Dante Gabriel Rossetti, Edmund Clarence Stedman, Stephen Phillips, and Tennyson.

Perhaps the finest two poems are Arnold's *The Strayed Reveler* and Tennyson's *Ulysses*.

In the former Arnold tells how a youth approaches the palace of Circe and there sees the enchantress and Ulysses. He recognizes the latter:

> How shall I name him—
> This spare dark-featured,
> Quick-eyed stranger?
> Ah! and I see too
> His sailor's bonnet,
> His short coat, travel-tarnished,
> With one arm bare!
> Art thou not he, whom fame
> This long time rumors

216

The favored guest of Circe, brought by the waves?
Art thou he, stranger—
The wise Ulysses,
Laertes' son?

Tennyson tells how Ulysses, in his old age, sickens of peace, and yearns for the turmoil of adventure, the zest of danger, the quest of the unknown; and sets forth, with a few comrades, in search of new experiences.

Specific Literary References

What do the following references mean? Where a word or phrase is italicized, explain only the word or phrase.

1. *Cassandra* at the gate,
   With wide eyes the vision shone in.
   —*Elizabeth Barrett Browning*
2. Then death came to old *Argus*, soon as he had lived to see Odysseus restored after twenty years.
   —*Homer*
3. I saw him on an island weeping, in the hall of the nymph Calypso, who holds him there by force.
   —*Homer*
4. Then wise Odysseus cast off his rags and sprang to the broad threshold, bow in hand.—*Homer*
5. Nor pour wax into the little cells of thy ears, with self mistrusting Ulysses.—*Lamb*
6. It was the mournful privilege of Ulysses to descend twice to the shades.—*Lamb*
7. As one that for a weary space has lain
   Lulled by the song of *Circe*.—*Lang*
8. A wond'rous bag with both her hands she binds,
   Like that where once Ulysses held the winds.
   —*Pope*
9. Not so great wonder and astonishment
   Did the most chaste *Penelope* possess
   To see her lord.—*Spenser*
10. In New Jersey our worst affliction is the "one-eyed car," the automobile with one headlight extinguished and the other glaring balefully like an angry *Cyclops*.—*Newark Sunday Call*.

Suggestions for Oral or Written Composition

1. The adventures of Ulysses are given in numbered order in this chapter. Copy the titles of the adventures in a list, memorize the list, and be able to describe each adventure in a well-constructed sentence.

2. Ulysses narrates his encounter with Polyphemus to Telemachus. Give the story in his own words. Let him emphasize how the prayer of Polyphemus was fulfilled.

3. Did Ulysses stay peacefully and contentedly at home after the slaying of the suitors? Did he have any further adventures? Give your idea of his life after his return home.

4. Why did the Greeks esteem Ulysses so highly? What good qualities did he have? Write a character sketch of Ulysses, with references throughout to his various adventures and the traits he displayed during them.

Word Study

1. Give the correct pronunciation of the following names:

    Hermione, Cassandra, Orestes, *Odyssey,* Cyclopes, Polyphemus, Eurylochus, Telemachus.

2. What is the meaning of the following expressions? "To go on an Odyssey," "to dally in a lotus-eaters' land," "Cassandra-like prophecies," "the spell of the sirens," "between Scylla and Charybdis."

3. What is a pun? Where in the story of Ulysses is a pun used?

Questions for Review

1. What happened to Menelaus and Helen? to Agamemnon?
2. How did Orestes find Iphigenia?
3. Where does Homer relate the adventures of Ulysses?
4. How many years was he away from home?

5. What befell him in the land of the Ciconians? in the land of the lotus-eaters? in the country of the Cyclopes? in the island of Æolus? in the land of the Læstrygonians? in the island of Circe? on his visit to Hades? on his voyage past the sirens? on his encounter with Scylla and Charybdis? in the island of the Cattle of the Sun? on the island of Ogygia? in the land of the Phæacians?
6. In what condition did he return home?
7. What situation did he find in his own palace?
8. Who helped him in his plans?
9. Who recognized him?
10. What was the trial of the bow?
11. What did Ulysses do to the suitors?
12. What, according to the legends, became of Ulysses?

Reading List

Poems and Plays

Arnold, Edwin: *Iphigenia*
Arnold, Matthew: *The Strayed Reveler*
Bridges, Robert: *The Return of Ulysses*
Buchanan, Robert: *Penelope*
Daniel, Samuel: *Ulysses and the Sirens*
Doolittle, Hilda ("H. D."): *At Ithaca—Odyssey*
Euripides: *Iphigenia among the Taurians*
Goethe, J. W. von: *Iphigenia in Tauris*
Homer: The *Odyssey*
Landor, Walter Savage: *The Last of Ulysses*
Lang, Andrew: *A Song of Phæcia—The Odyssey*
Lowell, James Russell: *The Sirens*
Mather, Frank Jewett: *Ulysses in Ithaca*
Ovid: *Hermione to Orestes* (in *Heroines*)—*Penelope to Ulysses* (in *Heroines*)
Phillips, Stephen: *Ulysses*
Rossetti, Dante Gabriel: *The Wine of Circe*

Prose

Halliburton, Richard: *The Glorious Adventure*
White, Edward Lucas: *The Song of the Sirens*

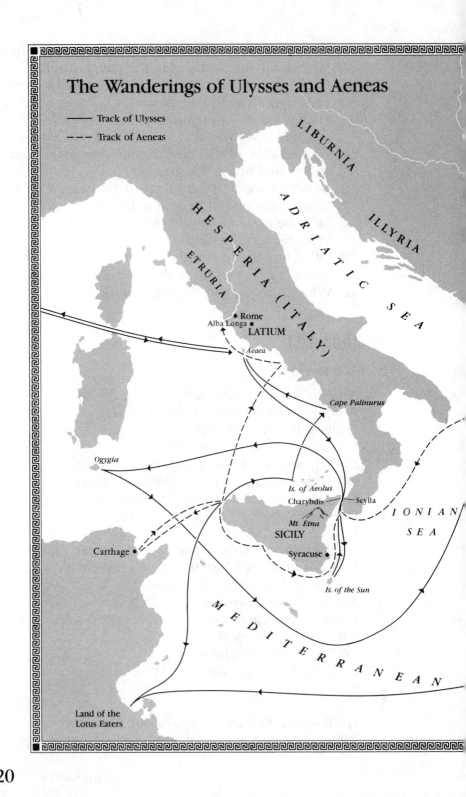

The Wanderings of Ulysses and Aeneas

—— Track of Ulysses

- - - Track of Aeneas

LIBURNIA

ILLYRIA

ADRIATIC SEA

HESPERIA (ITALY)

ETRURIA

Rome

Alba Longa

LATIUM

Aeaea

Cape Palinurus

Ogygia

Is. of Aeolus

Charybdis — Scylla

Mt. Etna

SICILY

Carthage

Syracuse

Is. of the Sun

IONIAN SEA

MEDITERRANEAN

Land of the
Lotus Eaters

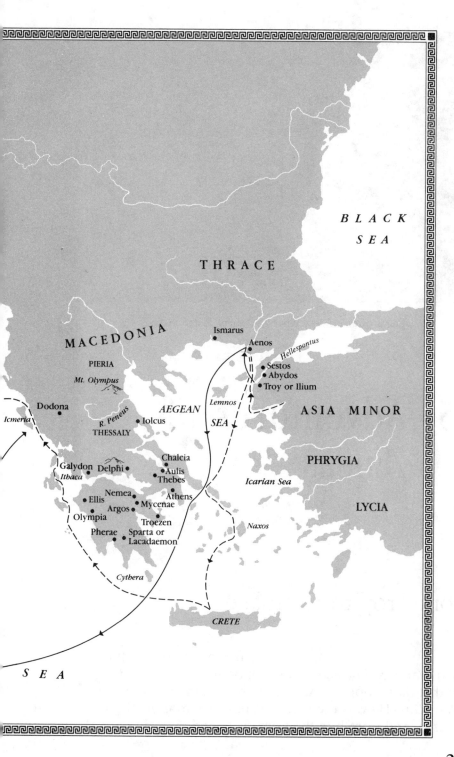

BLACK
SEA

THRACE

MACEDONIA

PIERIA

Mt. Olympus

Ismarus

Aenos

Hellespontus

• Sestos
• Abydos
• Troy or Ilium

ASIA MINOR

Dodona

Icmeria

R. Peneus • Iolcus
THESSALY

AEGEAN

Lemnos

SEA

PHRYGIA

Galydon • Delphi •
Ithaca

Chalcia
• Aulis
Thebes

Athens

Icarian Sea

Nemea
• Ellis •
Argos • Mycenae

Olympia
Troezen

Pherae • Sparta or
Lacadaemon

Naxos

LYCIA

Cythera

CRETE

S E A

221

Æneas offering a sacrifice—Altar of Peace, Rome

15 Adventures of Æneas

One speech in it I chiefly loved: 'twas Æneas' tale to Dido.

Shakespeare

From Troy to Carthage

One of the bravest heroes of the Trojan War was Æneas, who, it will be recalled, was the only man that dared oppose Achilles in his wrath after the death of Patroclus. He was the son of Venus by a mortal father, Anchises, and from him the Romans traced their descent. A great Latin poet, Virgil, told in one of the master epics of all times, the *Æneid*, how Æneas escaped from Troy and after many adventures came to Italy and founded the state of Latium.

When Troy fell, Æneas escaped from the conflagration. He carried Anchises out on his back, and with him went his wife and young son. But before they could get away, his wife perished. For a time Æneas lingered at a place nearby, and then set sail for some new land. He came first to Thrace, afterwards to Crete, but in neither place did the gods favor the idea of building a city. In a dream Æneas was told to seek a land in the west called Hesperia.

So Æneas and his companions sailed westward, but before they reached Hesperia (today called Italy) many adventures befell them. First they encountered the Harpies. They had landed on an island on which roamed many fat cattle. Some of these they killed for food. Just as they were sitting down to eat, a flock of evil-appearing and evil-smelling Harpies appeared and snatched the food from the tables. They beat at them with their swords in vain; and finally, left the island in disgust.

Later they came to the land of the Cyclopes, and from the shore they were hailed by a man in tattered garments, who implored them to take him on board. He was a Greek, he told Æneas, a sailor on the ship of Ulysses, who had accidentally been left behind when Ulysses had fled from Polyphemus. Even as the Greek was speaking, Polyphemus himself came stumbling along—a fear-inspiring monster, huge in bulk, with an angry red cavity where his eye had been. Hearing the voices, the terrible giant waded toward the ship of the Trojans, his immense height standing far above the waves. He shouted at them as he heard their oars fall in the water, and his voice brought the other Cyclopes to the shore, which they lined like a row of mighty pines. The Trojans were glad when their vessel was once more on the deep sea out of danger.

Æneas, warned by those familiar with the dangers of Scylla and Charybdis, avoided entirely the region where these monsters dwelt and skirted the coast of Sicily. At this time his father Anchises died. Juno, looking down from heaven, felt her resentment rise again at the success with

Æneas escaping from Troy

which this remnant of the Trojan people was making its way to a new land. So she caused a great tempest to arise, and the vessels were scattered far and wide. They were all in danger of shipwreck when Neptune became aware that a storm was raging without his consent. He saw the fleet of Æneas in the midst of the storm, and immediately guessed that Juno was at fault. He ordered the waves to cease from tumult and he sent the clouds scurrying back to their mountain homes. Such ships as had run on the rocks he pried loose with his trident. As soon as the sea had become calm, the whole fleet sought the nearest port to repair the damage that the winds and waves had done. They found themselves on the shores of Carthage—a Phœnician colony which lay opposite Sicily on the coast of northern Africa.

Here reigned Queen Dido. She received Æneas hospitably, held games in his honor, and listened entranced to the tale of his adventures. So attractive was the Trojan hero and so moving was the narrative of his exploits that Dido fell in love with him, and offered herself to him as a bride–with her kingdom as a dowry. Æneas might perhaps have been tempted to accept, but Jupiter sent Mercury to him with a message reminding him that his destiny would not be fulfilled until he had journeyed farther. Dido, assisted by her sister Anna, did her best to dissuade Æneas from actually setting out, but when all her allurements proved in vain and Æneas hoisted sail, she prepared a funeral pyre, mounted it, stabbed herself, and was consumed in flames. Æneas, looking back, saw the flames of the pyre mounting over Carthage.

Neptune, at the urging of Venus, now consented to let Æneas reach Italy in safety, but he demanded the sacrifice of one life. The pilot of Æneas, Palinurus, was the one whom fate selected as the victim. Neptune sent the god of sleep, Somnus, to him as he watched by the helm, and gradually slumber stole upon him. Then Somnus gently shoved him into the waves, but he continued to grasp the helm and it came away in his hands. Neptune guided the ship safely over the waves until Æneas saw that Palinurus had disappeared. Greatly grieved at his loss, Æneas himself took charge and at last they touched the Italian shore.

In the Underworld

In order to obtain further counsel,
Æneas visited the Cumæan sibyl. She dwelt in a grove
sacred to Apollo, and had been endowed with the gift of
prophecy. No sooner did she behold Æneas than she
seemed to recognize him. She prophesied that he would
still have to undergo many hardships and perils, but in the
end would conquer them. Æneas asked her to help him
enter the abode of the dead, in order to meet his father
Anchises, and hear from him what the future of the Trojans
would be in their new home. The sibyl warned him that the
descent to Avernus was easy, but that to retrace's one's
steps and come to the upper air again was very difficult.
First he must seek a certain tree on which grew a golden
bough. He was to pluck this bough and carry it along with
him as a gift to Proserpina. Æneas, with the help of Venus,
found the tree, plucked the branch, and sought the sibyl
once more.

Near Mount Vesuvius Æneas found the cavern of
Avernus, and, guided by the sibyl, descended into the
underworld. There, in deep terror, he beheld the Furies,
saw the dread forms of Death, Hunger, and Fear, heard
hydras hiss frightfully and shrank back as chimeras breathed
fire. At the sight of the Golden Bough Charon relaxed his
sternness and consented to ferry Æneas across the Styx.

On the opposite shore Cerberus came to meet them,
his three heads growling, but when he had devoured a
drugged sop that the sibyl threw him, he fell fast asleep.
Through the regions of the underworld Æneas then passed,
sometimes with great sadness as he beheld persons whom
he had known. Among others whom he encountered was
Dido, and Æneas realized that the flames that he had seen
when he left Carthage were those of her funeral pyre. He
asked her to forgive him and to bid him a last farewell, but
with eyes averted she vouchsafed him no word.

He saw, too, the warriors in whose company he had
fought and those others against whom his spear had many
times been cast. The Trojans thronged around him, but the
Greeks, as on the plains of Troy, fled when they beheld his

glittering armor. He saw and recognized Palinurus, and heard from him how he had been thrust into the sea and drowned. The pilot begged Æneas to take him back with him to the land of the living, but the sibyl told him that this was impossible, although the place where his body had been washed ashore should ever after be called Cape Palinurus. He also saw Ixion and Tantalus. Wandering through the Elysian Fields he heard Orpheus playing his lyre, and he gazed on heroes and bards feasting merrily or listening to strains of music.

At last he found Anchises, who showed him the Valley of Oblivion, where dwell the souls of those yet to be born. He enumerated to his son what heroes and statesmen would proceed from among these souls to establish the glory of the Trojan—later the Roman—state. Then Æneas and the sibyl made their way back to the mortal world.

In Italy

Æneas parted from the sibyl, to whom he promised eternal reverence, and continued to sail along the coast of Italy until he came to the mouth of the Tiber. The land of Latium, situated around this river, was ruled by King Latinus, who traced his descent from Saturn. He had no son, but his beautiful daughter Lavinia had many suitors. Of them all her parents favored Turnus, king of the Rutulians, although Latinus had been warned in a dream that the man whom Lavinia was destined to marry would come from another land, and that their offspring would one day rule the world.

When Æneas appeared in the land of Latium, he was hospitably received by Latinus, who immediately recognized in the Trojan hero the son-in-law destined for him. But Juno once more stirred up trouble for the Trojans, chiefly by arousing the wrath of Turnus against this possible rival. Finally King Latinus himself was persuaded to dismiss the strangers from his country; and Juno, descending from heaven, burst open the gates of the Temple of Janus—the sign of war.

To help Turnus, who was recognized as leader of the party opposed to Æneas, came Camilla, a favorite of Diana. She was a huntress and a warrior; and she had taken a resolution never to marry.

Other allies ranged themselves with Turnus. Æneas was troubled at the forces arrayed against him, but in a dream Father Tiber appeared to him and encouraged him. He told him, too, that he must seek Evander, chief of the Arcadians, who was an old enemy of Turnus's, and ally himself with him. Æneas awoke and immediately sought out King Evander, whose capital was situated where later Rome arose. Evander and his son, Pallas, welcomed Æneas and were glad to ally themselves with him; but Evander told Æneas that his own power was very slight. He proposed, however, that Æneas seek out the Etruscans, who had just ejected their king, Mezentius, for cruelty. Mezentius had taken refuge with Turnus, and the Etruscans would naturally be willing to join Æneas. The latter immediately set out for the Etruscan camp, and found that the Etruscan leaders rejoiced at the opportunity to conclude an alliance with him.

While Æneas was away on this business of winning allies for himself, Juno sent Iris to Turnus and urged him to take advantage of the fact that the leader of the Trojans was absent. Turnus accordingly attacked the Trojan camp, but the Trojans defended themselves skillfully and refused to be drawn out of their entrenchments. Night came on, and the army of Turnus withdrew in seeming triumph. Two Trojans, Nisus and Euryalus, offered to steal through the camp of their enemies and carry word of their situation to Æneas. They set out on their mission, and had actually passed through the army of besiegers when they were intercepted by a troop coming to join Turnus. Even then Nisus might have escaped, but seeing his friend in the hands of their foes, he slew as many as he could before he and Euryalus were killed.

Soon Æneas arrived on the scene with his Etruscan allies, and then the war raged in earnest. The two armies were pretty well matched, and for a time the advantage lay

How does this picture suggest Aeneas' visit to the underworld?

with neither. In a personal combat Æneas killed the tyrant Mezentius and his son Lausus, while in the same battle Turnus overcame Pallas. In another battle Camilla greatly distinguished herself, but while she pursued one man too ardently, she was slain by a javelin hurled by an Etruscan warrior named Aruns. Diana was angered at the death of her follower, and as Aruns stole away from the field in secret triumph, he was struck and killed by an arrow from the bow of a nymph in Diana's train.

Gradually Æneas seemed to be getting the upper hand, and when Turnus could no longer resist the murmurings and reproaches of his followers, he was obliged to seek out Æneas in single combat. The Trojan hero was assisted by his divine mother and by the Fates, and to protect himself he wore an armor specially fashioned for him by Vulcan. Turnus, on the other hand, was quite without the aid of the gods, for Jupiter, in obedience to the decrees of destiny, forbade Juno to interfere in his behalf against the might of Æneas. The spear of Turnus fell harmless from the shield of Æneas, but the spear of Æneas pierced the shield of Turnus and wounded the latter in the thigh. Turnus begged for mercy, and Æneas would have granted it to him gladly. But even as Turnus spoke the eye of the Trojan fell upon the belt of Pallas, a trophy of the slain prince that Turnus had taken from him when he slew him. Then Æneas was again filled with wrath and in the name of Pallas he killed Turnus.

Thus the war ended, Æneas triumphed, and the Roman state began. Æneas married Lavinia and founded a city in her name—Lavinium. His son, Ascanius or Iulus, founded Alba Longa. From him Julius Cæsar himself claimed descent.

Romulus and Remus

It was in Alba Longa that twins, called Romulus and Remus, were born to a descendant of Iulus, named Rhea Sylvia, and it was believed that they were her children by Mars. The branch of the family to which Rhea Sylvia belonged had, however, been excluded

This statue has become the most famous portrayal
of the founders of Rome.

from the throne, and she and her children, in order to
prevent any hostile demonstrations in their favor, were
condemned to be drowned in the Tiber.

But the cradle in which the children were exposed was
stranded on the shore before any harm had come to them.
There they were found by a she-wolf, which carried them to
her den and suckled them along with her own young. They
were found by the king's shepherd, who took the infants to
his own house and gave them into the care of his wife.

When they had grown to manhood Romulus and
Remus resolved to found a city of their own. This they did
on the banks of the Tiber. But a strife arose between the
brothers over the name of the city, each wishing it to be
called after himself; and a combat ensued in which Remus
was killed.

The numbers in Rome were so few that Romulus
invited all murderers and runaway slaves to take refuge in
it, and so he increased its population. But the inhabitants

The king's shepherds discover Romulus and Remus.

were mainly men, and to secure wives a large number of maidens were carried off from the neighboring tribe of the Sabines and brought to Rome. When their fathers angrily advanced on Rome with an army, the Sabine women themselves, now reconciled to their Roman husbands, intervened and begged them all to make peace. They not only did so, but agreed to form a single nation, over which Romulus ruled for thirty-seven years. At the end of that period he was snatched up to heaven in a fiery chariot by his father Mars. He was worshiped thereafter by the Romans, sometimes under the name of Quirinus. Rome itself became in time the ruler of the world.

PRACTICAL APPLICATIONS

References to Mythology in Literature

What do the following references mean? Where a word or phrase is italicized, explain only the word of phrase.

1. The word by seers or *sibyls* told,
   In groves of oak or fanes of gold,
   Still floats upon the morning wind,
   Still whispers to the willing mind.—*Emerson*
2. It was like *the golden branch* that gained Æneas and the sibyl admittance into Hades.—*Hawthorne*
3. They do not willingly seek *Lavinian shores.*—*Lamb*
4. Softer than the lap where Venus lulled *Ascanius.*
   —*Lamb*
5.   In such a night
   Stood *Dido,* with a willow in her hand,
   Upon the wild sea-banks, and waved her love
   To come again to *Carthage.*—*Shakespeare*

Suggestions for Oral or Written Composition

1. When Æneas takes on board the sailor of Ulysses who was left behind in the land of the Cyclopes, the marooned Greek has an interesting story to tell. Describe how Æneas questions him, and what replies he gives.
2. Æneas tells Dido about the fall of Troy, as a result of the stratagem of the wooden horse. Give the story as he tells it.
3. You have an opportunity to interview Æneas in the Elysian Fields. Tell him about Rome and Italy today, and report his comments.
4. Invent an adventure in which Camilla played a part, in the days before the coming of Æneas and of the war in which she fell.

5. Give a number of suggestions for effective scenes in a motion-picture play to be based on the story of Æneas.

Word Study

1. Tell something about the origin of the following words:

    sibylline—prophetic, mysterious
    harpy—a greedy, grasping person

2. Look up the following names in a mythological dictionary and practice the correct pronunciation. Æneas, Anchises, Cyclopes, Polyphemus, Phœnician, Dido, sibyl, Latinus, Lavinia, Camilla.
3. Which names of characters in the story of Æneas are still used today as given names? Select one that you would like to see revived and explain why.
4. What names of places are explained by the story of Æneas? How did Rome derive its name? What is meant by the expression "to cut up didoes"?

Questions for Review

1. Who was Æneas? Describe his parentage.
2. How did he escape from Troy?
3. Where was Hesperia?
4. What adventure did Æneas and his companions have with the Harpies? In the land of the Cyclopes?
5. How did Æneas escape Scylla and Charybdis?
6. Who was the enemy of Æneas among the gods?
7. What trouble did she cause as he was approaching his future home?
8. How did Neptune help him?
9. Where did Æneas find himself at the end of the storm?
10. Who was the ruler of the land?
11. Was she attracted to Æneas?
12. What happened when Æneas rejected her

proposals and set sail?

13. What sacrifice did Juno demand before Æneas was allowed to reach Italy?
14. What prophetess did Æneas visit?
15. What land did he visit with her assistance?
16. What did Æneas see on his trip to the underworld?
17. What figures of the future did Anchises show him?
18. What was the "Lavinian shore," and who was Lavinia?
19. Who was the rival of Æneas for the hand of the latter? What war ensued?
20. Who was Camilla?
21. Who were Evander and Pallas?
22. Why did the Etruscans help Æneas?
23. How did Nisus and Euryalus die?
24. How was Camilla slain?
25. Who was the victor in the combat between Æneas and Turnus?
26. Who were the descendants of Æneas, and how did they become the founders of the Roman state?
27. Who was the father of Romulus and Remus?
28. What happened to them?
29. What city did they found?
30. Why did they quarrel?

Reading List

Brooks, Edward: *The Story of the "Æneid"*
Church, A. J.: *Virgil's "Æneid" Retold*
Clarke, M.: *The Story of Æneas*
Dryden, John: *Virgil's "Æneid" in English Verse*
Howell, H. L.: *Stories from the "Æneid"*
Marlowe, Christopher, and Thomas Nash: *Dido*
Slaughter, M.: *The Story of Turnus*

The Roman Forum

16 Divinities Of Rome

Long ere Rome had gathered slowly
Round the sacred fane of Saturn

Sharp

Janus and Saturn

Just as some deities are found only in Hellenic worship, so others are found only among the Romans.

One such god was *Janus*. He was usually represented with two faces, and originally, it is said, this god was really two deities, representing the sun and the moon. Janus

236

occupied an important place in the Roman religion. He presided over the beginning of everything, and his name was always invoked first in every undertaking, taking precedence even over Jupiter. He opened the year, and hence the first month was named after him. He was the porter of heaven, and was called the "opener" and the "shutter." He was thus the guardian of gates—which look two ways. In Rome there was a covered passage dedicated to him. This was opened in time of war and closed in time of peace; during the great days of the Roman state it was rarely closed. On New Year's Day, which was the principal festival of Janus, people exchanged presents. These usually consisted of sweetmeats and copper coins with the double head of Janus on one side and a ship on the other.

Another Roman god was *Saturn,* whom some connect with Cronus, the Greek god of the beginning. But in his functions Saturn is much more closely connected with Demeter (Ceres) than with Cronus, and his worship continued at Rome alongside that of Zeus or Jupiter. The name of Saturn is probably connected with the Latin word for "sowing," and he was believed to be the deity who had introduced agriculture and with it civilization and government. Some legends identified him with an ancient king of Italy, and it was believed that during his reign, as in that of Cronus, had occurred a Golden Age, when all was well with mankind; we still speak of the "Golden Age of Saturn." His wife was *Ops,* the goddess of plenty.

The statues of Saturn were hollow, and were filled with olive oil, to denote the fertility of Italy in this product. The god was usually represented as holding in his hands a crooked pruning knife, and his feet were wrapped up in woolen ribbon. His temple at Rome was used as a treasury of the state, and in it were deposited copies of many laws. The chief festival of this god was called the "Saturnalia," and it was celebrated toward the end of December. Then all was mirth and festival; friends made presents for one another; schools were closed, and the Senate was not in session. No war was proclaimed, no criminal executed; slaves were permitted to jest with their masters, and the latter even waited on them at table. In the time of the emperors this festival extended over seven days.

Lesser Roman Deities

The *Camenæ* were nymphs endowed with the gift of prophecy, and in some legends they were identified with the Muses. The most famous of them was *Egeria,* who became the spouse of a great Roman king, Numa Pompilius, and imparted to him such wisdom that he became the real founder of the religious system of the Romans. He built the passage dedicated to Janus which has been mentioned, but during his thirty-nine-year reign, its gate remained shut, for he cherished peace.

Great reverence was paid in Italy to the goddess *Fortuna.* She was represented in different ways. Sometimes she was shown with a rudder, as the divinity who guides the affairs of the world. Again, she was shown with a ball, to indicate how unsteady and slippery fortune is. Occasionally she carried a horn of plenty.

Bellona was a goddess of war; she is sometimes spoken of as the sister or the wife of Mars.

Terminus, as his name indicates, presided over boundaries. His worship is said to have been instituted by Numa, who ordered that every one should mark the limits and bounds of his landed property by placing stones sacred to Jupiter, and that every year, at these boundary stones, sacrifices should be offered in the festival of the Terminalia. This festival took place on the twenty-first of February, and on that day the owners of the adjoining pieces of land met at the stones or posts of Terminus and placed garlands on them. Then they raised rude altars, on which were offered gifts of grain, honey, and wine. They concluded by singing a hymn in praise of the god. The roof over the altar of Terminus in the Capitoline temple at Rome was kept open, to show that this god was worshiped only in the open air.

Silvanus was a Roman god who in some ways resembled Pan. His name is connected with the Latin word *silva,* or "woods." He was the god of fields and forests, and, like Terminus, he also protected the boundaries of fields. He delighted in trees that grew wild, and was sometimes shown as carrying the trunk of a cypress. At other times he was represented as joyously bestriding a

Flora, goddess of flowers and springtime - painting by Botticelli

wineskin. Flocks were intrusted to the care of Silvanus; he made them fertile and protected them from wolves. The sacrifices offered to him consisted of grapes, ears of corn, milk, meat, wine, and pigs.

Another Latin deity who resembled Pan was *Faunus*, the protecting deity of agriculture, the god of shepherds, also a giver of oracles. Like Pan he was shown with horns and the feet of a goat. Later the idea arose of many *fauns*, usually represented as beautiful young men with tiny horns hardly visible. They lived joyous lives, haunting the woods with music.

Lupercus and *Luperca* were worshiped as the protectors of flocks from wolves and as deities of fertility. Their festival was called the Lupercalia, and was held on the fifteenth of February.

Pomona presided over fruit trees. *Flora,* on the other hand, was the goddess of flowers and of the springtime. Her festival, the Floralia, was celebrated at the end of April and the beginning of May. The poets said of Flora that she was the bride of the West Wind.

Hymen, god of marriage, was a winged youth, carrying a bridal veil and a torch.

Among the most striking of the purely Roman deities were their domestic gods, the *lares* and *penates.* The former presided over the house, fields, and roads. They were in reality the souls of the dead, who still hovered over the places in which they had dwelt. But only the spirits of good men were honored as lares. The head of them all was the *lar familiaris,* who was regarded as the founder of the family. Images of the lares stood in Roman houses, and upon joyful family occasions these images were crowned with wreaths. The penates were gods of the whole house, but especially of the storeroom. They had their images at the hearth of every house, and the table was sacred to them. On the table the saltcellar and the firstlings of fruits were regarded as connected with them. Collectively, the lares and penates represented a family through all generations and typified the family spirit and traditions.

The *manes* were shades that presided over places of burial.

A familiar deity of the Romans was *Father Tiber,* spirit of the important river that flowed through Rome.

The Romans deified their important heroes, particularly their emperors in later times. Thus both Julius Cæsar and Augustus Cæsar were worshiped as gods, and temples were erected to them.

PRACTICAL APPLICATIONS

Myths in Literature

The great contribution of the Romans to mythology as employed in modern literature has been in the matter of *names*. The Greek deities are more familiar to us by the titles of their Latin equivalents than in the original Hellenic form. We are more likely to think of Jupiter or Jove than of Zeus, of Juno than of Hera, of Minerva than of Pallas Athena, of Vulcan than of Hephæstus, of Hercules than of Herakles, of Cupid than of Eros.

This is true despite the fact that it is generally admitted that the Greek names are frequently both more beautiful in themselves and more significant in their associations. The Romans would have been the first to confess this, and it was the chief duty of an educated Roman to become well acquainted with Greek literature and with the stories of the gods as told by the Greeks. Latin has, however, been the mediator and interpreter for Greek literature and for Greek ideas; and of course for many centuries Greek was practically unknown, whereas Latin was the familiar second tongue of every educated person. It became very natural, therefore, to use the Latin rather than the Greek names of gods. As Hellenic influence increased, however, many writers began to use the Greek names, so it is necessary for us to be acquainted with both the Latin and Hellenic forms.

The fauns of Latin myth have impressed the modern imagination greatly, and have been joined with Pan and the satyrs to symbolize the forces of nature. The idea of the lares, penates, and manes, the conception of Janus and of Saturn's Golden Age, and the belief in Pomona and in Flora have all found their place in later literature.

Specific Literary References

What do the following references mean? Where a word

or phrase is italicized, explain only the word or phrase.

1. Oft do the *fauns* and *satyrs*, flushed with play,
   Come to my coolness in the hot
   noonday.—*Buchanan*
2. O, for a draught of vintage!that hath been
   Cool'd a long age in the deep-delved earth,
   Tasting of *Flora* and the country green.—*Keats*
3. Allan Cunningham vowed a memoir to his *manes.*
   —*Lamb*
4. When all the Tuscans and their *lars*
   Shouted, and shook the towers of Mars.—Landor
5. There let *Hymen* oft appear
   In saffron robe, with taper clear.—*Milton*
6. And shadows brown that *Silvan* loves.—*Milton*
7. Long ere Rome had gathered slowly
   Round the sacred fane of *Saturn.—Sharp*
8. *Faunus*, lover of the woods.—*Virgil*
9. Far from the fiery noon, and eve's one star,
   Sat gray-hair'd *Saturn*, quiet as a stone.—*Keats*
10. Those *Saturnalia* of two or three brief hours.—*Lamb*
11. *Janus* am I: Oldest of potentates!
    Forward I look and backward—*Longfellow*
12. When *Bellona* storms,
    With all her battering engines bent to raze
    Some capital city.—*Milton*
13. Since love our hearts and *Hymen* did our hands
    Unite.—*Shakespeare*
14. Bear me, *Pomona*, to the citron groves.—*Thomson*
15. Came *Silvanus* too,
    With rural glory crowned, and brandishing
    Fennels and giant lilies in his hand.—*Virgil*

Suggestions for Oral or Written Composition

1. You meet a faun while wandering in the wood, and he tells you of the joys of living close to the heart of nature and of knowing the ways of the little creatures of the wild. Give an account of your meeting.

2. Go to the front of the room. Say: "I am a god (or goddess)," but do not mention your name. Then go on and

242

describe your realm. See how many in the class can guess what your name is. Let others do the same with other deities. Go through the same process with the symbols of the gods.

Word Study

1. Explain how the following words came to have their present meanings:

   saturnalian—marking a period of riot and **indulgence**
   Saturnian—distinguished for peacefulness, happiness, content
   January—the first month of the year
   terminal—the end or boundary
   silvan—woodlike
   hymeneal—pertaining to marriage
   floral—pertaining to flowers
   janitor—a doorkeeper
   opulent—rich, luxuriant
   pomology—the science and practice of fruit growing

2. The following English words all have a mythological derivation. Identify their origin and use each of them in a sentence. (If you are not familiar with the meaning of any of them, consult a dictionary.)

Jovial	Saturday
mercurial	Bacchic
martial	plutocrat
March	panic
volcano	satire
vulcanize	satirical
June	music
cereal	museum
vestal	auroral
saturnine	chronology

3. Look up the following words in a mythological dictionary and practice the correct pronunciation.

Aphrodite	Silvanus
Poseidon	Pomana
Æneas	penates
Janus	lar familiaris
Saturnalia	manes

4. Give the Latin equivalents for *Zeus, Ares, Artemis, Pallas Athena, Hermes, Demeter, Herakles.*

5. What is meant when a woman is called an "Egeria"? What are "flora and fauna"?

Questions for Review

1. Do the Roman gods resemble those of Greece?
2. What was the attitude of the Romans toward the Greeks?
3. Who was Janus? Saturn?
4. What were the characteristics of the rule of Saturn?
5. What were the Saturnalia?
6. Who was the wife of Saturn?
7. Who was the most famous of the Camenæ?
8. Who was Fortuna? Bellona? Terminus? Silvanus?
9. Who were the fauns?
10. What gods protected flocks from wolves?
11. Which one presided over fruit trees?
12. Who was the god of marriage?
13. Who were the lares and penates? the manes?
14. To what river did the Romans pay reverence? Why?

Reading List

Poems and Plays

Corbin, Alice: *What Dim Arcadian Pastures*
Doolittle, Hilda ("H.D."): *Hymen*

Long, Haniel: *The Faun*
Macaulay, Thomas: *Lays of Ancient Rome*

Novels and Descriptive Words

Davis, W.S.: *A Day in Old Rome*
Fowler, W.W.: *Roman Ideas of Deity*
Fox, W.S.: *Greek and Roman Mythology*
Hawthorne, Nathaniel: *The Marble Faun*
Lamprey, Louise: *Children of Ancient Rome*
Shumway, E.S.: *A Day in Ancient Rome*
White, Edward Lucas: *Anduvius Hedulio—The Unwilling Vestal*

Greek Theatre at Delphi

17 Myths in Ancient Literature

*Oft of one wide expanse had I been told
That deep-brow'd Homer ruled as his
demesne.*

Keats

Homer, Hesiod, and Pindar

Among the ancient Greeks, as
among most other peoples, there was no definite body of
myths to which anyone could go as an authority on the
form and spirit of a particular story. Myths began among
the people. They grew and changed with the ages. In
different parts of Greece the same god was worshiped
under different names, the same myths told with variations.

The poets who told and retold the Greek myths through the course of the centuries came to play a very important part in giving a story a particular form. From the very earliest times the Greeks, like most other races, regarded the poet as a sacred person, one directly inspired by the gods and under their constant protection. The poet, according to the Greek belief, composed his songs in a kind of divine madness. The Muse entered into him, and it was the gods and not he that spoke in his poems. The poet was only an instrument of heaven—a pipe on whom the gods played. One of the most highly regarded of the Greek gods was Apollo, deity of song and music; and no greater compliment could be paid to the other gods than to record of them that they had invented a musical instrument and composed songs.

Such being the attitude of the Greeks toward their poets, it is easily understandable that great respect was paid to poets' versions of stories of the gods. In the misty beginnings of Greek literature certain of these poets were thought of as the sons of one or another of the gods—Orpheus was, for example, the son of Apollo; Musæus was the son of Orpheus, and Amphion was the son of Jupiter. Naturally such poets would be especially endowed by the gods with a vision of the truth, the nature of the universe, and the experiences of the deities.

But, although fragments of hymns were attributed to Orpheus, these first poets left no definite compositions to which later generations could turn. It remained for two later poets to provide some facts to which the Greeks could turn for information about their gods. These poets were Homer and Hesiod.

Possibly neither of these poets really existed, but around their names gathered a great mass of literature of a very significant kind.

In Homer's two great epics, the *Iliad* and the *Odyssey*, and in certain hymns attributed to him, many stories of the gods were told with surpassing skill; and from Homer's allusions and references other stories can be built up.

Hesiod, supposed to have lived not very much later than Homer, was a shepherd and poet to whom are attributed two long poems—*Works and Days* and *The Origin*

Scene from a comedy of an angry father chastising his son

of the Gods. In these writings Hesiod organized what is almost a definite system of the gods and their history.

In later Greek literature the most important poet, so far as the development of myth is concerned, was Pindar, of the sixth century B.C. Pindar was the most popular and greatest of the poets who were engaged to celebrate the victors in various athletic contests held in Greece. No matter what other honors were paid such a victor, his glory was felt to be incomplete unless a poem of praise was written in his honor. In writing such poems Pindar quite often concentrated on the victor's ancestors or on the glory of his city rather than on the athlete himself. While so doing he took occasion to relate or to suggest many exploits of early Greek heroes.

Greek drama frequently took as its subject the adventures of the gods, the events of the Trojan War or those that followed it, and other mythical subjects. The

248

dramatist treated his themes freely, and developed the story according to his own conception. It frequently happens, therefore, that the story as told by Æschylus and the story as told by Sophocles are by no means the same; and then Euripides may add his own variation. The great comic dramatist of Greece, Aristophanes, moreover, had his own viewpoint; and some of his remarks and some of the adventures in which his gods engage must have seemed very irreverent to many of his listeners.

Virgil

The genius of the Romans was not an inventive, original genius. Their strength lay rather in their ability to seize and comprehend what others had done, and to give it a more practical form. Through the Romans the ideas of other nations have often reached the rest of the world; and this is particularly true with reference to their adoption of Greek ideas. But the Romans gave many ingenious turns to the myths of the gods.

When the Romans became acquainted with the Greek gods and with Greek myths they perceived at once the remarkable similarities that existed between these and their own gods and myths. The more educated among the Romans were very proud of being as familiar with Greek literature and philosophy as with their own literature and philosophy; and they adopted the Greek pantheon, or system of gods, wholesale.

When we come to the Latin poets, especially to Virgil and Ovid, the two writers who did most for the growth of myths, we find that they were thoroughly familiar with all the stores and treasures of Greek myth. Whether they called the Greek gods by their own names or by the names of their Latin counterparts, these poets made constant use of them. But they did more than merely adopt Greek myth in a mechanical way. Both poets were endowed with a fine imagination, with a gift for beautiful phrasing, and with genius for telling a story.

Homer

It frequently happens, consequently, that the modern world is acquainted with a particular legend or with the career of a particular god through Virgil or Ovid rather than through a Greek poet. We think of the gods by the names these poets gave them; their descriptions of them occur first to us; and we accept their version of the myth.

Virgil, as has already been stated, is the author of the *Æneid,* a twelve-book account of the adventures of Æneas. In general Virgil follows Homer's scheme of narrative and treatment. His first six books, relating the journey of Æneas from Troy to Italy, correspond to the *Odyssey.* His last six books, relating the struggle of Æneas to found a state, correspond to the *Iliad.*

But although, as a writer, Virgil followed the Greek Homer, as a man he was an ardent Roman patriot, one deeply interested in the success of the empire newly founded by his patron Augustus Cæsar. This patriotism is reflected in his treatment of mythology. Most frequently he uses Latin rather than Greek names, and his purpose throughout is to show that Italy and the Roman state had always been under the protection of the gods. He seeks, moreover, to awaken in his reader a new reverence toward these gods, and a new devotion to them.

250

In general, one may express the changes which Virgil made in the Greek myths by saying that he refined them and made them more plausible, less childlike, and less primitive. He had, too, a gift for picturesque language, and often our memory of a mythical character or place comes from his vivid descriptions—Venus revealing herself a goddess by her gait, the blind and shapeless monster Polyphemus, the horrid sights of the underworld. He has, moreover, bound up the myths in history. He explains, for example, the long and bitter enmity between Rome and Carthage by telling the story of Æneas's rejection of Dido. The places mentioned in the *Æneid* are definitely fixed: unlike those in Homer, they have a "local habitation in modern geography."

In his narrative Juno is endowed with that same too human spirit of implacable vengeance toward Æneas which Homer shows Neptune as displaying toward Ulysses. The most pleasing aspect of Juno is, perhaps, her messenger Iris, who makes her way back and forth from heaven on the rainbow. A full-length picture is drawn of Minerva, and it is from Virgil that one gets the best account of the stratagem of the wooden horse. In connection with this episode occurs one of the most famous phrases in Virgil, spoken by a Trojan: *Timeo Danaos et dona ferentes.*

"I fear the Greeks, even though they come bearing gifts," exclaims the priest Laocoön; and then Virgil describes, with powerful vividness, how the serpents came and killed the priest and his children.

Venus is an important character in the *Æneid,* inasmuch as Æneas was her son. She helps him on many important occasions. Apollo figures in Virgil particularly as a giver of oracles and as a prophet, but one likes the glimpse of him in book iv as a god of war—the arms rattling on his shoulders as he walks along. Diana is called "brightest glory of the star land." Vulcan makes a shield for Æneas, just as in the *Iliad* he made armor for Achilles. Neptune is shown calming a storm as an orator calms a mob.

A host of minor deities appear in the *Æneid*—Triton, for example, blowing with skill his snail-shaped horn; many nymphs, Saturnus, Faunus, the two-headed Janus, hoar-headed Vesta (thought of as the oldest of the Roman deities), the friendly penates, the familiar lar who presided over the fortunes of the house, and others. When the Trojans come to Italy they invoke the gods in prayer and pay special tribute to the *genius loci*—the presiding spirit of the place. Æneas's visit to the underworld, although an imitation of that of Ulysses in Homer, is beautifully done. The "sop to Cerberus" which he prepares so the three-headed dog may not molest him has become famous as a symbol for placating monsters, physical and mental; and the lines which the sibyl, or prophetess, who assists Æneas uses to describe the journey are a favorite quotation:

> . . . facilis descensus Averno;
> sed revocare gradum superasque evadere ad auras,
> hoc opus, hic labor est.

> "Easy is the descent to the underworld," she
> explains, "but to retrace one's steps, to escape once
> more to the upper air, that is difficult, that is a task."

Three deities exert an influence upon the fortunes of Æneas—Jupiter, Venus, and Juno. But back of these three deities lurks a mysterious force to which these gods are themselves subject—the power of fate, to which Virgil refers sometimes as Fata, again as Parcæ, elsewhere as Fortuna. The gods recognize this force, as when Juno resolves to make Carthage a world power, "if the Fates permit." But, somewhat oddly, it appears that the gods, even if unable to thwart fate, are sometimes able to delay it. Just as Homer, for example, describes Neptune as holding back Ulysses from Ithaca for many years, so Juno places obstacles in the path of Æneas.

The gods in Virgil have communication with mankind in various ways. They sometimes appear directly, as when Venus, in the disguise of a huntress, talks to Æneas who does not recognize his mother until she turns to go: then her gait reveals her as a goddess. Again, the gods make their will known by signs, as when the serpents were sent to destroy Laocoön. Or mortals may consult oracles, such as that of Apollo at Delos which Æneas consults. Finally the

Portrait of Virgil in mosaic

gods speak to mortals by means of dreams; and Virgil has the allegory of the two gates by which dreams issue to the living world: the one of horn, through which truthful visions come; the other of ivory, through which come false and misleading apparitions. Mercury appears in a dream to Æneas, and bids him leave Carthage immediately.

Reference must be made to the famous "Golden Bough." In book vi of the *Æneid*, Virgil tell us about the attempt of Æneas to discover ways and means of reaching the underworld to visit his father Anchises. The sibyl tells him that if he is resolved to make the attempt, he must first find and pluck the Golden Bough, as a gift to Proserpina. Later two doves of Venus guide him to the mystic tree, and Æneas easily plucks the bough and bears it back to the sibyl. What was this tree? It was a tree guarded by a grim priest with sword in hand, ready to slay all comers. But any one who slew him became in turn guardian of the tree. The legend is such an odd one that it immediately attracted attention and has continued to do so. In 1890, however, appeared a famous book—*The Golden Bough,* by Sir James G. Frazer. Frazer took this legend and traced parallels to it in the mythology and folklore of all nations. He used his exposition of the mystery of the Golden Bough to cast light upon the growth and nature of mythology and magic everywhere. His book, thus suggested by a passage in Virgil, is the most famous work in any language on the subject of the early beliefs of mankind.

Ovid

Ovid was a contemporary of Virgil. Very early in life he devoted himself to poetry. When he was more than fifty years old, he offended Augustus Cæsar in some way no longer known and was banished to a desolate town on the Black Sea. There he continued to write, although in sad strain, for Ovid loved the gay life and gaudy pleasures of Rome.

Of Ovid's works those that are most important from the viewpoint of mythology are his *Metamorphoses,* or *Transformations;* his *Fasti,* a calendar of religious festivals; and his twenty-one *Epistolæ Heroidum—Letters of Heroines* of mythical times to their absent husbands or their faithless lovers—from Penelope to Ulysses, for example, and from Dido to Æneas.

The *Metamorphoses,* in fifteen books, contains more than two hundred stories of changes chronicled in myth; of Hyacinthus to a flower, for example. But Ovid does not adhere strictly to this theme and relates other stories in which transformations play no part. Thus he tells the story of Deucalion and Pyrrha, and of Æneas's voyage from Troy. He begins by telling how from chaos arose an ordered universe. He describes the sins of man and the great flood

Research this painting by Delacroix of Ovid among the Scythians.

which Jove sent and how Deucalion and Pyrrha escaped from this flood.

The slaying of the Python, the birth of the laurel, the slaying of Argus, the death of Phaëthon, the abduction of Europa, the carrying off of Proserpina, the vengeance on Niobe, the hospitality of Baucis and Philemon, the love of Orpheus and Eurydice, the greediness of Midas, and episodes of the Trojan War are among the subjects of other stories told by Ovid.

Ovid had a knack for storytelling. Frequently his tales are true short stories, which would now be told in prose, but with the details otherwise little altered. Very famous, particularly, was his story of Pyramus and Thisbe. Often there are sly touches of humor which show he did not take the stories too seriously.

Ovid immediately became popular with the Romans. They read his tales, and when they came to decorate their houses, they often employed suggestions from the *Metamorphoses* in their frescoes and works of art. During the Renaissance Ovid was the favorite Latin author of most

The Apotheosis of Homer with Zeus, Apollo and the Muses

readers, and the great Italian writers of this period were deeply influenced by him. We can, moreover, easily trace his influence on most English authors of this same period—Spenser, Shakespeare, and Milton, among others. John Macy, in his *Story of the World's Literature,* says of Ovid:

"His imagination is at its best in the *Metamorphoses,* in which he put together many of the Greek and Græco-Roman myths. This was the great source book of ancient legend for modern poets, the Italians of the Renaissance, Shakespeare and his contemporaries, and English poets of the eighteenth and nineteenth centuries. His work as a whole had an incalculable influence on the literature of modern countries, unsurpassed even by the influence of Virgil."

PRACTICAL APPLICATIONS

References to These Authors in Literature

What do the following references mean? Where a word or phrase is italicized, explain only the word or phrase.

1. *Pindar* sang horse races.—*Byron*
2.   Greece, sound thy *Homer's,*
   Rome thy *Virgil's* name.—*Cowper*
3. Oft of one wide expanse had I been told
   That deep-brow'd *Homer* ruled as his
   demesne.—*Keats*
4. They hear, like Ocean on a western beach,
   The surge and thunder of the *Odyssey.*—*Lang*
5. Roman *Virgil,* thou that singest *Ilion's* lofty temples
   robed in fire,
   Ilion falling, Rome arising, wars, and filial faith, and
   Dido's pyre.—*Tennyson*
6. He had not the slightest inkling of why the district
   attorney should have sent for him, and *he feared the
   Greeks bearing gifts,* particularly one who looked so
   wily a *Ulysses.*—*Twain*

Suggestions for Oral or Written Composition

1. Read any Greek play in an English translation and prepare a report on the way in which the gods are regarded in this play. Begin by making a list of references to the gods as they occur in your reading.

2. Write a supposed letter from Penelope to Ulysses, and then compare it with a translation of the letter that Ovid thought Penelope wrote (in the *Heroines*).

Word Study

1. What is the connection between the words *music* and *Muse?*
2. Is there any relation between *inspiration* and *spirit?* between *inspiration* and *respiration?*
3. Explain the following expressions:
   The great battle of the pitchers was Homeric.
   His ode, unrestrained and wild, was truly Pindaric.
   His smooth, happy style was Virgilian.
4. What are some famous phrases that come from Virgil?
5. How many synonyms can you find for *metamorphosis?*

Questions for Review

1. Was there a definite form for any particular myth among the Greeks?
2. What part did poets play in their development and transmission?
3. What was the Greek idea as to the way in which poetry was composed?
4. What two early poets are especially important in the history of Greek mythology? Name two works by each of these.
5. Why is Pindar important?
6. How did Greek dramatists treat themes from mythology?
7. What was the role of the Romans in the development of myths?
8. What two Latin writers did most for the growth of myths? Name one work by each.
9. In what ways is Virgil thoroughly Roman?
10. How did he treat the Greek myths?
11. What deities appear in his work?
12. What are some famous passages from his pen?
13. How do the gods in Virgil communicate with mankind?

14 What was the Golden Bough?
15. What is the reason for the title given to Ovid's chief work?
16. How many stories does it contain?
17. Why is Ovid important?

Reading List

Poems and Descriptive Works

Gibson, William Hamilton: *Virgil's Tomb*
Jobb, R.C.: *Homer*
Keats, John: *On First Looking into Chapman's Homer*
Kelsey, F.W., and J. W. Scudder: Introduction to *Selections from Ovid*
Lang, Andrew: *Homeric Unity—The Odyssey* (sonnet)
Murray, Gilbert: *The Rise of the Greek Epic*
Pindar: *To Hiero the Ætnæan, Victory in the Chariot Race* (Pythian I)—*To Hiero the Syracusan, Victor in the Horse Race* (Olympian I)
Tennyson, Alfred: *Virgil*

THE CHALLENGE OF THOR

I am the God Thor,

I am the War God,

I am the Thunderer!
Here in my Northland,
My fastness and fortress,

Reign I forever!

Here amid icebergs
Rule I the nations;

This is my hammer, . . .

Giants and sorcerers
Cannot withstand it!

These are the gauntlets

Wherewith I wield it,

And hurl it afar off;
This is my girdle;
Whenever I brace it,
Strength is redoubled!

The light thou
beholdest
Stream through the
heavens,
In flashes of crimson,
Is but my red beard
Blown by the
night-wind,
Affrighting the nations!

Jove is my brother;
Mine eyes are the
lightning;
The wheels of my
chariot
Roll in the thunder,
The blows of my
hammer
Ring in the earthquake!

Force rules the world
still,
Has ruled it, shall rule
it;
Meekness is weakness,
Strength is triumphant,
Over the whole earth
Still is it Thor's-Day!

Henry Wadsworth Longfellow

PART TWO:

OTHER MYTHS OF
THE OLD WORLD

A Valkyrie welcomes Odin to Valhalla.

18 Gods of the Northland

Where are in circle ranged twelve golden chairs,
And in the midst one higher, Odin's throne.

Arnold

Creation of the World

The peoples of the northland were allied in blood and language to those of the peninsulas of Greece and Rome; and consequently there are numerous resemblances between the myths of the North and of the South.

Yet, although the resemblances are striking, the gods of the North in a good many respects differed from those of the South. The latter were more joyous and sunny; the former reflected the gloom and the hard conditions of life in the forests and waters of northern Europe. The stories told about them likewise differed.

For the Northmen believed that at the beginning for long ages existed *Niflheim,* a world of mist and ice. In the midst of Niflheim was a deep well, and from this well flowed ten rivers. To the south lay *Muspellsheim,* which glowed with fire. Gradually, in the course of time, the warmer airs from Muspellsheim melted the frost of the North, and out of the clouds that resulted sprang the giant *Ymir* and a whole race of other giants. The ground became visible, and on it lay masses of stones. From the frost itself sprang the cow *Audhumla,* and her milk nourished Ymir. The cow herself, by licking the salty, frost-covered stones, created the gods. On the first day she licked the stones, a man's hair came forth. He was named *Buri,* and he was fair and tall. Then a female being was created, and from her and Buri came *Bor* and a number of goddesses. Bor's sons were the gods *Odin, Vili,* and *Ve;* and from them were descended the other gods.

These three gods slew the giant Ymir, and out of his body formed the heavens and the earth: from his flesh the earth, from his blood the sea, from his bones the mountains, from his hair the trees, and from his skull the sky. The earth was called *Midgard,* and over it the sky was made fast at its four corners. At each corner sat a dwarf.

From the sparks that Muspellsheim sent forth, the three gods made stars to illumine the earth, and set them in the sky; and there too they placed the sun and the moon and set a course for them. Around the earth flowed the great sea, and on its coast lived the giants, at *Jotunnheim.* Among the giants were Nor, with his daughter *Nat* and his grandson *Dag.* Nat was dark and swarthy, Dag was light and handsome. Odin gave them rule over the night and the day. Nat or Night drives first the horse *Hrimfaxi,* from whose bit the foam flies down over the earth and becomes dew. In her wake comes Dag or Day with his steed, *Skinfaxi,* and his mane throws radiance over land and water.

A stone picture describing one of the adventures of Odin

Toward the north, at the end of the heavens, sat
Hrœsvelg, a giant in eagle's form. With the violent strokes
of his wings he sent forth gales over the earth. Between the
land and the sky stretched the bridge of three hues, the
rainbow, called *Bifrost.* Over this rode the gods to their
places in heaven. At the end of the bridge dwelt *Heimdall,*
who guarded the bridge against the mountain dwarfs. These
were small, ugly, and surly creatures, endowed, however,
with great wisdom and skill. They were supposed to have
sprung from the blood and bones of two giants whom the
gods had slain. Quite different were the elves, handsome
and well disposed toward gods and men.

In the midst of the world stood a gigantic tree,
Yggdrasill, at the foot of which the gods held their
assemblies. It was an ash, the largest and best of trees: its
branches spread over the whole world and rose high into
the heavens. This tree had three immense roots: one
extended toward the race of men; the other toward
Niflheim or *Hel,* the underworld; the third toward

Jotunnheim, abode of the frost giants.

The root that extended into Midgard was guarded by the *Norns,* three sisters who had control over fate. Of them one was called *Urth* or *Wyrd,* the past; the second, *Verthandi,* the present; and the third, *Skuld,* the future. Sometimes they are called the *Wyrd,* or *Weird, Sisters.*

Once the three gods were walking along the beaches of the world, and saw two trees lying on the ground before them. Then the fancy came upon them to create human beings. From one they created a man and from the other a woman, and they called them *Ask* and *Embla.* The first of the gods gave them soul and life, the second endowed them with speech and the five senses, and the third bestowed on them understanding and the power of motion. From them came all the inhabitants of Midgard.

Gods of the North

Originally there were three chief gods, but in time all the power came into the hands of Odin, king of gods and men. He and the other gods dwelt in *Asgard,* which lay at the end of Bifrost, the rainbow. Asgard was divided into two realms—*Gladsheim* for the gods, *Vingolf* for the goddesses. Here were many palaces of gold and silver, but the most beautiful of them was *Valhalla,* the dwelling place of Odin. Before Odin had made his rulership secure, he had had to contend with another race of gods far to the north, but between them peace was finally effected, and they too came to live in Asgard. From among them Odin chose a wife, named *Frigg.*

Upon the shoulders of Odin, the All-Father, sat the ravens *Hugin* and *Munin*—Thought and Memory. They flew each day over the whole world, and brought back to him reports of all that was happening. At his feet lay two wolves, and to them Odin gave the meat that was set before him, since he himself needed no food; and he drank only *mead,* a drink made of honey. He was the fountainhead of wisdom, the founder of civilization, the patron of poetry, the watcher over kings, the lord of battle. To him was ascribed the invention of the runes, the alphabet of the Northmen; he set forth the decrees of fate, which were then inscribed by the Norns upon a shield. Sometimes his name was spelled *Woden;* and in his honor Wednesday was named.

When a hero died in battle his soul was carried off to Valhalla by the *Valkyries,* martial maidens clad in armor and mounted on winged steeds. In Valhalla all such heroes feasted perpetually with Odin, and the roasted boars on which they fed each day were at night miraculously renewed, and the mead which they drank was always replenished. Sometimes, for amusement, the heroes fought one another with savage fervor, but their wounds were immediately healed.

Next to Odin on his throne sat his wife Frigg, queen of the gods, who knew all things.

Thor, son of Odin and Frigg, was the thunderer, the god of war. He was the strongest of gods and men. In the palace wherein he dwelt were five hundred and forty rooms, for it was the largest house that was ever built. Two goats drew the wagon of Thor. He had three wonderful treasures in his keeping. One was the hammer *Mjollnir,* of which even the frost giants lived in dread, for he had slain many of them. The second was the *girdle of strength.* When Thor put this around his body, his great strength was at once doubled. The third was a pair of *iron mittens* with which to grasp the hammer handle. With these weapons Thor engaged in perpetual battle with the enemies of the gods and of mankind, for he was a good friend to human beings. He was a blunt, somewhat hot-tempered god, without fraud or guile, using few words and preferring actions to speech. Thursday was named in his honor.

Another son of Odin was *Balder.* He was the best of the gods, and in him all was perfect. He shone with such radiance that light came from him. He was the wisest, most eloquent, most gracious of the gods, and in his dwelling nothing was impure. He was the god of sunlight, spring and gladness. Yet it was prophesied of him that he should die.

Frey governed the rain and the sunshine, and made all the things of the earth grow. Men called upon him to

Detail from a 12th century tapestry showing Odin, Thor, and Frey.

obtain prosperity and times of peace and happiness. His sister, *Freya,* was the goddess of love, music and flowers, and she ruled over the fairies in Alfheim. Her wagon was drawn by two cats. She owned a costly necklace, called *Brisingamen,* and she was called "she that shines over the sea." Friday was dedicated to her.

Tyr or *Tiu* was the most courageous of the gods and delighted in war. Brave men called upon his name in battle. His day was Tuesday.

Bragi was the god of poetry and the best of all the "skalds" or minstrels. His wife was *Ithunn,* goddess of the early spring. She was the guardian of certain golden apples, which the gods eat to become youthful again when they feel themselves growing old.

The punishment of Loki, god of evil

Among other gods were *Höthr*, or *Hoder*, who presided over winter, and who was blind; *Ull*, unrivaled as an archer and ice skater, whose favor was invoked by those engaged in single combats; and *Forseti*, god of justice.

Of a different sort was *Loki*, the god of evil. He was a god who liked to bring about quarrels, originated all frauds and deceits, and was the disgrace of the gods. He was handsome to look upon, but malicious in disposition and very fickle. He was very ingenious, and again and again by his cleverness, managed to escape the punishment that was due him. He was the father of the wolf *Fenrir*, of the *Midgard Serpent*, which encircled the earth, and of the goddess *Hel*, or Death. The latter was confined in Niflheim, and her home was called Sleet-Den. Among her followers were Hunger, Care, and Stumbling-Stone.

Adventures of the Gods

For a time the wolf Fenrir dwelt in Asgard. But as he increased in size the gods perceived his evil nature, and they resolved to bind him. No bands that they could place around him, however, held fast; twice he broke forth from their strongest fetters. Finally, the mountain spirits made a chain that would hold him. This was strangely contrived out of the noise of a cat's paw, the beard of a woman, the roots of a mountain, the sinews of a bear, the breath of a fish, and the spittle of a bird. The chain looked so slender and worthless that the wolf would not let the gods place it upon him, for he suspected some fraud, some hidden power in it. At last he consented to have it placed around him if one of the gods would place his hand inside the wolf's mouth as a pledge. The gods feared to do this, but at last Tyr carried out the wolf's condition. Then the fetter was placed upon Fenrir and held fast, but in revenge the wolf bit off the hand of the god.

Once a mountain giant assumed the form of a man and came to the gods with the suggestion that he build a wall for them that would protect them forever against the frost giants. But he asked in return that Freya be given to him as a bride, and the sun and moon as a dowry. The gods consented to these conditions, provided he finish the whole work without assistance in one winter. The giant agreed, but asked that he be allowed the use of his horse, Svadilfari. Again the gods, on the advice of Loki, consented, and he began work. Then the gods saw that it was really the horse, capable of drawing stones of immense size, that was doing the greater part of the work. Soon the fortification approached completion, and the gods in despair dreaded the time when Freya would no longer give them love and music and flowers, and when the world would be darkened without sun or moon. So they laid hands upon Loki, and told him that unless he could prevent the giant from completing his work, he himself would be killed. Loki promised to use his wits against the giant. That night he managed to entice the steed into the forest to keep him from assisting the giant. The giant did his best to work

Bronze statuette of the God Thor

alone, but it was in vain. Just then Thor returned from an expedition, and he slew the giant and hurled him to the underworld.

Thor himself not long afterward lost his hammer, which fell into the possession of the frost giants. Their king refused to return it unless Freya became his bride. She refused his proposal, but Loki persuaded Thor to dress himself in women's clothes and accompany him to Jotunnheim, as if he were Freya. In Jotunnheim a splendid feast was prepared for the supposed bride, but the king of the giants was amazed at the huge quantity of food which the coy goddess consumed—a whole roasted ox, eight great salmon, three tuns of mead, thirty hams, besides an immense quantity of sweetmeats. When he lifted up the veil to kiss the bride, he was terrified by her eyes shining like fire. But Loki reassured him. The bride, he said, had been so anxious to see him that for eight days she had neither eaten nor slept. At last the favorable moment arrived. Thor seized his magical hammer, slew the king and his followers, and returned to Asgard.

At another time Thor, accompanied by his servant Thialfi and Loki, set out for the land of the giants. On the way they passed through an endless forest, and came at last to a great but deserted hall, in which they lay down to rest. In the night the ground shook as if from an earthquake, and in the morning when they crawled out they found a giant of mountainous size sleeping nearby, whose snoring still made the ground tremble. He awoke, and told Thor that his name was Skrymir.

"Where is my glove?" he cried, and looking around he picked it up. The glove was the hall in which Thor, Loki, and the servant had slept. The giant suggested that they all travel together, but Thor was hard put to it to keep up with him. At nightfall the giant lay down to sleep, but handed Thor his wallet and bade him take food from it. Thor could not open the wallet, and after struggling in vexation with the strings, he lost his temper and hit the giant a terrific blow with his hammer. The giant yawned and opened his eyes.

"Did a leaf fall on my head?" he asked, and fell asleep again. Again Thor struck him, and once more he awoke.

"Did some birds perch on my head?" he inquired, and again he fell asleep. Thor resolved that the third time he would slay the giant, and struck his skull with all his might, but the giant merely roused himself uneasily and grumbled at the acorn that had dropped on his head.

The giant told Thor that he himself was but a small person among the giants that lived in Jotunnheim, and he advised him to be careful when he reached that city. Then he left them and departed on a way of his own.

At last Thor, Loki, and the servant reached the city of the giants, over which Utgard-Loki ruled. This king looked at them scornfully, and asked them in what feats they were skilled.

"I can eat," rejoined Loki, "faster than any one else can, and I am ready to compete with your heartiest eaters."

The king made one of his followers named Logi come forward, and place an immense trough filled with food between him and Loki. Loki began at one end, Logi at the other and they ate their way toward each other. They met in the exact middle of the trough, but inasmuch as Logi had eaten everything, whereas Loki had left the bones, Logi was called the victor.

Then the king asked Thor's servant what he could do. Thialfi replied that he could outrun any one who might compete with him. Thereupon they all adjourned to a far-spreading plain, and there a young man named Hugi was matched against Thialfi. Three times they ran, and always Hugi far outstripped Thor's servant.

Finally the king turned to Thor and inquired of him what feat he would perform. Thor claimed he could drink as no one else could. So the king bade them bring forward a horn, which seemed of moderate size.

"A good drinker," said Utgard-Loki, "can empty this in a single draft, but a moderate one may need two. Anyone can empty it in three."

So Thor lifted up the horn, and he drank and drank until every bit of breath had left his body. He looked in the horn, and the liquid seemed scarcely to have been touched. Again he drank deeply, and still it seemed not to be diminished. A third attempt brought no better results, and in sullen anger Thor handed the horn back to the king.

Now the king proposed another test to Thor—to lift his cat from the ground. Thor tugged and tugged, but was just able to stir one of the animal's legs. When Thor angrily proposed that some one wrestle with him, the king smiled and called forward an old woman.

"Wrestle with my old nurse Elli," he bade Thor.

But the stronger the grip of Thor upon Elli, the more she resisted; and she was even able to bring him down upon one knee. At that moment the king commanded that they cease.

The next morning Thor and his companions departed, and Utgard-Loki accompanied them to the gates of the city. As they were about to set forth on their journey, he stayed them, and said to Thor:

"Now I will tell you the truth, because I know that never again shall you enter my city. Mighty and marvelous is your strength, and throughout all these trials I have deceived you. I was the giant in the forest. The wallet was tied with iron wires, that you could not tear. The three blows of your hammer never touched me: I skillfully evaded them, and if you will look on the mountainside, you will find three glens that your blows created. Logi, with whom Loki competed, was Fire; and who can consume more than Fire? Hugi was Thought; and what is swifter than Thought? The end of the horn wherefrom you drank reached into the sea, and to my marvel you almost emptied it. That cat was not really a cat, but the Midgard Serpent, and when you lifted its leg, it was almost loosened from the earth. As for Elli, she is Old Age; and what man or god is there whom Old Age will not, sooner or later, overcome?"

So saying Utgard-Loki disappeared, and the city with him.

Death of Balder

The death of Balder came about in this way. It was known that sooner or later he would be killed, and to avert his doom his mother Frigg went around to all things on heaven and earth and made them swear that they would never harm Balder. But one thing she overlooked—the mistletoe, hidden in the oak leaves.

Now the gods, knowing what had happened, amused themselves by hurling at Balder their swords and battle-axes, stones and limbs of trees, huge masses of earth and metal. But nothing would touch him, and he remained unharmed. Loki was vexed at this, and he searched everywhere for something with which he might harm Balder. At last he came to an insignificant plant, the mistletoe, from which Frigg had exacted no oath. He cut a sprig of it eagerly, and then persuaded Höthr, the blind god, to hurl it at Balder. He did so, and the beautiful god fell to the ground dead. All mourned for him, as men mourn for the departed springtime. One of the gods even sought Balder in the underworld, and was told there that if all things lamented for Balder, he would return. But this could not be. Loki was punished by being bound in chains, and above his head was a serpent whose venom fell on him continually.

Pendant representing Balder, the best of the gods

According to these Northern legends, there was to
come a time when all the world would be destroyed—when
the rulers of heavens would themselves be brought to
judgment. This age was called *Ragnarok,* the judgment of
the gods or the twilight of the gods. First would come three
years that would be all winter, month after month of
continuous snow and tempest. Then would come disastrous
earthquakes. Men would die in hordes. The wolf Fenrir
would snap his chains, the Midgard Serpent arise from his
bed. Then Loki would escape and join the enemies of the
gods. Over the twilight bridge the hostile hosts would
advance against heaven, and a great combat would ensue in
which all would perish. The sun would sink from the sky,
flames would consume the earth, time would come to an
end. But the Father of All, greater than Odin or his
enemies, would make a new heaven and a new earth, set in
a Golden Age.

PRACTICAL APPLICATIONS

References to Mythology in Literature

What do the following references mean? Where a word or phrase is italicized, explain only the word or phrase.

1. And the stars came out in heaven,
   High over *Asgard.—Arnold*
2. Of *Frigga*, honored mother of the gods.—*Arnold*
3. But in his breast stood fixt the fatal bough
   Of *Mistletoe.—Arnold*
4. Thou camest near the next, O warrior *Thor*,
   Shouldering thy hammer.—*Arnold*
5. For this thing also had been appointed by *Urd* and
   Verdandi and *Skuld* as they sat weaving under
   Yggdrasil.—*Cabell*
6. *Balder* the Beautiful
   God of the summer sun!—*Longfellow*
7. But *Odin* spoke in answer, and his voice was awful
   and cold.—*Morris*
8. The *Weird Sisters*, hand in hand,
   Posters of the sea and land,
   Thus do go about, about.—*Shakespeare*
9. Their radiant palace is *Valhalla* called.—*Wagner*
10. And *Freya* next came night, with golden tears;
    The loveliest goddess she in heaven.—*Arnold*
11. Where are in circle ranged twelve golden chairs,
    And in the midst one higher, *Odin's* throne.
    —*Arnold*
12. And the *Valkyries* on their steeds went forth
    Toward earth and fights of men.—*Arnold*
13. There goes *Thor's* own Hammer,
    Cracking the dark in two!—*Kipling*
14. *Hoeder* the blind old god,
    Whose feet are shod with silence.—*Longfellow*
15. The *Norns*, the terrible maidens.—*Scott*

Suggestions for Oral or Written Composition

1. Go to the front of the room. Say: "I am a goddess (or god)," but do not mention your name. Then describe your realm. See how many in the class can guess what your name is. Let others do the same with other deities.
2. Which gods do you find more interesting, those of the Greeks and Romans or those of the Northland? Why?
3. Invent another adventure of Thor, in imitation of those given in this chapter.
4. Pretend you were one of the gods present when Balder was killed. Tell how he died.

Word Study

1. Give the origin of the following names: Tuesday, Wednesday, Thursday, Friday.
2. Give the correct pronunciation of the following: Ymir, Hræsvelg, Mjollnir, Valkyries.
3. Look up in the dictionary the word *weird,* both the noun and the adjective, and note how its present meaning is connected with that of *wyrd,* fate.
4. The Norsemen had a drinking saltuation, "Skoal!" (See Longfellow's *The Skeleton in Armor.*) With the name of which of the Norns is this salutation connected? Would *Valhalla* be an appropriate name for a "Hall of Fame" for heroes? (See the dictionary's definition of the word.) What were the runes? How many synonyms can you find for *skald?*

Questions for Review

1. How do the gods of the North and South differ?
2. What, according to the men of the Northland, was the way the world originated?
3. How did the stars and the sun and the moon come into existence?
4. Where did the gods hold their assemblies?
5. Who were the Norns?

6. Who was the king of gods and men?
7. What was the name of his dwelling place?
8. Who was his wife?
9. What was his food?
10. Who were the Valkyries?
11. Who was the strongest of gods and men?
12. What three wonderful treasures did he possess?
13. Who was Balder? Frey? Freya? Tyr? Bragi? Ithunn? Höthr? Ull? Forseti?
14. Who was the god of evil? of death?
15. How was the wolf Fenrir bound?
16. How was the giant outwitted who was promised Freya as a wife?
17. How did Thor contend with the frost giants?
18. How did the death of Balder come about?
19. What was the belief of the Norsemen as to the final destiny of the gods?
21. What was Ragnarok?

Reading List

Poems and Prose Epics

Arnold, Matthew: *Balder Dead*
Bellows, H.A.: *The Poetic Edda*
Brodeur, A. G.: *The Prose Edda*
Buchanan, Robert: *Balder the Beautiful*
Gray, Thomas: *Ode on the Descent of Odin—Ode on the Fatal Sisters*
Kipling, Rudyard: *Song of the Red War-Boat*
Longfellow, Henry Wadsworth: *Tagner's Drapa—The Saga of King Olaf*
Scott, W.B.: *The Norns Watering Ygg-drasil*

Novels and Descriptive Works

Anderson, R.B.: *Norse Mythology*
Asbjörnsen, P.C.: *Popular Tales from the North*
Colum, Padraic: *The Children of Odin*
Dahn, Felix: *A Captive of the Roman Eagles*

"The Viking Sea Raiders"—painting by Albert Goodwin

19 Heroes of the North

Stout in battle, he slew the dragon.

Beowulf

Siegfried

Near Xanten on the Rhine lived a king and a queen named Siegmund and Sieglinde, to whom was born a fair prince named Siegfried. As Siegfried grew older, the Netherlands, the kingdom over which his parents ruled, was threatened by invaders, and the young prince was sent away from the castle, for fear that he might fall into the hands of the foe. His parents intrusted him to the care of a blacksmith named Mimer, who lived in the secret thickets of a great forest.

Now Mimer was a dwarf or troll, and belonged to a strange race of the little people, called Nibelungs. For the most part these Nibelungs dwelt underground, in a dark little town which they had built. This town was named Nibelheim. The great majority of the Nibelungs were very skillful smiths, who would hammer all day at their tiny anvils. But at night the Nibelungs, both men and women, would make merry with dance and music. Mimer was a Nibelung who lived on the surface of the earth, and built his forge under the trees of the forest.

Siegfried was delighted to join Mimer and his apprentices, and he learned in a little while how to swing the heavy hammer. Indeed, his strength soon became too great, for so resounding and powerful were the blows he struck that often the anvil would be shattered to pieces. Then Mimer would scold him sarcastically, and Siegfried, angrily leaving the smithy, would stride off into the woods and listen to the cheerful caroling of the birds.

One day, while Siegfried was wandering through the forest, the whim came upon him to blow his mighty silver horn. He did so, and before the sound had died away, he saw suddenly before him a huge shaggy bear. He was not in the least frightened. Rather it occurred to him that here was a good chance to pay Mimer back for his numerous rebukes. He rushed at the great beast, seized it in his arms, and in the twinkling of an eye had muzzled the animal with his belt. Then he led the bear back to the forge.

There Mimer was sharpening a sword at the anvil. As he heard the laughter of the prince, he turned around and saw the bear. Instantly he dropped the sword with a clang and ran off to the darkest corner of the smithy, trembling with fear. For a time Siegfried continued to tease the little man, then he unmuzzled the bear and set him free again.

This was but one of the many pranks which the young prince played upon Mimer, for he did not care very much for the cunning and ill-tempered troll. Finally, the latter grew tired of the trouble that Siegfried was causing him, and determined to get rid of him.

One day, therefore, he sent him deep into the forest to bring home from a certain storehouse some charcoal for the forge. He did not tell the lad that on the road he would have to pass a terrifying dragon, named Fafnir. Siegfried strode merrily along. Once more the impulse came on him to blow a few notes on his beloved horn, and as he did so, once more danger appeared. At the sound of the blast the dragon roused himself in his lair and began to spout fire. The trees swayed and trembled as the dragon made his way underneath them toward Siegfried, and the little birds and beasts of the forest scurried away in fear.

Yet when Siegfried beheld the dragon he was not at all frightened. In fact, after a few moments, he began to laugh, for he welcomed the break in his too peaceful life that the dragon was bringing him. The dragon sat down on a hill and glared at Siegfried. But Siegfried remarked cheerfully:

"I am going to kill you, for you are too ugly to live."

At these bold words Fafnir opened his huge jaws and showed his teeth, extending in triple rows like a forest. But again Siegfried laughed. Then Fafnir, wild with anger, crept nearer and nearer and lashed his tail furiously. But Siegfried drew his sword, that he himself had forged with care at the anvil of Mimer. Leaping upon the dragon's back, he plunged the blade into his heart. In dreadful convulsions the dragon fell dead.

Siegfried was not yet done with the dragon, however. As the dragon lay at his feet, he remembered that while working in Mimer's smithy he had heard some of the Nibelungs talk of this very dragon. He recalled that they had said that whoever bathed in the blood of the dragon would be forever after invulnerable. For his skin would grow so tough and horny that no sword or arrow could pierce it. So Siegfried flung aside his dress of deerskins and plunged into his dragon bath. From top to toe he washed himself with the magical red fluid. Yet, as he bathed, a linden leaf dropped unseen right between his shoulders, and there alone the dragon blood did not touch him, and consequently, there alone he was vulnerable.

This duty performed, Siegfried returned swiftly to the forge. He realized that Mimer had wished to kill him, so without more ado he slew the treacherous dwarf.

Afterward Siegfried wandered to many places, and after a while he came to a country called Iceland, over which reigned a queen named Brunhild, who was both beautiful

Siegfried killing the dragon

and warlike. Her castle stood by the sea, and was guarded by seven gates; and her marble palace glittered in the sun. He inquired of passers-by who might dwell here, and they not only told him her name, but also spoke to him of her strange refusal to marry anyone unless he could vanquish her in the tests she set him.

When Siegfried entered the castle, Brunhild, who marveled at his handsome face and his mighty muscles, received him favorably and even allowed him to see her magic horse, Gana. Yet Siegfried somehow had no love for Brunhild, and refused to undertake the tests she set. But to prove to her that it was no lack of skill or strength that made him decline her proposals, Siegfried calmly threw down the seven gates of her castle and even enticed the horse Gana to accompany him. Brunhild never forgave Siegfried for his scorn of her.

Siegfried, continuing on his travels, came to an immense cavern where lay outspread the treasure of the Nibelungs: gold and silver, jewels of all kinds, most marvelous riches. Two Nibelung princes, surrounded by twelve foolish giants, their counselors, were quarreling over the treasure. For the king of the Nibelungs had died, and now his sons could not divide their heritage peacefully. When the little princes saw Siegfried, they asked him to act as arbitrator, promising him as a reward the sword Balmung, which could overcome the strongest warriors. He consented, and began to make a division, but soon the dwarfs in dissatisfaction began to mock him and scold him in their harsh voices. At last Siegfried in anger slew both the dwarfs and the giants, and laid the treasure aside in a secret place.

Now seven hundred knights came to bar his way, but Siegfried conquered them, and made them swear to be his liegemen thereafter. In a little while he had need of them, for the dwarfs of Nibelheim, under the leadership of a chieftain named Alberich, took the field against him, anxious not only to avenge the death of their princes but also to recover the lost treasure of the Nibelungs. But Siegfried had little trouble with them. He chased them all into a great cave on the mountainside, and from Alberich himself he stripped the Cloak of Darkness, which rendered the wearer invisible and invincible. He made Alberich and his army of dwarfs likewise swear allegiance to him, and then he placed them in charge of his treasure.

When Siegfried returned to his own country he was most warmly welcomed. Great feasts were held in his honor, and he received knighthood from the hands of the king. But he could not rest in quiet, and shortly he set forth on a new quest. For he had heard of a beautiful princess named Kriemhild, who dwelt at the Court of Worms in Burgundy, and from her description she seemed to him the ideal maiden of his dreams. He journeyed to Burgundy, accompanied only by eleven stalwart knights, and he was graciously welcomed by King Gunther, brother of Kriemhild, and by the latter's uncle and chief councilor Hagen, who was a cunning and cruel man. Not long after Siegfried arrived, two kings threatened Burgundy, but

"The Wooing of Brunhild"—painting by Arthur Rackham

largely by Siegfried's valor they were overcome and
conquered.

Then a great feast was held, which Kriemhild attended.
For the first time Siegfried gazed upon her, and thought her
more lovely even than her fame. But when Siegfried sought
to have her as a bride, King Gunther, at the advice of
Hagen, would by no means grant him her hand unless
Siegfried first accompanied Gunther to Iceland and helped
him win Brunhild for wife. Siegfried consented, and
accompanied only by a small band they set out for the
country of Brunhild.

They were gayly welcomed, although Brunhild was
angry that Siegfried came to assist Gunther rather than try
to win her himself. With the help of Siegfried, who was clad
in his Cloak of Darkness, Gunther passed the three
trials—to overcome Brunhild in combat, to cast a stone

Carving from a church portal illustrating the slaying of Hagen

farther than her cast, and to jump a greater distance than
she did. Then did Brunhild yield to Gunther and wed him,
and Siegfried was given Kriemhild as his bride.

But the story does not end here. Siegfried and
Kriemhild in time became rulers of the Netherlands, and
after a while were invited to Worms to take part in a
tournament and its accompanying festivals. As the two
queens sat together and watched their husbands in the
combat, each began to boast of the prowess of her spouse.
By a slip of the tongue Kriemhild revealed that her husband
was vulnerable in one place. Later, goaded to anger by
Brunhild's remarks, Kriemhild revealed the stratagem by
which Siegfried had aided Gunther to win Brunhild, and the

284

latter determined on revenge. With the aid of Hagen, Kriemhild was persuaded to make a garment for Siegfried in which a silken cross was embroidered above the spot on which the linden leaf had fallen; and there one day, as he was bending over a brook to drink, Hagen thrust his spear and killed him.

The Burgundians then came into possession of the treasure of the Nibelungs, but Kriemhild always plotted vengeance. In the course of time she married again, and her husband, King Etzel, was willing to aid her schemes. She invited her brothers and Hagen to visit her. Quarreling rose, and a fierce battle took place, in which many were killed, Hagen dying by the hand of Kriemhild and she herself slain by the knight Hildebrand.

Beowulf

In Denmark there once ruled a king named Hrothgar, who built for himself a magnificent hall, in which his warriors feasted by day and slept by night. For a time the monarch and his subjects rejoiced in their fine dwelling place, but suddenly their rejoicing was turned to lamentation. For in a dreary and noxious fen nearby there lived a monstrous creature named Grendel. Each night Grendel entered the hall and seized some of the warriors, whom he carried off to his home in the fen and devoured.

Night after night this slaying continued, and nothing seemed of any avail to check the monster. The tidings of what was happening went far and wide, and at last came to the land of the Goths toward the north, where there lived a young hero named Beowulf. Beowulf resolved to go to Denmark to rid King Hrothgar of the monster who troubled him. He set sail and in a few days reached Denmark. When King Hrothgar heard of the purpose of the hero, his heart was glad. That night Beowulf and his men went to the great hall, and although his comrades slept, Beowulf kept watch. At midnight the monster crawled into the hall and, before Beowulf could stop him, he had seized and killed one of the Goths. But then Beowulf grasped him in his mighty arms, and a terrible struggle took place. Grendel managed to tear himself free, leaving his arm in Beowulf's irresistible grip. Mortally wounded, the monster plunged into the waters of the fen and died.

Great was the rejoicing on the following morning in the heart of Hrothgar and his people, and Beowulf was loaded with thanks and gifts. But still the Danes could not sleep in peace in the great hall they had built, for that very night the mother of Grendel came forth and, full of wrath, seized some of the king's best warriors and carried them off to the fen. Now once more Beowulf steeled himself for combat, and when Grendel's mother took refuge in the waters of the fen, the hero plunged in and continued diving until he came to the cave of the monster. He fought fiercely with her and at last slew her. In the cave he found the body of Grendel, and cutting off his head, he rose with it to the surface and returned to the hall of the Danes.

Then Beowulf prepared to return to his own land and to report to his ruler, King Hygelac, what he had accomplished. Hrothgar thanked him again and again, and gave him many presents to carry back with him. In Gothland Beowulf did valiant service for his king year after year, and when that monarch died, Beowulf became ruler of the land. For fifty years he governed with wisdom and courage, beloved by his people, and he looked forward to closing his years in peace and honor.

Such was not, however, to be his fate. For now it happened that a runaway slave came upon a great hoard of treasure, guarded by a fearsome dragon. The slave's eyes were dazzled by the vast wealth he saw before him. He knew that if he but bring some proof of what he had seen to his master, he would be forgiven for having run away. Fortunately for him, the dragon was asleep. Stealthily he took a great golden cup from the hoard and stole away with it.

His master, as he had foreseen, was pleased. But the dragon awoke and missed the cup, and resolved to exact immediate punishment. He followed the track of the slave, lashing his tail in fury. He came at last to a stream and lost the trail. Then, because he could not take vengeance on the thief himself, he resolved to punish the slave's fellow men.

This ancient Nordic carved head bears a striking resemblance
to a 20th century "extra-terrestrial creature."

High over the town he flew; and spitting forth flame, he set
fire to many a home and slew many a man and woman.

News of this raid was carried to King Beowulf, and he
immediately made preparations to fight the monster. Of all
his followers only one young man, named Wiglaf, dared to
accompany the aged king. They sought the cave where the
dragon brooded. At the sound of their approach the dragon
rushed forth in wrath. Beowulf met him with a blow of his
trusty sword. Back and forth wavered the fortune of battle,
and Beowulf, fatally scorched by the flames of the monster,
knew his last hour had come. But with a final mighty effort,
he pierced the dragon to the heart.

There, as Beowulf lay dying, his other warriors came to
him, and he intrusted to them the great treasure the dragon
had guarded, bidding them use it for the welfare of the
kingdom. He appointed Wiglaf as his successor. Having
spoken these commands Beowulf died. His followers
erected a huge funeral pyre and burned his body. Mariners
far off at sea saw the leaping flames and marveled.

PRACTICAL APPLICATIONS

Myths in Literature

It is a singular tribute to the power of classical—Greek and Latin—mythology that it has exerted a much more definite and pervading influence on English literature than has the mythology of the ancient Germans. References to the ancient Teutonic gods and heroes in our writers are few and far between, and only a few authors in English have gone back to the fine old stories told by their forefathers in the primitive forest or in their first settlements. William Morris, among others, has excellently retold some of the old tales, particularly in *Sigurd the Volsung* and in parts of *The Earthly Paradise*.

The influence of *Beowulf* can be seen in what is without question the finest of all renderings of the old Teutonic myths in more modern literature—Matthew Arnold's *Balder Dead*. Arnold was so imbued with the spirit of ancient Germanic mythology that his poem is almost a manual to that mythology. In his poem one sees the gods vividly: their power, their weakness, the eerie surroundings amid which are transacted the slaying of Balder, and the vain efforts to bring him back.

Thomas Gray and Henry Wadsworth Longfellow have likewise retold some of these ancient tales, and the "Three Weird Sisters" of Shakespeare's *Macbeth* are an interesting survival of the three Norns or Fates of Teuton myth. A famous German musical composer who displayed considerable literary ability in the composition of the librettos of his operas, has perhaps given the modern world the most brilliant version of the Siegfried story—Richard Wagner in *The Ring of the Nibelung*.

288

Specific Literary References

What do the following references mean? Where a word or phrase is italicized, explain only the word or phrase.

1. Now will I, *O Beowulf*,
   Best of warriors, even as a son
   Love thee in my heart!—*Beowulf*
2. Stout in battle, he slew the dragon, keeper of the treasure-hoard.—*Beowulf*
3. Grendel's mother kept thought of her sorrow.
   —*Beowulf*
4. Wiglaf in wrath upbraided his comrades.—*Beowulf*
5. Then uprose the king of the *Nibelungs*, and was clad in purple and pall.—*Morris*
6. With what joy and gladness welcomed were they there!
   It seemed when came dame *Brunhild* to Burgundy whilere.—*Nibelungenlied*
7. Now, as he spake, came Siegfried rushing in,
   In wanton merriment he urged along
   A great bear he had bridled for his sport.—*Wagner*

Suggestions for Oral or Written Composition

1. In what ways do the stories of Siegfried and Beowulf resemble each other? How do both remind you of ancient Greek or Roman tales? Do the Germanic heroes display qualities not to be found in the heroes of Greece and Rome?

2. Siegfried relates to a comrade his exploit with the bear. How does he tell the story?

3. When Beowulf returns home, he makes a report to his king. What would he say? Would he boast, or would he be modest? Try to give an old-fashioned flavor to his remarks.

4. Give an account of Wagner's famous group of music dramas, *The Ring of the Nibelung*. If you can do so, present a recording of some of the music.

Word Study

1. Give the correct pronunciation of the following names:

    Siegfried, Brunhild, Kriemhild, Hrothgar, Beowulf.

2. Ask an instructor in German to select three or four lines of the medieval German in which the epic of the *Nibelungenlied* is composed, and explain what they mean. Does the language resemble English in any way?

3. Similarly, try to get a fragment of the Old English epic of *Beowulf*. How close does this come to modern English?

4. The word *dragon* is an interesting one. Look up the following words in Webster's dictionary: dragon (especially the derivation), dragon fly, dragoon, dragonnade, dragon's blood.

Questions for Review

1. Of what country were the parents of Siegfried the rulers?
2. Into whose care was he intrusted?
3. Who were the Nibelungs?
4. What qualities did Siegfried develop?
5. What was his adventure with a bear?
6. How did he incur Mimer's ill will?
7. How did Mimer determine to get rid of him?
8. What creature did he slay?
9. How did he make himself invulnerable?
10. What revenge did he take on Mimer?
11. Who was Brunhild?
12. What was Siegfried's attitude toward Brunhild?
13. How did he win the treasure of the Nibelungs?
14. What condition was laid upon him when he sought Kriemhild as a bride?
15. How did he fulfill it?
16. How did Siegfried meet his death?
17. What revenge did Kriemhild take?

18. Whose subjects did the monster Grendel harry?
19. From what land did Beowulf come to help Hrothgar?
20. What was the issue of the battle between him and Grendel?
21. How did Beowulf overcome Grendel's mother?
22. How did Hrothgar reward him?
23. What monster did Beowulf fight in later years?
24. What was the result of the battle?

Reading List

Baldwin, James: *Story of Siegfried*
Child, C.F.: *Beowulf*
Hackel, Oliver: Wagner's *Siegfried*
McSpadden, Walter F.: *Stories from Wagner*
Morris, William: *The Fostering of Aslaug* (in *Sigurd the Volsung)*
Motherwell, William: *The Battle-Flag of Sigurd*
Shumway, D.B.: *The Nibelungenlied*
Wagner, Richard: *The Ring of the Nibelung*
Whittier, John Greenleaf: *The Norsemen*

The Book of Kells, an illuminated Celtic manuscript of the four gospels, is considered one of the most beautiful books in the world.

20 Celtic Fairyland

Sage beneath a spreading oak
Sat the druid, hoary chief.

Cowper

The Ancient Celts

Once a great empire stretched across the whole northern part of Europe, from the Black Sea to the British Isles. At one time the inhabitants of this empire were powerful enough to sack Rome itself. They conquered Spain from the Carthaginians and waged other great wars and often they were in alliance with the Greeks and Romans. This empire was the empire of the Celts.

Today but little visible trace remains of this mighty empire. The Celts left no written records of their own, and our direct literary knowledge of them comes only from the histories of their foes and allies. A few of their coins have survived and a few ornaments and weapons in bronze. The names of many places, moreover, bear testimony to the fact that once the Celts possessed them, and in oral tradition and legend may be found definite traces of the stories and the myths of this ancient people.

Where are the Celts themselves today? Just as when they conquered the various sections of Europe, they mingled with the peoples whom they overcame, so in turn the Celts have in many sections completely mingled with those that conquered them. In France, Spain, and England, for example, the Celtic intermixture is marked; and as to the last country in particular some historians argue that its people ought to be called, not "Anglo-Saxon," but "Anglo-Celtic."

There exists, moreover, what is known as the "Celtic fringe." As the Germanic peoples conquered the Celtic empire, the Celts retreated to the edges of various lands. Thus, in France, Brittany is predominantly Celtic; and in the British Isles one may find an almost unmixed Celtic population in Wales, in the Highlands of Scotland, in certain islands, and in Ireland. Ireland was never even visited by the Roman legionaries, and so was able to retain some of its early Celtic characteristics.

In such Celtic countries one finds that many of the ancient Celtic traits, as recorded in history, are still visible in their modern inhabitants. Physically, the Celts of the British Isles were mostly a tall, fair, red-haired race. By much intermixture with those who conquered them and those whom they conquered, these traits have somewhat changed, and one finds dark as well as light Celts. They were a warlike, masterful race, eager for battle, says Cæsar, but easily dashed by reverses. Another Roman remarked that there were two things to which the Gauls (or Celts) were devoted—the art of war and craft in speech. They were always eager to hear news, besieging merchants and travelers for gossip; easily influenced, optimistic, wavering in their opinions, fond of change. They were at the same time very quick and intelligent. They loved display. Their weapons were richly ornamented, their horse trappings were wrought in bronze and enamel, and their raiment was embroidered with gold. They had great respect for their poets and learned men, and (to judge by what has come down to us through tradition) they were rich in fancy, delighted in color and in the beauty of nature, and created stories that have deeply influenced all later literature.

Celtic Gods

Our direct knowledge of the old Celtic gods is very scanty, and for information concerning them we must depend chiefly on Roman chroniclers and on archaeological excavations. Probably their beliefs in many ways resembled those of the Romans, Greeks, and Germans. Cæsar, speaking of the five chief divinities of the Gauls, gives them Roman names. He says that these divinities were Mercury, Apollo, Minerva, Jupiter, and Mars; and of these the Gauls regarded the first most highly.

Excavations, showing temples and statues dedicated to these gods, have borne out what Cæsar says. Lucan, another ancient writer, mentions a triad of gods, all cruel in character—Teutates, Esus, and Taranis; and here, once more, excavations have been found to verify his statement. Pluto, too, according to Cæsar, was worshiped among the Celts; and elsewhere one finds mention of Lugh, a god of light. Traces of other deities have survived in the legends of Celtic lands.

One very important feature in ancient Celtic religion was *stone worship,* although the veneration of rivers, trees, mountains, and other natural objects was also common. Everywhere in the countries once part of the Celtic empire may be found inscribed stones, arranged in certain mystical forms. These were once objects of worship among the Celts. They believed some stones had magical powers: such as a certain "coronation stone" among the Irish. Stones were associated too with the holy places of the dead.

Celtic descendants have never forgotten their Druidic heritage and still celebrate it with seasonal festivals.

The priests of the ancient Celts were called *druids*. The druids ruled their people with tyrannical power, and some writers have attributed the downfall of the Celtic empire to the misuse of this power. Cæsar says that they had power of excommunication and were therefore greatly feared. All affairs, public and private, were subject to their authority. They were free from military service and paid no taxes. Great schools were maintained by them, and in these schools their disciples learned by heart a great number of verses, for it was not lawful to commit any of their doctrines to writing. The principal point in their teaching, according to Cæsar, was that the soul does not perish, but that after death it passes from one body into another. All through history, one finds, the Celt has had an intense faith in another world.

The druids also taught many things regarding the stars and their motions, the extent of the universe and the earth, the nature of things, and the power and might of the immortal gods. They were supposed to have magical powers and to be able to give or withhold sunshine, to cause storms, to make fields fertile, to exercise invisibility, and to produce sleep. According to some, they regarded the mistletoe as sacred, especially when it grew on an oak; and they often performed their rites in oak groves.

Celtic Cycles of Legends

When the Celtic empire was swept away, when the power of this ancient people crashed in ruin, the orderly worship of their gods fell into confusion. In different parts of the old Celtic world, and especially in Ireland and Wales, new legends were born and new gods were worshiped. We have a large store of knowledge about these legends and gods, for some of this material was ultimately written down in old manuscripts, and some of it continued to be handed down orally from generation to generation until it too was duly recorded.

These stories fall, to a large extent, into cycles or groups. Of them the principal ones are, first, the *Cycle of the Invasions of Ireland;* second, the *Ultonian* or *Conorian Cycle;* and third, the *Ossianic* or *Fenian Cycle.* To these must be added the account of the *Voyage of Maelduin* and, most famous of all, the *King Arthur Saga.* From Wales come the beautiful stories of the *Mabinogion.* Many of these tales of gods and heroes are current not only in Ireland or Wales, but also in Scotland; and some of the King Arthur stories penetrated all over the European world. In addition, there are many miscellaneous legends, some of great beauty.

In these Celtic tales we come to a new realm of the imagination, and to a certain extent we find ourselves more at home there than in any other group of national legends. For these ancient Celts loved nature and spoke of it lovingly and gracefully. They displayed, too, a chivalry and a tenderness toward women. They had a keen sense of words and their shades of meaning, and often their phrases have an unsurpassed delicacy that makes one understand why many critics have tried to find Celtic ancestors for such masters of style as Shakespeare and Keats.

Cycle of the Invasions

In the legends the invasions of Ireland are divided into several sections: the coming of Partholan, of Nemed, of the Fomorians, of the Firbolg, of the Tuatha De Danann, and of the Milesians.

Of these the Tuatha De Danann, the people of the goddess *Dana*, were most important.

Among the ancient Celts, Dana (whose name appears in other forms—*Don, Ana, Danu*) was regarded as the mother of the gods. Sometimes, too, she is called *Brigit*. She was an earth goddess, a goddess of plenty. As Brigit she was a goddess of knowledge and presided over poetry; she was particularly a patron of women.

The *Dagda* (called too the *Dagda Mor*) was the father and chief of the people of Dana. He was pictured as huge and mighty. To feed him, a pit was dug in the ground and filled with porridge, and the spoon he used was big enough for a bed. He called the seasons into being with his harp, and from the caldron of his plenty, called *Undry,* he fed the whole earth. He was usually represented as wielding a large club or a fork, symbol of his dominion over food. He owned a harp, which came flying through the air at his call.

His son *Angus* was the god of love. Four bright birds hovered forever around his head, which were supposed to be his kisses taking shape in this lovely form. At their singing love sprang up in the hearts of mortals.

Midir the Proud was another son of Dagda, renowned for his splendor and personal beauty. *Lir* was god of the sea, but his son *Manannan* in later times was regarded as the deity of the waves and was one of the most popular of Celtic gods. Beyond his ocean lay the Land of Youth, the

Island of the Dead, and to that land Manannan guided the spirits. He was a master of tricks and illusions and owned many strange objects: a boat which obeyed the thought of those who sailed in it and went without oar or sail; a steed which could travel alike on sea or land, and a sword (called *Answerer*) which no armor could resist. White-crested waves were called the horses of Manannan (just as Neptune was god of the sea and of horses). He wore a great cloak which was capable of taking on every kind of color, just as the sea does when looked at from a height. The Isle of Man was his home and took its name from him.

The *Morrigu* was an extraordinary goddess, who embodied all that was perverse and horrible. It was her delight to set men at war, and she fought in battles herself, often taking the shape of a crow hovering over the dead.

Bran (or Bron) was represented as a man of gigantic size. No house or ship which was ever made could contain him, and when he laid himself across a river, an army could march over him as if over a bridge. He was the patron of minstrels and bards and himself claimed to be a skillful musician on many kinds of instruments. He was a king of the underworld, and there guarded the treasures of Dana against aggressors.

In many stories appears the god *Gwydion*, a son of Dana, who was a teacher of the arts and a giver of great gifts. He was skilled in war and in poetry, and suffered many strange experiences. He was kindhearted, for when the punishment was laid on Lleu that he should never have a wife of the people of the earth, Gwydion "enchanted a woman out of blossoms" for him. This Lleu or Lug is identified with Lugh, the god of light, mentioned earlier. Such was the radiance of his face that it seemed like the sun, and none could gaze steadily at it. He was a master of all the arts of war and peace. Among his possessions was a sword that slew of itself. His sling was seen as the rainbow, and the Milky Way was called "Lug's Chain."

In four great fairy cities—Falias, Gorias,Finias, and Murias—the people of Dana were reared, and sages taught them science and craft. They brought four great treasures to the invasion of Ireland: the Stone of Destiny, on which kings were crowned, and which today is England's

Celtic crown

Coronation Stone; the invincible sword of Lugh, a magic spear, and the Caldron of the Dagda. They were transported into the land on a magic cloud. For a time, however, the fortunes of the Tuatha De Danann wavered, and the Firbolg and the Fomorians ruled over them. Lug the sun god came to the aid of the Tuatha De Danann. A great battle took place and the people of Dana were victorious.

For a long time they ruled in Ireland, but at length they too were overthrown by a race of men who, it was fabled, came from Spain—the Milesians. The three kings of the people of Dana were defeated and slain by them, and the children of Miled became the rulers of the land.

But although many of the Tuatha De Danann were slain, they did not withdraw from the Green Island. They exercised their magic arts but were thenceforth invisible; and in Ireland may be found two peoples: the earthly and the elvin. The Dogda still rules over the latter, and to each of his subjects he assigns a place. On green mounds and ramparts, among the broken stones of ruined fortresses and sepulchers, in lonely woods, or by deserted pools, the fairy divinities dwell, and there their palaces rise. In eternal sunshine they hold their revels, and they feast forever on magic meat and magic ale, and draw therefrom everlasting youth and beauty. Sometimes they mingle with mortal men. Of their mingling we shall speak later.

Ultonian or Conorian Cycle

Many tales are told of the Milesians at Tara and especially of their High King Conary, but in time the scene of the story shifts to Ulster, to King *Conor,* and to his great vassal *Cuchulain.*

The deeds of Conor and Cuchulain are told in three manuscripts—*The Book of the Dun Cow, The Book of Leinster,* and *The Yellow Book of Lecan.* In these volumes it is related how Conor was granted the throne of Ulster for a year, but so wise and prosperous was his reign that at the year's end the people insisted that he remain their king.

Now there was at this time an order of knights called the "Red Branch," noted for their daring and chivalry. Greatest of these knights was Cuchulain, whose father was Lug and whose mother was a mortal maiden. It was prophesied of him during his infancy by the druid Morann:

"His praise will be in the mouths of all men. Charioteers and warriors, kings and sages will recount his deeds. He will win the love of many. This child will avenge all your wrongs. He will give combat at the fords. He will decide all your quarrels."

Originally he was called Setanta, but at a very early age he slew, in self-defense, a huge and ferocious dog that guarded the home of a wealthy smith named Cullan. To soothe the sorrow of Cullan at the loss of his faithful dog the boy promised to guard the home until one of the hound's puppies had grown up. Because of this, he was thereafter called Cuchulain—the "Hound of Cullan."

At the age of seven Cuchulain assumed the arms of a man and slew three champions who had defeated all the warriors of Ulster. He traveled to Scotland to learn skill in arms from a warrior witch. When at his full strength, no man could look him in the face without blinking. His body heat melted snow. He was a champion without equal.

Now over Connaught ruled a queen named Maev, and her heart was bitter against Ulster. She coveted for her own a famous Brown Bull of Quelgny, the mightiest in all Ireland. His back was broad enough for fifty children to play on. He was like both a savage lion and a dragon.

300

So all the mighty men of Connaught were gathered together and there was despair, for a curse lay upon the warriors of Ulster and no hand in all that realm could lift a spear. Only Cuchulain was free from the curse. All alone he withstood the great army of the enemy. In single combat he met their most valiant champions, and for three months he defended the marches against them. Every day he fought a bitter duel, and often he had to combat not only the natural strength of his foes but magic arts as well. His father came at night to heal his wounds, and the fierce goddess of war, the Morrigu, was so enchanted with his deeds that she wished to marry him.

Once, with much reluctance, Cuchulain was compelled to fight his old friend, Ferdiad, who while overcome with wine had been lured into a rash pledge to fight the Ultonian champion. For three days they engaged in combat, always treating each other with knightly courtesy, and at last Cuchulain gave his friend the death wound. The hero burst into passionate lament:

"It was all a game and a sport until Ferdiad came. Now the memory of this day will be like a cloud hanging over me forever."

Finally the curse was lifted from the men of Ulster, and joyfully they hastened into battle. They drove back the men of Connaught, and Maev herself cowered under her chariot and begged for mercy as Cuchulain came upon her.

"I am not accustomed to slay women," said Cuchulain scornfully, and he protected her until she had crossed the Shannon at Athlone. The famous Brown Bull so coveted by Maev had been seized and sent into Connaught. There it met the white-horned Bull of Ailell, and the two beasts fought bitterly. The Brown Bull was victorious, but it ran about madly until at last it too fell dead.

Though Maev made peace with Ulster, she vowed the death of Cuchulain, and in order to bring it about more readily, she sent her followers far and wide over the earth to learn evil magic. Then they attacked Cuchulain in every possible way—deceived his eyes, lured his mind and deprived him of his weapons. Still he fought desperately, and even when he was mortally wounded, he bound himself with his belt to a pillar, so that he might die standing. After he had drawn his last breath, his sword, falling from his grasp, cut off the hand of an enemy about to seize his body.

Not long after the passing of Cuchulain his master, King Conor, was likewise slain; and with them passed the glory of the Red Branch.

Ossianic Cycle

With the Ossianic cycle of stories we go back to an earlier age. Whereas the knights of Conor, like the warriors of Homer, dwell in fortified cities and drive forth in chariots, the followers of Finn live the lives of nomad hunters in primitive forests. The deeds of Finn's heroes are still a living reality to the peasants of Scotland and Ireland. There is a proverb that if the Fenians found that they had not been spoken of for a day, they would rise in wrath from the dead.

This cycle deals with the adventures of a band of warriors who formed a Fianna or a standing army, in the pay of King Cormac of Tara, to protect Ireland from both internal and external foes. At their head was *Finn* (also called *Fionn*), whose name means the "white" or "fair."

Under Finn, the Fianna of Erin reached its highest glory. He ruled them wisely and strongly, and bore no grudges. Even his enemies sometimes came into his service and were loyal and valiant. Chief of his friends was Dermot of the Love Spot, who was so fair and noble that all women fell in love with him.

Finn's son *Ossian* (called also Oisin) was both warrior and bard, and it is his songs of the deeds of the Fianna that are said to have been handed down. Ossian's own son was *Oscar*, the fiercest of all the fighters of the Fenians. He slew three kings in his maiden battle, and thereafter through his short life he fought with intense bravery. Ossian himself, it was fabled, escaped the fate of mortals by being taken to the Land of Youth by the fairy Niam of the Golden Hair, daughter of Manannan. He went with her to this Celtic

302

The ancient Monument of Stonehenge in England was used
by the Druids for sun worship.

paradise, and there enjoyed three hundred years of divine youth. But then there came upon him the longing to see his own country again. Niam set him upon a magic horse, but warned him not to set foot on the soil. As he rode, a saddle girth broke suddenly, and Ossian fell to the ground. When he rose up, he was a pitiably blind and decrepit old man, stripped of all the gifts of the gods. Soon thereafter he passed away.

Yet another tradition says that Finn, Ossian, Oscar and all their great clan never died, but lie spellbound in a magic cave, awaiting the appointed time when they shall awaken and redeem their land from all tyranny and shame.

What tests did a man have to undergo to be permitted to join the Fianna? The candidate had to be versed in the *Twelve Books of Poetry* and had to be skilled in making original verse in rime and meter. Then he was buried to his middle in the earth, and with a shield and a hazel stick he had to defend himself against nine warriors who cast spears at him. He had to leap over a narrow strip of wood level with his brow, and run at full speed under one level with his knee. A thorn was placed in his foot, and he had to pull it out while running and never slacken speed. He was permitted to take no dowry with his wife. Here were some of the maxims which were impressed on the Fianna:

"So long as thou shalt live, thy lord forsake not; neither for gold nor for any other reward in the world abandon one whom thou art pledged to protect.

"Be more apt to give than to deny, and follow after gentleness. Be especially gentle with women and with them that creep on the floor and with poets, and be not violent to the common people.

"Be no tale-bearer, nor utterer of falsehoods; be not talkative."

Voyage of Maelduin

Maelduin was the son of a great hero, who was slain in battle by plunderers from over the sea. His mother fled with her babe, and took refuge with a neighboring queen. Maelduin was reared with the sons of this queen. He grew up as a tall and fair youth, well skilled in the use of weapons. Then there came one who reproached him because he did not avenge the death of his father, and so Maelduin resolved to set out across the sea and find the pirates who had slain his sire.

But first he sought counsel from Nuca the wizard. Nuca instructed Maelduin what kind of boat to build, when to begin, and at what time he must put to sea. Nuca charged him strictly that there should be seventeen men in his crew, no more or less.

So the boat was built and the voyage began. But as they moved away from the shore and the wind filled their many-colored sails, Maelduin's three foster brothers came running down to the shore and implored him to take them along. As he paid no heed to their entreaty, they threw themselves into the water and swam after the boat. So Maelduin could not do otherwise than take them aboard, although he remembered the injunction of the wizard with foreboding.

Soon they came to the two islands from which the pirates had sailed, but a great wind drove them far away. They drifted many days, and then one day at dawn they heard the sound of waves breaking against the shore. They were about to land when they saw before them huge ants, each the size of a small horse; and they swarmed on the beach ready to seize whatever should land. So in great fright they hoisted sail and speeded forth.

Then for many more days they voyaged on, until they came to another island. On the shore frolicked a great beast, shaped like a horse but with legs of a hound with long, sharp talons on its feet.

"I do not like this beast," said Maelduin, so they turned the boat away once more toward the ocean. Shortly they came to another land, where they seemed to hear the fierce shouting of demons, so they dared not stay. A little later they came to a house on an island which had two entrances—one from the sea and one on the land. Into the fomer, great salmon swam and were captured. Maelduin and his men went into the house by way of the island, took of the salmon and ate, but the inmates of the house did not make themselves known. Once more they sailed on, and hunger came upon them. As they passed another shore, Maelduin seized a huge branch from a tree. He held it upright for many days, and at last it bloomed and the blossoms turned to fruit like apples. Maelduin and his men feasted on these apples for many days.

They had many other adventures also. In some places there were strange monsters. In others the ground was hot beneath their feet. Elsewhere they found a wondrous feast made ready for them in a house rich with jewelry and precious things. Only a cat guarded the mansion, but when one of the men attempted to carry off a necklace, he was immediately consumed to ashes. Once they came to a region of the underworld, where frightful creatures and terrible ogres confronted them. In one place all the inhabitants were wailing, and when a member of Maelduin's crew landed on the island he too began to wail and knew not why. On another island there was eternal laughter and rejoicing. The dweller on one lofty island entertained them well. She gave them a sweet wine to drink, and they slept for three days and then found themselves on their own boat, far from sight of land. In similar fashion a fortress in which dwelt a fairy lady suddenly disappeared from view, and once they saw beneath them in the sea a beautiful country where lived a dreadful beast that devoured whomever it could lay its claws upon.

They beheld many other marvels, and at last they came back to the place where dwelt the slayers of Maelduin's father. But the inhabitants welcomed them, and Maelduin took no vengeance. He returned to his own district again and there related the wonders he had seen. And Aed, the chief poet of Ireland, wrote down the adventures of Maelduin, that men might wonder at them forever.

King Arthur

Of all the heroes of the Celtic race none has won renown so great as has King Arthur, who (as the legends tell us) ruled over Britain. He was the son of Uther Pendragon, and for a time lived unknown. Yet when the appointed day arrived, he pulled forth a great sword from a stone wherein it seemed fixed immovably. So he proved himself worthy and destined to be king.

He took as wife the beautiful Guinevere, and around him he gathered many brave and noble knights. Each day they assembled at the Table Round, where might be seated fifty knights sworn and true. All the seats were assigned to warriors saving only one—the Siege Perilous. On that was written the warning that none should sit there except a knight altogether pure in heart; and in time Sir Galahad dared seat himself there.

Day by day King Arthur held court, and to him came many with favors they sought or with wrongs they wished to have righted. Then Arthur would listen to their plea, and if it seemed just to him, he would send forth a knight with the petitioner and the knight would continue on his task until all was well again. So went forth the greatest of King

Ancient manuscript showing an adventure
of King Arthur's knights

Arthur's knights—Sir Lancelot; and so too went forth on
quests Sir Gareth, Sir Percival and many another.

Greatest of the quests of King Arthur's knights was the
quest for the Holy Grail. This was a chalice from which
Jesus was said to have drunk at the last supper, and the
legend said that only to the eyes of the wholly pure would
it ever be revealed. Many knights went in quest of it,
although Arthur opposed their journeyings, for he felt that
only to a few of them could the sight of the Grail be
granted. The rest only wasted their time. Galahad indeed
beheld it, but to most of the others the quest was a vain
one. Meanwhile the kingdom of Arthur fell into disorder.

At last, after many brave wars and after many great and
noble deeds, the rule of Arthur came to an end. By the
treachery of his own nephew, Sir Modred, and by the
disloyalty of Lancelot, came ruin. In a mightly battle at
Lyonnesse all the Round Table fell, save one knight, Sir
Bedivere. King Arthur himself was severely wounded. He
bade Sir Bedivere cast his famous sword, Excalibur, into a
lake near by; and a fairy hand came forth and grasped it.
Shortly afterwards a wonderful barge, with three queens
sitting silent on the deck, came and took Arthur away. It
was believed that he dwelt in the paradise called Avalon (or
Avilion), and that some day he would come and rule once
more.

Arthur learns of Excalibur—
painting by Aubrey Beardsley

The Mabinogion

Most of the stories that have just been told are current chiefly in Ireland, although that of Ossian may be heard in Scotland. However, that of Arthur is to be found all over the Celtic world. Variations of these tales occur also in Wales; and from this district of Britain comes the *Mabinogion*—a great storehouse of legends. A "mabinogi" was a story which every apprentice bard was required to know. This particular volume contains the "four branches of the mabinogi"—that is, four such tales.

The first of the stories tells how Pwyll became a king in Annwn, the land of chaos, the Other World of the Welsh; how, by a clever trick, he won his bride; how their son, Pryderi, was born, and mysteriously stolen; how his mother was falsely punished for having brought about his disappearance, and how he was recovered and restored on the night of the first of May. In the second "branch" Pryderi is grown up and married. He joins himself to Bran at Harlech and assists that god and the king in an attack upon Ireland, at the close of which the Irish are defeated, although only a few of the Welsh remain alive. Bran himself is wounded with a poisoned spear, and in his agony orders the others to cut off his head and bury it under a tower in London. It is interred with the eyes facing France, that no foreign foe may come unobserved to Britain. Arthur in later years, however, removes it, scorning to hold the island other than by valor.

In the third division a friend of Pryderi marries the latter's mother, apparently ever youthful. Then they and Pryderi and his wife become fugitives, for their kingdom has been taken from them by the Children of Don (Dana). They live a nomadic life, and Pryderi and his mother are spirited away by magic, but are brought back by the craft of Manawyddan (Manannan).

The fourth "branch" deals chiefly with the Children of Don, who are ruled by Math, the brother of Don. Gwydion, who has already been mentioned, plays an important part in the story. He is a kindly character who helps his friend and his people. Yet at the end it is he that is responsible for the death of Pryderi.

In other portions of the *Mabinogion* tales of King Arthur and his court are told, with many variations from those that are told elsewhere.

The Little People

When one people is conquered by another, a curious phenomenon sometimes takes place. As the conquered people shrink into the background they take their gods with them. Instead, however, of being mighty and powerful, as they once were, these deities shrink in glory even as their worshipers shrink—and they become the "Little People," as the Irish call them. In other words, they diminish from gods dwelling on high mountains or in great palaces and dwindle into the fairy folk, so minute as not to be visible at all, except to eyes specially endowed to see them. Their home is a tiny mound in a meadow or a hollow in a green glen.

Almost all lands have their fairy folk, but nowhere do they dwell in greater number and variety than in Ireland, where the imagination of the people has always lovingly cherished them. The special name they have in Gaelic is *sheehogue,* a diminutive of *shee* in the more familiar term, *banshee.* One hears of them under other skies as elves, brownies, gnomes, goblins, kobolds, kelpies, nixies, peris, pixies, sylphs, and trolls. One special kind of Irish fairy is the *leprechaun,* or fairy shoemaker, who has by his trade grown very rich. Occasionally one may catch a glimpse of him in a cellar or out on the fields. If you can manage to steal up on him and snatch away his cap, he will grant you any wish to get it back. But he is very sly, and has often been known to fool mortals who have stolen his cap and to get away without granting a wish.

Sometimes a circle of withered grass may be seen on a lawn. There, the night before, the fairies probably danced merrily. Sometimes bright sparks are seen in the woods by

"Fairy changeling"

night. It is only the fairies lighting up their revels. The fairies have three great festivals during the year—May Eve, Midsummer Eve, and November Eve. The first two are gay holidays; the last is a time of gloom, and then they dance only with ghosts.

Sometimes mortals may associate with the Wee Folk, but usually only at great peril. Once in a while, according to legend, the fairies steal a mortal child and substitute one of their own infants for it—a "fairy changeling," who may at any time return to its own people.

PRACTICAL APPLICATIONS

Myths in Literature

The myths of the Celts have fared much more fortunately in English and American literature than have the myths of the Germans. Their influence has been more powerful and more apparent. One portion of Celtic mythology, that dealing with King Arthur and the quest of the Grail, has figured in English literature since the time of Geoffrey of Monmouth, whose book on the kings of Britain in the twelfth century was the first of a still unclosed series of works to handle this theme. Since his time Spenser, Tennyson, William Morris, Lowell, Swinburne, Richard Hovey, Edwin Arlington Robinson, and many others have treated it. At one time Milton meditated writing an epic on King Arthur, and even made an outline for the proposed poem. So "mystic Uther's son" is in many ways the most important single theme in English literature.

Celtic myth may be regarded as fortunate in another respect. For more than a century there has been a Celtic renaissance or revival. In large part this is due to the fact that in the eighteenth century an extraordinary book by James Macpherson appeared—his account of Ossian. This deeply influenced not only English literature, but all the literatures of Europe, even though it has been shown that Macpherson himself invented stories that he attributed to ancient bards.

The attention which Macpherson directed to Celtic literature has resulted in a remarkable series of historical studies, in the writing down of many stories hitherto handed on from generation to generation only by word of mouth, and in the composition of innumerable poems, dramas, and romances.

Among the most illuminating of the studies were Matthew Arnold's lectures *On the Study of Celtic Literature*. Arnold showed that English literature owed to Celtic

312

influence much of its gift for style, considerable of the melancholy spirit that pervades it, and nearly all of what he called the "natural magic" of its poetry. This last quality is to be found particularly in the ability to render with wonderful felicity the magical and weird charm of nature. He contrasted Saxon names of places (Weathersfield, Shalford), with the penetrating, lofty beauty of Celtic names (Velindra, Tintagel, Carnarvon). He contrasted, too, the gift of being, sometimes Greek in his clear realism, and other times Celtic in aërialness, magic and charm.

Ireland witnessed a truly extraordinary rebirth of this Celtic spirit, and Irish poets have gone back eagerly to the old myths of their race and retold them in English (some of them in Gaelic) in a very beautiful way. William Butler Yeats may especially be mentioned among the leaders in this revival.

As has been suggested, nowhere are the fairy folk more enticing and delectable than in Ireland and in Irish poetry, but the story-tellers and poets of many other lands have written excellently of the Little People. In our own literature, for example, we have had quaint fancies from Joseph Rodman Drake and William Cullen Bryant. In English literature Shakespeare created sprites that dance forever in his *A Midsummer Night's Dream* and *The Tempest*. Milton has references to the fairy people in *L'Allegro* and *Il Penseroso*. An odd use of tiny spirits of the air and water, fire and earth was made by Alexander Pope in *The Rape of the Lock*. Further amusing and beautiful details about fairies have been gathered by Robert Herrick in a number of his poems.

Specific Literary References

What do the following references mean? Where a word or phrase is italicized, explain only the word or phrase.
  1. Lay your ear close to the hill.
     Do you not catch the tiny clamor,
     Busy click of an elfin hammer,
     Voice of the *leprechaun* singing shrill
     As he merrily plies his trade?—*Allingham*
  2. Sage beneath a spreading oak
     Sat the *druid*, hoary chief.—*Cowper*

3. To the island-valley of *Avilion*,
   Where falls not hail, or rain or any snow,
   Nor ever wind blows loudly.—*Tennyson*
4.   *Lancelot* came,
   Reputed the best knight and goodliest man.
                     —*Tennyson*
5. Arm'd knights go forth to redress wrongs; some in
   quest of the *Holy Grail.—Whitman.*
6. Altar-fires twinkle at *Stonehenge.—Allen*
7. Up the airy mountain
   Down the rushy glen,
   We daren't go a-hunting
   For fear of *Little Men.—Allingham*
8. Gleams like a glorious emerald *Guinevere.*
                     —*Swinburne*
9. So all day long the noise of battle roll'd
   Among the mountains by the winter sea;
   Until *King Arthur's Table,* man by man,
   Had fall'n in Lyonnesse about their lord,
   King Arthur.—*Tennyson*
10. It was before the time of the great war
    Over the *White-Horned Bull* and the *Brown
    Bull.—Yeats*

Suggestions for Oral or Written Composition

1. Which of the cycles summarized in this chapter do
you like best? Why? Tell the episode that particularly
pleased you.

2. Select a hero of Celtic myth and imagine him visiting
the world of today. Of what things would he approve or
disapprove? What aspect of our life, in your opinion, would
astonish him most?

3. Write another incident for the voyage of Maelduin
and describe some wonder he beheld.

4. Sketch the character of Achilles and that of
Cuchulain. Compare and contrast the two heroes.

5. Compare King Arthur's knights and the state
troopers of our own day.

Word Study

1. Look up the following words in a mythological dictionary and practice the correct pronunciation.
   Ossian, Fenian, Manannan, Cuchulain, Maev, Connaught, Guinevere, Modred, *Mabinogion*, leprechaun.
2. The "Siege Perilous" in which Galahad sat is obviously an odd term. Look up *siege* in the dictionary and give the meaning of the word as it is used here.
3. *Titan* and *Titaness* in Greek mythology refer to gigantic, superhuman beings; and that is how the adjective *Titanic* gets its meaning. But Titania, in Shakespeare's *A Midsummer Night's Dream*, was a tiny creature, queen of the fairies. What passage in this chapter explains the change in size?
4. What does *cycle* mean when applied to stories? What is the meaning of *saga*? What is the meaning of *Mabinogion*?

Questions for Review

1. Who were the Celts?
2. Where may their descendants be found today?
3. What were the traits of the ancient Celts?
4. How has information as to their gods come down to us?
5. What is stone worship?
6. Who were the druids?
7. What did they teach?
8. Name the six groups of Celtic legends that still survive.
9. Who were some of the gods and heroes that appear in the *Cycle of the Invasions?*
10. Who were the Tuatha De Danann?
11. How do they still survive?
12. In which cycle appears the hero Cuchulain?
13. To what order did he belong?

14. Why was he so called?
15. Who was Queen Maev?
16. What possession of Ulster did she desire?
17. What great deeds did Cuchulain perform?
18. How was he slain?
19. Who was Finn?
20. What was the name of his son? of his grandson?
21. What were the latter's great achievements?
22. What were the tests set a man who wished to join the Fianna?
23. Who was Maelduin?
24. Why did he set out on his voyage?
25. What were some of the marvels he beheld?
26. Where did King Arthur reign?
27. Who was his wife?
28. What was the Table Round?
29. Who was the greatest of his knights? the purest?
30. On what quest did his knights set forth?
31. How did the rule of Arthur come to an end?
32. To what land does the *Mabinogion* belong?
33. Who are some of the characters in its stories?
34. How is the existence of fairies sometimes explained?
35. What is a leprechaun?
36. By what signs may one know where the little people have been?
37. What are their three great festivals?

Reading List

Descriptive Works

Arnold, Matthew: *On the Study of Celtic Literature*
Cæsar, Julius: *The Gallic War*, book v, 11-20
Curtin, Jeremiah: *Myths and Folklore of Ireland*
MacCulloch, John A.: *Celtic Mythology*
Rolleston, T.W.: *Myths and Legends of the Celtic Race*
Squire, Charles: *The Mythology of Ancient Britain and Ireland*

Poems and Plays

Ferguson, Samuel: *Lays of the Western Gael*
Robinson, Lennox: *The Golden Treasury of Irish Verse*
Tennyson, Alfred: *The Voyage of Mældune*
Wordsworth, William: *Glen-Almain*
Yeats, W.B.: *Baile and Aillinn—On Baile's Strand—The Old Age of Queen Maev—The Song of Wandering Ængus—The Wanderings of Oisin—Under the Moon*

Novels and Tales

Bishop, Farnham, and A.G. Brodeur: *The Altar of the Legion*
Colum, Padraic: *The Voyagers*
Jacobs, Joseph: *The Book of Wonder Voyages*
Kipling, Rudyard: *Puck o' Pook's Hill—Rewards and Fairies*
Lamprey, Louise: *Children of Ancient Britain*
O'Duffy, Eimar: *King Goshawk and the Biros*
Stephens, James: *The Crock of Gold*
Yeats, W.B.: *Irish Fairy and Folk Tales*

The Arthurian Cycle

Emerson, Ralph Waldo: *Merlin*
French, Allen: *Sir Marrok*
Hovey, Richard: *The Birth of Galahad*
Lowell, James Russell: *The Vision of Sir Launfal*
Millay, Edna St. Vincent: *Elaine*
Morris, William: *The Defense of Guinevere*
Robinson, Edwin Arlington: *Lancelot*
Swinburne, Algernon Charles: *The Tale of Balen*

Fairy Lore

Bryant, William Cullen: *The Little People of the Snow*
Drake, Joseph Rodman: *The Culprit Fay*
Herrick, Robert: *Oberon's Feast*
Hopper, Nora: *The Fairy Fiddler*
Pope, Alexander: *The Rape of the Lock*
Shakespeare, William: *A Midsummer Night's Dream*
Yeats, W.B.: *The Land of Heart's Desire*

Why could Easter Island be a myth-maker's paradise?

Conclusion: Other Applications of Mythology

*The gods, the goddesses, and the demigods
the heroes, Titans, and spirits of good
and evil are the pageant of eternity.*

Haniel Long

Early Theories

Although we know that myths were
the attempts of primitive peoples to explain the world
around them, scientists have been trying to find a more
specific explanation of mythmaking and to classify the
myths of all nations according to the themes they treat and
the basis of their plots. The ancient Greeks, the earliest
people to develop a true sense of science, in very early

318

times began to investigate the origin of the myths which were their religion. As far back as the fourth century B.C. a Greek named Euhemerus, a native of Messene, arrived at some conclusions concerning the nature of the gods, but did not dare express them directly. So he invented a story. He said that in the course of a voyage he had discovered an island called Panchaia in the Indian Ocean. Here he had found a number of inscriptions which showed that the principal gods of Greece were really only earthborn beings, who had performed such heroic deeds that they had been deified after death. This theory of Euhemerus brought down upon him many reproaches and accusations from those who still piously worshiped the old gods.

But his theory has persisted through the ages, and is sometimes called "euhemerism." It was adopted in ancient times by many eminent men, among whom were the historian Polybius and the great church father St. Augustine. Following the thought of Euhemerus, Greek writers said that Æolus was an ancient mariner, the Cyclopes were savages inhabiting Sicily, Atlas was an astronomer, and Scylla a fast-sailing pirate. During the eighteenth century French writers made similar applications of euhemerism. In the nineteenth century Gladstone employed it in his treatment of Greek mythology.

Another theory was advanced by the famous philologist and Orientalist, Friedrich Max Müller; namely, that mythology was only a disease of language. That is, the gender or sex of words in time created in the mind of primitive peoples an idea of personality, which was gradually extended into the notion of godhood. Thus *der Mond* in German is masculine, *luna* in Latin is feminine. A moon masculine in gender would give in time an idea of a male deity of the moon; a moon feminine in gender would suggest a female deity. He also showed that there was a close connection among the Greeks, Romans, Germans, Celts, and Hindus, whose languages and mythologies resembled one another.

Later mythology was explained largely in the light of what is called *anthropology*: the study of man in all his relations and aspects. The anthropologist makes a detailed study of uncivilized life to help him learn what the beginnings of mankind were. Anthropology has shown that the myths of the Greeks and Romans, and many others with a high state of culture are not essentially different from those of other cultures, and that all mythologies arise out of the same needs and often employ similar plots.

It is generally thought today that myths go back to the time when early man, looking around his universe with awe, endowed trees, stones, mountains, and clouds with the same sort of life which he himself possessed. This earliest faith is called *animism,* and was found in many parts of the world. Another early belief was *fetishism:* the notion that certain inanimate objects are inhabited by spirits who have power to ward off evil, destroy enemies, and produce prosperity. Fetishism, in the worship of stones, wooden figures and beads, still exists among some African tribes.

Totemism is also widely spread among primitive peoples. A totem is an animal, bird or plant worshiped by a family or clan who regard it as its original ancestor. Many peoples, all over the surface of the earth, show the influence of totem-worship, although it is best known in connection with the American Indian, from whose language the word *totem* is derived.

These various ideas—hero-worship, gender in language, belief in spirits, worship of inanimate objects, and the deification of totems—probably account for the existence of the gods and goddesses of most mythologies. Possibly another element is deliberate invention by poets, whose imagination enlarged upon the mythical stories, and by moralists, who found lessons and allegories in such myths.

Scientists have classified myths. Among almost all peoples are found myths which explain the creation and origin of man, myths which tell of a place of reward and a place of punishment, myths which describe a great flood, the sun, the moon, important heroes, beasts, the soul and death, and myths of journeys through the underworld. There is a similarity, too, in the myths which account for arts and inventions, customs and rites.

There are, also, well-defined groups of deities. In almost all mythologies we find war gods, weather gods, wind gods, thunder gods, gods of agriculture, gods of the chase, and gods of death. Often one set of deities is described as being displaced by another set, and the displacement is accounted for in various ways—by one nation's conquering another, by the change from the hunting stage to the agricultural stage, and by a general advance in the power to reason.

Later Mythmaking

The mythmaking faculty did not cease after primitive or ancient times. Poets still love to make myths, and often create figures equal to the best of the ancient world.

No poet, for example, has made more beautiful figures of a mythical sort than did Shelley in *Prometheus Unbound*. In this great drama he mingled deities of the Greeks and some of his own imagining. Another mind strongly endowed with the mythmaking faculty was that of William Blake, who with mystic fervor created a whole pantheon of superhuman persons. Some fanciful moderns have endowed this or that city, or this or that river with a presiding deity. Milton, in his *Comus,* tells how a gentle nymph, named Sabrina, fleeing the mad pursuit of her enraged stepmother, sought refuge in the Severn River, and how the god Nereus transformed her out of pity into a goddess of the stream. She often helps the herds that stray along her banks, and is filled with kindly thoughts of maidens such as herself. To her the good Spirit sings:

> Sabrina fair,
> Listen where thou art sitting,
> Under the glassy, cool, translucent wave,
> In twisted braids of lilies knitting
> The loose train of thy amber-dropping hair;
> Listen for dear honor's sake,
> Goddess of the silver lake,
> Listen and save!

A myth of a city is to be attributed to Washington

Walt Disney's animated cartoon, "Peter Pan"

Irving, whose character Diedrich Knickerbocker (appearing in *The Sketch-Book* and in *Diedrich Knickerbocker's History of New York*) is the original of *Father Knickerbocker,* that well-known figure who typifies the metropolis of America, and who has been the model for many similar patron saints of other American cities. Irving, moreover, is responsible for still another myth, that of Rip Van Winkle, the old Dutchman who sleeps twenty years at a stretch and awakens to find the world altogether changed. Maeterlinck has created the myth of the *Bluebird of Happiness,* and Sir James M. Barrie the appealing figure of *Peter Pan.*

Among other myths that are widely known may be mentioned two more: that of the *Fountain of Youth,* which Ponce de León and many others have sought through the ages; and that of Santa Claus or Kris Kringle, who was brought over from "the old country," and who has become the patron saint of children.

Just one other author may be described here—Lord Dunsany, who has shown an astonishing gift for creating a whole company of gods, all most plausibly pictured. For the most part these gods belong to a group which Dunsany calls the "Gods of Pegana." It is thus, for example, that his tale of *When the Gods Slept* begins:

> **All the gods were sitting in Pegana, and Their slave, Time, lay idle at Pegana's gate with nothing to destroy, when They thought of worlds, worlds large and round**

and gleaming, and little silver moons. Then (who knoweth when?), as the gods raised their hands making the sign of the gods, the thoughts of the gods became worlds and silver moons. And the worlds swam to Pegana's gate to take their places in the sky, to ride at anchor forever, each where the gods had bidden. And because they were round and big and gleamed all over the sky, the gods laughed and shouted and all clapped their hands. Then upon earth the gods played out the game of the gods, the game of life and death, and on the other worlds They did a secret thing, playing a game that is hidden.

Mythology and Scientific Terms

To scientists, always in need of good descriptive terms for the new things they are constantly discovering, mythology has been a gold mine. Again and again they have gone to these old legends for the names of birds, butterflies, insects, fishes, minerals, and animals. The following list will give a brief idea of the influence of mythology on the field of science.

Amazon: (1) Amazon ant—a kind of ant (2) Amazon stone—a bright green feldspar, used as a gem
Apollo: A variety of butterfly found in Europe
Argonaut: A cuttlefish (paper nautilus) found in the Mediterranean
Balder: Balder's-blood—the name of a flower found in Norway
Calliope: A humming bird of the western United States and Mexico
Cyclops: Cyclopidæ—a family of crustaceans, with a large eye
Diana: (1) A West-African monkey, with a white mark across the forehead (2) A variety of butterfly, found in North America
Europa: One of the satellites of the planet Jupiter
Freya: Freyalite—a mineral found in Norway

Hamadryad: Another name for the king cobra
Helen: (1) Helenium—a genus of the aster family, bearing yellow flowers (2) Helenin—a drug obtained from elecampane root
Hercules: (1) A large northern constellation (2) Hercules beetle—found in America (3) Hercules'-club—another name for the pepperwood tree
Juno: (1) Juno's-tears—name of a European flower (2) Junonia—a genus of butterfly, found in the U.S.
Jupiter: (1) One of the planets (2) Jupiter fish—the gibbar (3) Jupiter's flower—the columbine
Medusa: (1) A jellyfish (2) Medusa's head—a cluster of stars (3) Medusa's-head—a species of fungus
Mercury: (1) One of the planets (2) A silver-white liquid metal, often used in thermometers (3) Dog's mercury—the name of a plant
Odin: Odinite—the name of a mineral
Penelope: Penelopinæ:—a subfamily of birds, related to the curassows
Phaëthon: The genus of tropic birds
Tantalus: Tantalum—a white metallic element, which was isolated only after great difficulty; hence the name
Thor: Thorium—a gray metallic element, used in the manufacture of gas mantles
Titan: (1) Titanic acid (2) Titanite—a mineral used sometimes as a gem (3) Titanium—a gray metallic element, used in making certain kinds of steel

Mythology in Advertising

Examples have already been given to show that it is not only the poets and other authors who have made use of the ancient myths of Greece and Rome or the tales of Germany and Ireland. The modern advertising person has frequently found in these narratives a stimulus to his or her imagination, an impetus to invention, and a storehouse of apt reference and allusions.

However, mythology in advertising is not confined to the modern space age or the electronic age of television,

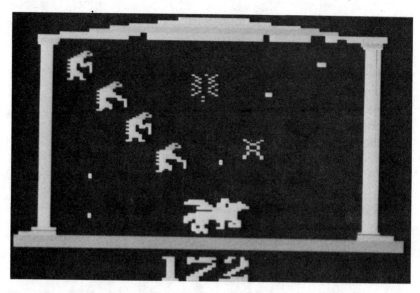

"No Escape," a new video game for *Imagic* steps right out of mythology.
It shows the winged horse Pegasus carrying Jason
from one dangerous encounter to another.

computers, calculators, and video games. Copywriters of
big business firms have always been aware that educated
persons are familiar with such myths and stories, and they
have often used them to point out a business moral or drive
home a selling point. If you were to go to a library and
research newspapers and magazines of several different
periods, you would see how numerous such references to
mythology have always been.

For example: an advertisement for the Atlas Portland
Cement Company opened with these words:

> **A thousand years before Helen brought disaster to
> Troy, a Sea King of Crete built himself a lordly palace at
> Knossos. The architect, in a moment of sentiment, forgot
> the procession of warriors and scenes from the arena with
> which the stucco walls were decorated and, in a panel of
> the great hall, he painted a picture of a little Minoan boy
> gathering flowers. The colors are as fresh as if laid on
> yesterday; the stucco is smooth and unbroken, although
> the hand which smoothed its surface has been dust for
> three thousand years.**

Other Applications of Mythology **325**

Or again, somewhat modifying the ancient story:

> HESPERIAN APPLES: **In Greek mythology the Garden of Hesperides was the abode of the setting sun. There golden apples grew on a tree guarded by a sleepless dragon. To secure the coveted fruit Herakles risked his life in mortal combat with the monster. This was a risk worth taking if the apples were as delicious as those served at** CHILDS.

The Colonial Fireplace Company used the Greek tale of the origin of fire to make its implements for the hearth more attractive:

> **In the beginning only the Immortals had Fire. Prometheus looked with compassion on the cheerless creatures of earth. In defiance of the gods he stole Fire from the heavens and brought it to earth in the pith of a reed.**
> **"Now will man overthrow us," said the Immortals. And they chained Prometheus to Mount Caucasus and sent a vulture to feed forever on his liver. But man from that day has treasured this miracle that lifted him above the shivering brutes.**

Postage stamps of all countries have often been adorned with mythological persons. Mercury appears again and again, especially on Greek stamps, but one may also find Apollo, Penelope, Ulysses, Ceres, and other mythological figures on various stamps.

Myths and the Constellations

All peoples on the face of the earth, filled with wonder at the stars and seeking to explain their existence and curious groupings, have told mythical stories about the heavenly bodies, and have by various legends attempted to account for the presence of the sun by day, and of the moon and stars by night.

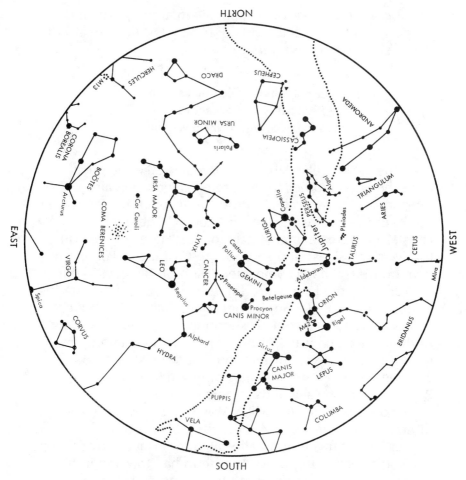

Stars and Planets—(a map of the sky)

Most numerous, of course, are the stories of the sun and moon, some of which have already been referred to—in particular, the legends of Apollo and Diana. The magnificent constellation Orion, for example, with the three blazing stars that make a belt, will be recalled as connected with the giant whom Diana unwittingly slew.

The legend of Perseus was used by the Greeks to account for several constellations and stars. The hero was so loved by the gods that on his death they transported him and Andromeda and the latter's mother Cassiopeia to the heavens as stars. Cassiopeia appears in a group which is supposed to be her chair. It is of her that Milton speaks in *Il Penseroso* when he refers to

> **That starred Ethiop queen that strove**
> **To set her beauty's praise above**
> **The sea nymphs, and their powers offended.**

Often the twelve labors of Hercules, like the great achievements of other heros, are explained as really representing the traveling of the sun through the year: one thinks of the twelve signs of the Zodiac. There is a constellation, incidentally, named after Hercules. Pegasus, too, is in the skies; and so, too, are Castor and Pollux, the twin brothers who accompanied Jason on his quest—they are called by the Latin word for "twins," *gemini.* Sagittarius, a southern constellation, is sometimes called *The Archer,* and is pictured as a centaur shooting an arrow. According to the Greeks, he was Chiron, placed by Jove among the stars. Orpheus' lyre, Europa's bull, and the ship *Argo* are also remembered in the names of heavenly bodies. The Pleiades were the seven daughters of Atlas.

In ancient times the Milky Way was believed to lead directly to the throne of Zeus-Jupiter. One legend accounted for this bright pathway in the heavens by saying it was the road along which Phaëthon had traveled in his mad course over the sky. Both the Chinese and the Japanese regard the Milky Way as a silver celestial river. The Norsemen believed that it was the path along which the souls of the departed went to Valhalla. To the Algonquin Indians it was "the path of souls," leading to the villages in the sun—the stars were bright lights and campfires guiding the spirits on their journey to the Happy Hunting Grounds. In northern India it was the "path of the snake," and in ancient Wales it was the "silver street leading to Caer Groyden," the castle where dwelt the king of the fairies.

PRACTICAL APPLICATIONS

References to Mythology in Literature

What do the following references mean? Where a word or phrase is italicized, explain only the word or phrase.

1. Or keeping watch among those starry *Seven*,
   Old Atlas' children.—*Keats*
2. A dignity equivalent to *Cassiopeia's chair*.—*Lamb*
3. The centaur, *Sagittarius*, am I. . . .
   With sounding hoofs across the earth I fly.
   —*Longfellow*
4. These be the great *Twin Brethren*,
   To whom the Dorians pray.—*Macaulay*
5. Those three stars of the airy giant's zone
   That glitter burnished by the frosty dark.—*Tennyson*

Suggestions for Oral or Written Composition

1. Give a talk on "Origins of Myths."
2. Invent a "modern myth," dealing, for example, with the origin of some invention, the name of a country, or some allegorical figure like Uncle Sam or John Bull.
3. Select a group of stars. Try to think of some object the group resembles (like an automobile or a steam engine), and then devise a myth to account for its presence in the skies.
4. Rewrite an advertisement in your favorite magazine so as to introduce an effective reference to mythology.
5. Prepare a talk on the use of myths by musical composers, or on the use of myths in art.

Word Study

1. Look up the following words in a mythological dictionary and practice the correct pronunciation.

Euhemerus, anthropology, fetishism, Sabrina, Maeterlinck, Ponce de León, Pleiades, Gemini.
2. Tell what *euhemerism* is.
3. Look up the word *mythopœic* in the dictionary. See if you can then explain this sentence by Fiona Macleod: "The mythopœic faculty is not only a primitive instinct, but a spiritual necessity." Does it mean that people still ought to make up myths?

Questions for Review

1. How did Euhemerus endeavor to explain myths?
2. How did Max Müller explain myths?
3. What science has recently studied mythology?
4. What has it shown?
5. What is animism? fetishism? totemism?
6. What are some classes of myths? of gods?
7. Who are some modern authors of myths?
8. How is mythology employed in advertising?
9. How are the stars connected with mythology?

Reading List

Bacon, Francis: *The Wisdom of the Ancients*
Barrie, Sir James M.: *Peter Pan and Wendy*
Butterworth, Hezekiah: *The Fountain of Youth*
Dunsany, Edward John: *Book of Wonder*
France, Anatole: *Putois*
Grahame, Kenneth: *The Wind in the Willows*
Hudson, W.H.: *Green Mansions*
Irving, Washington: *Rip Van Winkle*
Olcott, W.T.: *The Star Lore of All Ages*
O'Neill, Eugene: *The Fountain*
Procter, Mary: *The Young Folks' Book of the Heavens*
Ruskin, John: *The Queen of the Air*
Thomas, Edith M.: *Ponce de León*

REVIEW MATERIAL

References to Mythology in Literature

What do the following references mean? Where a word or phrase is italicized, explain only the word or phrase.

1. 'Tis Apollo comes leading
   His choir, the *Nine.—Arnold*

2. They see the *centaurs* . . .
   Reared proudly, snuffing
   The mountain wind.—*Arnold*

3. Hans Sachs, in describing *Chaos,* said it was so pitchy dark that even the very cats ran against each other!—*Coleridge*

4. She heaved a sigh—indeed, her breast was a very cave of *Æolus* that morning—and stepped across the room on tiptoe.—*Hawthorne*

5. O'er the long hills of folded Arcady
   Fleets *Artemis,* a-hunting of the deer.—*Hewlett*

6. In gulfs enchanted, where the *siren* sings,
   And coral reefs lie bare,
   Where the cold sea maids rise to sun their streaming hair.—*Holmes*

7. Meanwhile before the palace of *Odysseus* the suitors were making merry.—*Homer*

8. *Zeus* that rolls the clouds of heaven.—*Homer*

9. I will not have the mad Clytie,
   Whose head is turn'd by the sun.—*Hood*

10. Nor does *Apollo* keep his bow continually drawn.
    —*Horace*

11. Of *Pan* we sing, the best of leaders Pan,
    That leads the *naiads* and the *dryads* forth.—*Jonson*

12. Like a *Silenus* on an antique vase.—*Keats*

13. Ah, *Zephyrus,* art here, and *Flora* too!—*Keats*

14. Dame *Helen* caused a grievous fray.—*Kilmer*

15. Silence stiller than the shore
    Swept by *Charon's* stealthy oar.—*Knowles*

16. *Gorgons,* and *hydras,* and *chimeras* dire may
    reproduce themselves in the brain of superstition,
    but they were there before. The archetypes are in
    us, and eternal.—*Lamb*
17. Visions of love, of *Cupids,* of *Hymens!*—*Lamb*
18. Had he asked of me, what song the *sirens* sang, or
    what name *Achilles* assumed when he hid himself
    among women, I might have hazarded a "wide
    solution."—*Lamb*
19. We occasionally caught glimpses of *Tartarus.*—*Lamb*
20. *Cerberus* held agape his triple jaws.—*Landor*
21. To the two powers that soften virgin hearts,
    Eros and *Aphrodite.*—*Landor*
22. [Hermes to Pluto:]
    From Zeus who rules with you the threefold realm I
    come.—*Ledoux*
23. Let not our town be large, remembering,
    That little Athens was the *Muses'* home.—*Lindsay*
24. *Fauns* with youthful *Bacchus* follow.—*Longfellow*
25. *Pomona* loves the orchard,
    And *Liber* loves the vine.—*Macaulay*
26. Apollo hunted Daphne so
    Only that she might laurel grow;
    And Pan did after Syrinx speed
    Not as a nymph, but for a reed.—*Marvell*
27. With all the grisly legions that troop
    Under the sooty flag of *Acheron,*
    Harpies and *hydras.*—*Milton*
28. *Bacchus,* that first from out the purple grape
    Crushed the sweet poison of misused wine.
    —*Milton*
29.   I have oft heard
    My mother *Circe* with the *sirens* three,
    Amidst the flowers-kirtled *naiades,*
    Culling their potent herbs and baleful drugs,
    Who, as they sang, would take the prison'd soul,
    And lap it in *Elysium: Scylla* wept,
    And chid her barking waves into attention,
    And fell *Charybdis* murmur'd soft applause.
    —*Milton*

30. Rough *satyrs* danced, and *fauns* with cloven heel
From the glad sound would not be absent
long.—*Milton*

31. Or the unseen *genius* of the wood.—*Milton*

32.   Nature breeds,
Perverse, all monstrous, all prodigious things,
Gorgons, and *hydras,* and *chimeras* dire.—*Milton*

33. As when the wrath of *Jove*
Speaks thunder and the chains of Erebus
To some of *Saturn's* crew.—*Milton*

34.   Hovering dreams,
The fickle pensioners of *Morpheus'* train.—*Milton*

35. What the sage poets, taught by the heavenly *Muse,*
Stories of old in high immortal verse,
Of dire *chimeras* and enchanted isles.—*Milton*

36. With flower-inwoven tresses torn
The *nymphs* in twilight shade of tangled thickets
mourn.—*Milton*

37. That *Orpheus'* self may heave his head
From golden slumber on a bed
Of heap'd *Elysian* flowers, and hear
Such strains as would have won the ear
Of *Pluto* to have quite set free
His half-regain'd *Eurydice.*—*Milton*

38. Straightway he shuts the north wind up in the cave
of *Æolus.*—*Ovid*

39. Her hair was changed to leaves, her arms to
branches.—*Ovid*

40. Then Pallas assumed the form of an old woman.
             —*Ovid*

41. The sea holds the dark-hued gods: tuneful *Triton*
and changeful *Proteus.*—*Ovid*

42. I was wont to behold Queen Elizabeth riding like
Alexander, hunting like *Diana,* walking like *Venus,*
the gentle wind blowing her fair hair about her
pure cheeks, like a *nymph;* sometimes singing like
an angel, sometimes playing like *Orpheus.*—*Raleigh*

43.   Highest queen of state,
Great Juno, comes: I know her by her gait.
             —*Shakespeare*

44.   Now, by *two-headed Janus,*
Nature hath framed strange fellows in her time;
Some that will evermore peep through their eyes,
And laugh, like parrots, at a bagpiper;
And others, of such vinegar aspect,
That they'll not show their teeth in way of smile,
Though *Nestor* swear the jest be laughable.
—*Shakespeare*

45. As huge as high Olympus.—*Shakespeare*

46. Oh Phœbus! hadst thou never given consent
That Phaëthon should check thy fiery steeds,
Thy burning car never had scorched the earth.
—*Shakespeare*

47. To *Phœbus* was not *Hyacinth* so dear,
Nor to himself *Narcissus,* as to both
Thou, Adonais.—*Shelley*

48.   *Bellona,* in that warlike wise
To them appeared, with shield and armor fit.
—*Spenser*

49. Foolhardy as th' *Earth's children,* the which made
Battle against the gods.—*Spenser*

50. Foolish *Narcisse,* that likest the wat'ry shore.
—*Spenser*

Composition Work

A. Brief Descriptions

Describe each of the following in about twenty-five to thirty-five words. (Choose six groups.)

1. Zeus, Hermes, Poseidon, Pluto, Minerva, Daphne, Calypso, Cupid, Venus, Proserpina, Odysseus, Helen.
2. Menelaus, Hyacinthus, Arachne, Atalanta, Meleager, Ceres, Narcissus, Hero, Agamemnon, Argus, Æneas.
3. Charybdis, sirens, Baucis, Phaëthon, Hephæstus, Eumæus, Achilles, Patroclus, Hera, Ganymede, Iris, Dido.

334

4. Pan, satyr, faun, Pomona, Ares, Jupiter, Liber, Telemachus, lotus-eaters, Æolus, Anchises, Polyphemus.
5. Circe, Scylla, Penelope, Ithaca, Troy, Phæcia, Neptune, naiad, Graces, Muses, Niobe, Jason.
6. Pallas Athena, Artemis, Psyche, Pluto, Rhadamanthus, Icarus, Meleager, Mount Olympus, Elysium, Clytie, Æsculapius, Theseus.
7. Tithonus, Orpheus, Herakles, Perseus, Minotaur, Pygmalion, Eros, Leander, Thisbe, Hades, Menelaus, Thetis.
8. Cassandra, Clytemnestra, Medea, Europa, Admetus, Hesperides, Bacchus, Saturn, Father Tiber, Marpessa, Hestia, Echo.
9. Eros, Pyramus, Minos, Cadmus, Diana, Chaos, Epimetheus, Cyclops, Apollo, *Argo*, Nemean lion, Eos.
10. Tantalus, Hebe, Anchises, Hecuba, Nestor, Medusa, Andromache, Andromeda, Romulus, lares, wooden horse, Python.
11. Balder, Thor, Niflheim, Odin, Freya, Loki, Norns, Yggdrasill, Asgard, Valhalla, Siegfried, Beowulf.
12. Druids, King Arthur, Holy Grail, leprechaun, Tuatha De Danann, Manannan, the Dagda, Cuchulain, Ossian, Queen Maev, Oscar, Maelduin.

B. Short Stories

See how well you can tell the following stories.

1. The Theft of Fire and the Coming of Pandora
2. The Disappearance of Proserpina
3. A Visit to Mount Olympus
4. A Visit to the Underworld
5. Aurora and Tithonus
6. The Great Flood
7. Zeus Visits the Earth
8. A Story of Apollo
9. Admetus and Alcestis
10. The Golden Apples
11. The Calydonian Hunt
12. The Slaying of a Monster
13. One Labor of Hercules

14. The Marriage Feast of Thetis
15. The Judgment of Paris
16. The Trojan War
17. The Stratagem of the Wooden Horse
18. An Adventure of Ulysses
19. The Golden Fleece
20. The Wanderings of Æneas
21. Romulus and Remus
22. An Ancient Romance
23. A Tale from Northern Mythology
24. A Tale from Celtic Mythology

C. Factual Presentations

Prepare a report on each of the following.

1. The Origin of Myths
2. Myths and the Stars
3. Myths and Advertising
4. Myths in Art
5. Myths in Literature
6. Do We Make Myths Today?
7. Customs of the Ancient Greeks
8. Customs of the Ancient Romans
9. The *Æneid* of Virgil
10. The Poems of Ovid
11. The Ancient Germans
12. The Ancient Celts
13. Myths in Music
14. The Meaning of Myths
15. The Story in This Book I Like Best

D. Creative Writing

Use your imagination freely and present each of the following:

1. The Diary of Pandora
2. A Speech of Prometheus to Zeus
3. A Monologue of Tantalus
4. A Ghost is Brought before the Three Judges of the Underworld
5. A Letter from Telemachus to Menelaus, after the Slaughter of the Suitors
6. A Thirteenth Labor of Hercules
7. An Adventure of Ulysses that Homer Did Not Chronicle

8. A Conversation of the Sailors about the Bag of Winds—While Ulysses Is Asleep
9. If Pan (or some other god or some goddess) Came to Earth Today
10. A Mythology of My City

E. Advanced Composition

1. If you have any talent in verse writing, compose a poem on a subject selected from mythology—an ode to Mercury, a sonnet to Psyche, a narrative of the adventures of Jason, a monologue of Eurydice, an elegy for Adonis, etc.
2. Tell in the first person, from the point of view of one of the characters, a story from the *Bible,* the *Odyssey,* or the *Æneid.*
3. Discuss the two sides of the character of Achilles as shown in the *Iliad.* Illustrate each and tell whether there is anything like this contrast in the character of Hector.
4. Describe the parting of Hector and Andromache.
5. Describe Helen watching the combat between Menelaus and Paris.
6. Tell about Odysseus among the Phæacians.
7. Narrate the slaying of the suitors.
8. Was the desertion of Dido by Æneas justified?
9. Describe the performance of *Pyramus and Thisbe* before Duke Theseus.
10. Write brief explanations, of not more than a few sentences each, for *Dido, Achilles,* and the *sirens.*
11. State in a few sentences what you know about Medusa, Parnassus, and Pegasus.
12. Write a theme entitled "Riding Pegasus."
13. The ancient idea of a hero.
14. Have you, in your reading from the Greek and Latin classics, found any story that you think especially suitable for modern literary treatment? If you have, explain your choice and suggest how the story might be treated by a modern author. If not, tell what differences you see between ancient and modern life that make it difficult for you to understand the ancients.

15. What interest do you find in the ancient Greek narratives as compared with the modern fiction that you have read? Answer in one or two well-constructed paragraphs, referring to specific narratives.

Word Studies

1. From what names of gods are the following English words derived? Jovial, mercurial, vulcanize, cereal, Herculean, vestal, volcano, martial.
2. What is meant by the following expressions? "An Adonis," "the Midas-touch," "halcyon days," "a sop to Cerberus," "an Elysium," "the riddle of the Sphinx."
3. Find in Greek or Latin mythology names suitable for the following: a rowing club, a debating society, a dramatic society, a literary club, an athletic club, a polo team, a new high school, an outdoors club, a park, a swimming pool, a dog, a cat.
4. Find similar names taken from other mythologies.
5. Explain the following expressions, all common in modern speaking and writing: *a.* cleansing the Augean stables *b.* the heel of Achilles *c.* in the arms of Morpheus *d.* between Scylla and Charybdis *e.* rich as Midas *f.* she was an Amazon. *g.* a follower of Æsculapius *h.* fair as Helen *i.* sly as Ulysses *j.* strong as Hercules
6. Make up lists of the following: *a.* towns named after mythical persons or places *b.* persons part of whose names is that of some mythical person *c.* ships named after classical persons, places, or objects *d.* advertisements that refer to mythology

Comprehension Exercises

A. Questions for Review

1. What story explains the coming of spring? Which

338

explains the origin of a flower? of a star? of diseases? of an insect? of the color of skin of the Ethiopians? of the echo? of a tree?

2. What were some ideas that prevailed among ancient people as to the origin of the world?
3. Give examples of some strange transformations described in myths.
4. In what stories were gods friendly with mortals? In what other stories did they try to harm them?
5. What caused the death of Meleager? Why did Echo speak the last word? What were the Olympic Games? What sons of Apollo were slain by Jove? Who saved Alcestis from death? What were the twelve labors of Hercules? How did Theseus cause his father's death? How did Perseus save Andromeda? Who was the slave of Admetus? How did Orpheus twice lose his wife?
6. Mention five kinds of nymphs. What other deities appear in groups?
7. What gods fought on the side of the Greeks? of the Trojans? Who rendered the greatest service to Ulysses—a god, a goddess, or a mortal? What happened to Agamemnon after the war? to Helen? Who was Telemachus?
8. What are some differences between Greek and Northern mythology? What gods were especially worshiped in Rome?
9. What poets have been especially fond of Greek and Roman myths?
10. Against whom did Apollo have a grudge? Against whom did Apollo and Diana have a grudge? Neptune? Mars? Juno? Venus?
11. In what stories in this volume does a dragon appear?
12. What heroes go on long voyages or quests?
13. What heroes visit the underworld while still alive?
14. In what stories does the influence of women play an important part?
15. In how many stories do the Golden Apples of the Hesperides appear?
16. Why would Argus make a good traffic policeman?

What character in mythology was able to change his appearance at will, and therefore might have made a good actor? Which exploit of Hercules shows that he might have been put in charge of health work?

17. What ancient deity would you pick out to preside over television? bicycle riding? motion pictures? Why?

18. Tuesday, Wednesday, Thursday, and Friday were named after old Germanic deities. What Greek or Roman gods correspond to these deities? Name the days after them, and see if they sound as well.

19. The ancient Greeks had nine Muses, each presiding over her own realm. What new Muses would the present day need, for realms the Greeks knew nothing about?

20. What athletic games of the Greeks are still celebrated today?

B. True/False

1. Prometheus was glad to receive Pandora as his wife.
2. Minerva was the goddess of weaving.
3. As a symbol of his authority, Apollo carried the caduceus.
4. From the very beginning, Venus favored the idea of Cupid's marriage to Psyche.
5. The children of Latona were twins: Apollo and Diana.
6. Proserpina was the goddess of the springtime.
7. It was Juno who changed Io into a heifer.
8. Narcissus rejected the advances of Echo.
9. Sisyphus was tormented in Hades by being chained perpetually to a wheel.
10. Jupiter placed Orpheus among the stars.
11. The mother of Perseus was named Danaë.
12. Ariadne helped Theseus when he set out to battle with the Minotaur.
13. Minerva helped both Jason and Ulysses.

14. Achilles was the son of Thetis and Jupiter.
15. Ulysses proposed an oath to the suitors of Helen.
16. Iphigenia died as a sacrifice on Diana's altar.
17. Patroclus was slain in battle by Æneas.
18. Ulysses reached Ithaca two years after leaving Troy.
19. The father of Æneas died on the journey to Italy.
20. Æneas married the princess Lavinia.

C. Multiple Choice

1. The mænads were followers of Apollo, Pan, Bacchus, Neptune.
2. Pan was the son of Jove, Mercury, Mars, Vulcan.
3. The satyrs had some of the characteristics of a goat, horse, lion, bird.
4. During her stay in the underworld Proserpina ate of a golden apple, a pomegranate, nectar, grapes.
5. Daphne was changed into an oak, a birch, a beech, a laurel.
6. The river of forgetfulness was the Acheron, the Cocytus, the Styx, the Lethe.
7. Perseus rescued Andromeda from a sea monster, a dragon, a lion, a giant.
8. Pegasus was in the service of Apollo, the Muses, Neptune, the wood nymphs.
9. The name of Hercules was used by the ancients for Sicily, Gibraltar, Crete, Sparta.
10. Boreas was the ruler of east, west, north, south wind.
11. Pelias gave up the throne to Jason willingly, by force, on Jason's return with the fleece, because of the wiles of Medea.
12. Paris gave the Golden Apple to Juno, Venus, Minerva.
13. Achilles quarreled with Ajax, Ulysses, Agamemnon, Patroclus.
14. Ulysses tarried seven years with the lotus-eaters, Circe, Calypso, King Æolus.
15. An ally of Æneas was Turnus, Camilla, Evander, Mezentius.

Special Projects

1. Make a mythological scrapbook in which you paste pictures of the gods, each with a line of verse underneath. Include any useful facts about them as well as any advertisements containing references to them.

2. Prepare a "Symposium of the Gods." Imagine that you are on Mount Olympus, and that each member of the class represents a deity. Zeus speaks first, and tells who he is—what powers he has, what his symbols are. Then in turn he calls on each of the others to give a brief soliloquy of description. Perhaps the three Graces will dance, the Muses sing.

3. Similarly, tableaux or living pictures can be prepared, with well-known pictures (like those in this volume) as models.

4. A ballet of the ancient gods of Greece may be performed. Enlist the help of the music teacher, and give your performance before the school. "Echo and Narcissus," for example, would make a fine subject.

5. Many of the old stories, of Greek and other mythologies, offer excellent material for original plays—as writers through the centuries have been well aware. A one-act play (or a good short story) may readily be based on this material. Try writing a simple play on the following themes: *a.* Alcestis and Admetus *b.* Apollo and Marpessa *c.* Pallas Athena and Arachne *d.* The Slaying of the Suitors *e.* Pygmalion and Galatea *f.* Thor in the Home of the Giants

342

Index

cycles, Celtic, 296
Cyclopean (sī-kluh-pē'un), 22
Cyclopes (sī-klō'pēz), 13, 14, 78, 207, 217, 223, 233, 319, 323
Cyclopidæ (sī-klop'ih-dī), 323
Cynthia (sin'thē-uh), 71
Cynthus (sin'thus), 71
cypress of Pluto, ix
Cyprus (sī'prus), 60
Cythera (si-thir'uh), 28
Cytherean (sith-ir'ē-un), the, 28, 31

Dædalus (ded'uh-lus), 37, 47, 48
Dag, 263
Dagda (dag'dah), the, 297, 299
Dahn, Felix, 277
Damon (dā'mun), 155, 157, 158
Dana (dā'nah), 297, 298, 299, 309
Danaë (dan'uh-ē), 142, 143, 148, 157
Danaë, Lament of, Simonides', 157
Danaïdes (duh-nā'uh-dēz), 131, 139
Danaüs (dan'ē-us), 132
Daniel, Samuel, 123, 216, 219
Dante (dan'tē), 6, 137, 141
Danu, 297. See Dana
Daphne (daf'nē), 115, 116, 124, 332
Dardanelles (dar'duh-nelz), 175
David, 158
Davis, W.S., 23, 245
dawn, gods of the, 101-102, 124
Days, the, 75
Dead Pan, The, E.B. Browning's, 123
Death, 81, 134, 226. See Mors and Hel
Deianira (dē-uh-nī'ruh), 168
Deiphobus (dē-if'o-bus), 195, 196
Delos (dē'los), 252
Delphi (del'fī), 30, 82
Delphic sibyl (del'fik-sib'l), 29
Demeter (dē-mē'ter), 14. See Ceres
Dermot, 302
Deucalion (doo-kal'y-on), 19, 254
De Vere, Aubrey, 49, 122
Diana (dī-an'uh), viii, 28, 31, 32, 51, 58, 71, 76, 82, 88, 89, 92, 94, 95, 97, 114, 118, 131, 190, 205, 206, 228, 229, 252, 323, 327, 333
Dido (dī'dō), 124, 222, 225, 233, 234, 251, 254, 257
Dike (dī'kē), 29
Diomedes (dī-ō-mē'dēz), mares of, 164; the Greek hero, 190, 195
Dione (dī-ō'nē), 28
Dionysius (dī-ō-nish'i-us), 155, 156
Dionysus (dī-ō-nī'sus), 99. See Bacchus
Dis, 108. See Pluto
Disraeli (diz-rā'lē), Benjamin, 47
Divine Comedy, Dante's, 137

Dobson, Austin, 216
Dodona (dō-dō'nah), 30
dog's mercury, 324
dogs of Mars, 26
Doliones (dō-lī'ō-nez), 176
Don, 297. See Dana
Doolittle, Hilda ("H.D."), 35, 69, 87, 107, 127, 200, 203, 216, 219, 244
doves of Venus, 253
Dowden, Edward, 46, 141, 157, 159
Dr. Faustus, Marlowe's, 198
dragons, 38, 82, 129, 154, 165, 175, 180, 181, 278, 280, 286, 289, 290, 300, 326
Drake, J.R., 313, 317
drama, Greek, 248
Drayton, Michael, 20
Dream of Fair Women, Tennyson's, 199
druids (droo'ids), 292, 295, 313
Drummond, William, 87, 157
dryads (drī'ads), ix, 101, 105, 331
Dryden, John, 47, 50, 123, 200, 235
Dunsany, Lord, 7, 322, 330
Duty, 162
dwarfs, 263, 279
Dyer, John, 183

eagle of Jupiter, viii, 25, 27
Earthy Paradise, The, Morris', 157, 288
Earth-Mother, the, 3, 334
East Wind, 102
Echo (ek'oh), 118, 124
Egeria (ē-jē'ri-ah), 238
Electra (i-lek'trah), 206
Elis (ē'lis), 164
Elli (el'lē), 272
elves, 264, 310, 314
Elysian (i-lizh'un) Fields, 227, 233; Islands, 99. See Elysium
Elysium (i-lizh'ē-um), 129, 132, 137, 138, 139, 227, 332
Embla, 265
Emerson, R.W., 49, 107, 233, 317
Endymion (en-dim'ē-un), 89, 95, 96, 97
Endymion, Keat's, 31
Eos (ē'os), 101, 105. See Aurora
Epeus (ē'pē-us), 196
Epimetheus (ep-i-mē'thus), 14, 15
Epistole Heroidum, Ovid's, 254
Erato (er'uh-tō), 28
Erebus (er'uh-bus), 129, 333. See Hades
Erin (er'in), 302
Eris, 187
Eros (ir'os), 28. See Cupid
Erymanthian (er-uh-man'thē-un) boar, 164

351

356

ACKNOWLEDGMENTS

Cover photo: "The Horses of Neptune" - Walter Crane/ARTOTHEK
Color photos: Jupiter, Aurora, Jupiter/Ganymede, Satyr, Prometheus, Mercury, Bacchus, Perseus, Medusa, Centaur - Editorial Photo Archives; Diana, Pluto - Ronald Sheridan; Venus - The Bridgeman Art Library; Hercules, Sybil, Aeneas, Round Table, Lancelot - Aspect Picture Library; Theseus, Guinevere - Robert Harding Picture Library; Odin - American Heritage Picture Collection/Universitts Oldsakamling, Oslo; detail of head of Odin - American Heritage Picture Collection/ Musée des Antiquities Nationales, St. Germain en-Laye, Guiley, Lagache; head of Celtic god, Valkyrie pendant- Werner Forman Archive -

Photos within text: Editorial Photocolor Archives; 9, Paul Conklin; 12, National Gallery of Art, The Feeding of the Child Jupiter, Nicolas Poussin, date: c. 1640, Samuel H. Kress Collection; 17, Mary Evans Picture Library; 18, Editorial Photocolor Archives; 24, Photoresources; 27, National Gallery of Canada, Ottawa; 36, Isabella Stewart Gardner Museum; 39, American Heritage Picture Collection; 43, Mary Evans Picture Library; 44, Photoresources; 50, Museum of Art, Carnegie Institute; 52, Editorial Photocolor Archives; 54, Metropolitan Museum of Art; 57, 59, Editorial Photocolor Archives; 61, 61, 64, Museum of Modern Art/Film Stills Archives; 70, Photoresources; 72, 77, Editorial Photocolor Archives; 83, top, Editorial Photocolor Archives; 83, bottom, Wide World; 88, Metropolitan Museum of Art; 91, Ronald Sheridan; 92, 98, 100, bottom, Editorial Photocolor Archives; 103, Ronald Sheridan; 104, Robert Harding Picture Library; 108, Mary Evans Picture Library; 110, Editorial Photocolor Archives; 113, The Bridgeman Art Library; 114, Metropolitan Museum of Art; 117, Editorial Photocolor Archives; 121, Photoresources; 128, Editorial Photocolor Archives; 133, 135, Photoresources; 136, Museum of Modern Art/Film Stills Archives; 142, 145, 147, Editorial Photocolor Archives; 148, Ronald Sheridan; 152, Mary Evans Picture Library; 155, Photoresources; 160, Editorial Photocolor Archives; 163, Photoresources; 167, Editorial Photocolor Archives; 172, Miltiades Karamechedis; 174, Ronald Sheridan; 177, Mary Evans Picture Library; 181, Editorial Photocolor Archives; 182, Mary Evans Picture Library; 186, 189, Editorial Photocolor Archives; 191, Photoresources; 193, Ronald Sheridan; 196, Editorial Photocolor Archives; 204, The Bridgeman Art Library; 206, Editorial Photocolor Archives; 209, 211, Photoresources; 212, American Heritage Picture Library/British Museum; 222, Photoresources; 224, 229, 231, 232, 236, 239, Editorial Photocolor Archives; 246, Photoresources; 250, Editorial Photocolor Archives; 255, The Bridgeman Art Library; 256, Photoresources; 261, Martin Rogers/Woodfin Camp; 262, Werner Forman Archives; 264, Werner Forman Archive; 267, Photoresources; 268, Werner Forman Archive; 270, Photoresources; 274, Werner Forman Archive; 278, The Bridgeman Art Library; 281, Werner Forman Archive; 283, The Bridgeman Art Library; 284, Werner Forman Archive; 287, Werner Forman Archives; 292, Editorial Photocolor Archives; 295, Mary Evans Picture Library; 299, 303, Miriam Butts; 307, Robert Harding Picture Library; 308, Mary Evans Picture Library; 311, Michael Aryton/Harmony Books-Division of Crown Publishers 318, Editorial Photocolor Archive; 322, Museum of Modern Art/Film Stills Archive; 325, "No Escape" by Imagic; 327, Museum of Science, Boston; 311, taken from "The Leprechaun s Kingdom," by Peter Haining. Copyright © 1979 by Peter Haining and Pictorial Presentations. Used by permission of Harmony Books, a division of Crown Publishers, Inc.
All Photographs not otherwise credited belong to the Allyn and Bacon collection.